Fan or Follower of
Jesus Christ

Fan or Follower of
Jesus Christ

Vinu V Das

Tabor Press

© 2025 Tabor Press. All rights reserved. No part of this publication may be reproduced, distributed, or transmitted in any form or by any means without the prior written permission of the publisher, except in the case of brief quotations embodied in critical reviews and certain other noncommercial uses permitted by copyright law.

ISBN 978-1-997541-35-6

Table of Contents

Chapter 1 — Setting the Question: Fan Culture vs. Costly Discipleship 9

    1.0 Prologue: Why This Question Matters 10

    1.1 The Modern Phenomenon of "Fanhood" 12

    1.2 Biblical Background for the Language of Following .. 17

    1.3 Diagnostic Markers: Am I a Fan or a Follower? 20

    1.4 The Cost of Discipleship 25

    1.5 Cultural Pressures and False Metrics 28

    1.6 Case Studies: Fans Who Became Followers 32

Chapter 2 — Fans in the Gospels: Crowd Enthusiasm without Commitment 37

    2.0 Setting the Scene: Crowds and Christ 38

    2.1 Galilean Spectators and Miracle Seekers 40

    2.2 Political Aspirants Hoping for a Revolt Leader 42

    2.3 Curious Nicodemus under Cover of Night 45

    2.4 Sign-Demanders and Spectacle Seekers 51

    2.5 From Adoration to Rejection: The Crowd before Pilate 55

Chapter 3 — Old-Testament Typology: Spectators of God's Works 59

    3.0 Setting the Stage: Typology and Testimony 60

    3.1 Israel at Sinai: Acclaim without Obedience 62

    3.2 Wilderness Generation: Manna Fans, Mission Failures 67

    3.3 Prophetic Warnings against Lip-Service Religion 71

3.4 Judges' Cycle: Short-Lived Zeal and Deepening Apostasy 75

3.5 Royal Pageantry vs. Covenant Fidelity 78

3.6 Exile and Return: Echoes of Spectator Spirituality.... 82

3.7 Typology Fulfilled: From Shadow to Substance in Christ 86

Chapter 4 — The Cost of Being Merely a Fan 91

    4.0 Counting the Hidden Price 92

    4.1 Spiritual Superficiality and Shallow Roots................. 94

    4.2 Emotional Volatility and Disillusionment.................... 97

    4.3 Ethical Inconsistency and Witness Damage 101

    4.4 Isolation from Transforming Community................. 104

    4.5 Missed Mission Opportunities 108

    4.6 Eternal Stakes of Fan-Level Faith............................. 111

    4.7 Crossing the Line: From Fan to Follower 114

Chapter 5 — Crisis Encounters That Separate Fans from Followers 119

    5.0 Threshold Moments: Why Crises Clarify Commitment 120

    5.1 The Hard Sayings of Jesus 122

    5.2 Trials and Persecutions as Refining Fires 126

    5.3 Post-Resurrection Challenges to Belief.................... 129

    5.4 Moral Failures that Force a Fork in the Road 133

    5.5 Intellectual Crises and Cultural Pressures 135

    5.6 Suffering that Births Mission 138

Chapter 6 — Portraits of Authentic Followers in Scripture.. 143

    6.0 Framing Authentic Discipleship 144

6.1 Peter: From Impulsive Admirer to Commissioned Shepherd 146

6.2 Mary of Bethany: Worship over Work 150

6.3 Saul to Paul: Radical Re-Orientation 154

6.4 Ruth: Loyal Love That Transcends Ethnic Boundaries 158

6.5 Daniel: Integrating Conviction with Cultural Influence 162

Chapter 7 — Marks of the Follower: Identity, Intimacy, Imitation 166

7.0 Laying the Groundwork for Christ-Shaped Growth 167

7.1 Identity in Christ over Social Labels 169

7.2 Intimacy through Spirit-Formed Disciplines 173

7.3 Imitation Shaped by the Cross 177

7.4 Integrated Maturity: Head, Heart, and Hands 182

7.5 Obstacles and Aids on the Journey 184

Chapter 8 — Contemporary Obstacles to Wholehearted Discipleship 189

8.0 Mapping Today's Discipleship Landscape 190

8.1 Consumer Christianity and Spectator Worship 192

8.2 Digital Distraction and Fragmented Attention 196

8.3 Cultural Pressures and Ethical Compromise 200

8.4 Identity Fluidity and the Quest for Self-Definition ... 203

8.5 Skepticism, Deconstruction, and Post-Truth Realities 206

8.6 Exhaustion, Burnout, and Hurry Sickness 208

8.7 Disembodied Faith in a Post-Pandemic World 211

Chapter 9 — Spiritual Practices for Crossing the Line 215

9.0 Moving From Intention to Transformation 216

9.1 Repentance: Re-Aligning the Heart's Affections 218

9.2 Surrender: Offering the Whole Self 221

9.3 Obedient Action: Faith Expressed in Works 224

9.4 Perseverance: Habits that Survive Dry Seasons 228

9.5 Discernment: Hearing God amid Competing Voices 231

9.6 Missional Overflow: Practices that Turn Outward .. 233

Chapter 10 — Community of Followers: The Church as Discipleship Hub 238

10.0 Why Discipleship Flourishes Best in Community ... 239

10.1 Mutual Encouragement and Loving Accountability 240

10.2 Sacramental Rhythms that Shape Identity 245

10.3 Spiritual Gifts Deployed for Mission 249

10.4 Intergenerational and Intercultural Tapestry 254

10.5 Missional Communities and Kingdom Outposts 257

10.6 Cultivating a Culture of Ongoing Formation 261

Chapter 1 — Setting the Question: Fan Culture vs. Costly Discipleship

In our media-saturated age, devotion often takes the form of fleeting admiration rather than enduring commitment. People eagerly follow celebrities, influencers, and trends, cultivating a fervent attachment that revolves around charisma and momentary highs. Yet when similar patterns creep into our faith, the result is a diluted gospel and a shallow spirituality. Jesus did not call His followers into a theatre of applause but into a life of radical surrender that transcends entertainment or popularity. The allure of instant gratification and the validation of social-media metrics can obscure the serious demands of true allegiance. Beneath the bright lights of modern worship services and viral online ministries, the heart of discipleship—self-denial, cross-bearing, and covenant loyalty—can easily be eclipsed. The stakes are high, for the decisions we make about who or what shapes our devotion ultimately determine whether we stand firm when trials come. By examining contemporary tendencies toward "fanhood," contrasting them with the biblical model of costly following, and reflecting on real-life examples from Scripture, we aim to discern whether we have settled for superficial engagement or are pressing into authentic, lifelong submission to Christ. This chapter invites readers to move beyond passive reception and emotional highs, urging a deeper evaluation of what it truly means to follow the crucified and risen Savior.

1.0 Prologue: Why This Question Matters

1.0.a The Gospel Call in an Age of Entertainment The contemporary world is saturated with entertainment options that vie for our attention. From streaming platforms to social media algorithms, people are constantly inundated with content that competes for their focus. This entertainment culture shapes how individuals view engagement with any message, including the gospel. When the message of Christ is presented in a format that resembles a show or performance, it risks being consumed as mere amusement. The Great Commission, however, calls for transformation rather than transient fascination (Matt 28:18–20). Jesus did not fashion His message as theatrical spectacle but as an invitation to a kingdom that demands allegiance. In an age where people expect immediate gratification and emotional highs, the patient and costly journey of discipleship can feel slow and unsatisfying. Worship services that mimic concert experiences may draw large crowds but can also inadvertently foster a mentality of "consumer Christianity." When attendees treat sermons like entertainment, they may applaud emotional moments yet neglect calls to obedience. The apostles modeled a different approach, preaching a gospel that often led to persecution rather than popularity (Acts 5:41). Such preaching stands in contrast to today's polished production values that prioritize audience retention over truth. As ministers and church leaders navigate this entertainment-saturated landscape, they face the challenge of presenting Jesus as Lord rather than star (Phil 2:9–11). The prologue of this book highlights that the stakes are high when the gospel is reduced to another form of diversion. Jesus warned that following Him entails taking up one's cross daily (Luke 9:23), a concept at odds with the comfortable experience offered by modern worship venues. The challenge for Christians today is to discern whether they are craving an emotional rush or a transformative encounter with the living Christ. If Christian gatherings become mere variety shows, the radical message of surrender and obedience can be dulled. Yet even amid entertainment-driven culture, there remain opportunities to offer the gospel's depth. Authentic worship can and must resist the pull of consumerist impulses, allowing Spirit-empowered transformation rather than fleeting enthusiasm. As we transition to consider discipleship's primacy in the church, it is vital to remember that entertainment must serve the gospel, not eclipse it.

1.0.b Discipleship as the Church's First Mandate From the moment Jesus instructed His disciples to "go and make disciples of all nations," the church's identity became intrinsically linked to discipleship (Matt 28:19). Discipleship is not an optional add-on to Christian identity but the very essence of following Christ. In the early church, believers devoted themselves to the apostles' teaching and fellowship, intentionally cultivating spiritual growth (Acts 2:42). Every dimension of church life—worship, fellowship, communion—was filtered through the lens of making and sustaining followers of Jesus. Over centuries, however, institutional structures and programmatic approaches have sometimes shifted the focus from wholehearted following to merely maintaining congregational routines. When discipleship becomes transactional—attend this class, check this box—the radical call of Christ is domesticated. Genuine discipleship involves a lifelong process of conforming to the image of Christ (Rom 8:29). It implicates the whole person: mind, heart, soul, and strength. Such transformation does not happen by accident; it requires intentional cultivation of spiritual disciplines, community accountability, and sacrificial service. The apostle Paul envisioned the church as a body growing "up to the mature measure of the fullness of Christ" (Eph 4:13). This image underscores that discipleship encompasses both individual growth and corporate unity. In practice, however, churches can inadvertently prioritize numerical growth, programmatic efficiency, or cultural relevance over true spiritual formation. When this happens, believers can feel like customers of a religious service rather than apprentices of a teacher. The Great Shepherd's mandate to "feed my sheep" (John 21:17) challenges church leaders to shepherd God's flock toward maturity rather than simply attract large crowds. Discipleship demands cost. It calls for teaching that addresses sin, suffering, and surrender, not merely encouraging and entertaining messages. Jesus Himself exemplified this model when He said, "If anyone would come after me, let him deny himself, take up his cross, and follow me" (Luke 9:23). There is no short-cut to bearing the cross. In the early church, believers risked persecution because their allegiance to Christ went beyond Sunday attendance. The Subversive King they followed demanded exclusive devotion (Phil 3:8). For modern readers, the question becomes: has discipleship been reframed as a menu of options rather than total submission? If so, the church must repent of reducing Christ's call to a one-hour program. As we turn to examine how "fanhood" can masquerade as discipleship, recall that the church's first and greatest mandate remains making and sustaining learners of Jesus.

This exploration of the gospel call and discipleship's primacy sets the stage to examine how modern "fan culture" interacts with faith. With that foundation, we turn next to consider the phenomenon of fanhood in our present age.

1.1 The Modern Phenomenon of "Fanhood"

1.1.a Celebrity Fascination in Popular Culture Society today obsesses over public figures in a way that previous generations rarely did. Celebrity magazines, social media feeds, and 24-hour news cycles elevate entertainers, athletes, and influencers into almost mythical figures. People track every move of famous individuals, from their career decisions to their personal relationships, viewing them as aspirational models. This fascination reflects a deep human desire for connection with those who seem larger than life. When fans witness celebrities on red carpets or stages, they project ideals onto them—success, beauty, wealth, or perceived wisdom. Social media intensifies this by offering curated glimpses behind the scenes, creating an illusion of intimacy. Fans can comment on posts, share content, and even feel a sense of "knowing" the person, despite no real relationship existing. Marketers and talent managers capitalize on this craving by packaging celebrities into consumable brands. Merchandise, endorsements, and sponsored content blur the line between admiration and commerce. In many cases, fans feel loyal to a celebrity's brand rather than to the person behind it. Emotional investment becomes intertwined with consumer behavior: streaming a song, buying a jersey, or using a product simply because a favorite star endorses it. The effect is that fandom often becomes a passive relationship—enthusiasts consume content without any reciprocal investment from the object of their admiration. Yet fans speak as if they intimately know the celebrity's heart, motivations, or struggles. Reality TV and documentary-style programming feed the illusion that viewers "walk alongside" these stars. This dynamic fosters a culture in which identity can be borrowed from celebrated figures: "I am a Swiftie," "I Stan Beyoncé," or "I'm in the Marvel fandom." Even in secular contexts, the behavior patterns of fandom reveal how easily admiration can substitute for authentic relationship. Before moving on to faith contexts, keep in mind that the pattern of celebrity fascination primes hearts to treat leaders—spiritual or otherwise—as objects of worship rather than submitting to truth on its own terms. As we transition to explore fandom within faith contexts, note how persuasive this allure of celebrity can be when transferred to religious arenas.

1.1.b Transferring Fandom to Faith The dynamic of fandom readily extends into the spiritual realm when churchgoers begin to treat pastors, worship leaders, or Christian celebrities as the primary draw. Just as secular fans curate social media feeds to follow every update of a favorite actor, religious fans can subscribe to every sermon podcast, quote every devotion from a trusted teacher, and measure their spiritual growth by how many times they've viewed that leader's content. When this mindset takes hold, the gospel itself can become a side note: what matters most is being associated with a popular Christian brand. In some cases, churchgoers evaluate a congregation's worth based on how "big name" the preacher is.

Success metrics shift from transformed lives to social-media engagement, as if gospel fruit can be quantified in likes and shares. The irony is that although followers of Christ are called to worship the invisible God in Spirit and truth (John 4:24), many adopt a mentality that worship Jesus by proxy—through the mediating presence of a human personality. While Christian teachers and musicians can rightly shepherd and equip the flock, their role is to point people to Christ, not to themselves (John 5:39). When the messenger eclipses the message, hearts drift toward idolatry without realizing it. Distinctives of biblical faith—confession of sin, humility, repentance—become secondary to the allure of belonging to a "tribe" aligned with a popular leader's brand. Conferences and events market themselves based on headlining speakers, promising attendees an "experience" that centers more on personality than on deep engagement with Scripture. The result is that some believers know pastors' personal stories, favorite Bible verses, and vacation destinations more intimately than they know the gospel itself. Disillusionment follows when the celebrity falls short of expectations, revealing that faith was anchored in personality rather than in the Person of Christ (Eph 2:20). A true follower of Jesus, by contrast, finds identity in the unchanging Rock of Ages rather than in any human vessel (1 Cor 3:11). As we delve further into neural networks of fandom within church life, remember that transferring secular fan patterns to spiritual contexts can seriously compromise discipleship. This recognition leads us to examine additional dimensions of modern fan culture before contrasting them with ancient models of following.

1.1.c Social-Media Amplification and Influencer Religion Social media platforms have democratized both fame and ministry in unprecedented ways. Posts can go viral in minutes, elevating individuals from obscurity to wide recognition almost overnight. When Christian influencers gain large followings, they wield significant power over opinions, trends, and even theological discourse. While this can be used for good—spreading the gospel quickly and connecting disparate communities—it also introduces dangers inherent to any online fan subculture. Algorithms privilege content that generates engagement, often rewarding controversy, sensationalism, or charismatic presentation over careful exegesis and theological nuance. In the digital realm, engagement metrics—likes, shares, comments—become currency, incentivizing creators to craft content that appeals to the masses rather than challenging them toward deeper obedience. In many cases, influencers package their faith into digestible "sound bites," promising quick fixes for complex spiritual struggles. These bite-sized messages can help with awareness but fall short of equipping believers to navigate seasons of doubt, suffering, or theological complexity. Moreover, fans who attach their identity to online personalities risk becoming disoriented if that influencer's platform unexpectedly collapses or if their content changes direction. The instability of online "faith providers" contrasts sharply with the unchanging character of Christ. When followers realize their spiritual well-being depended more on trending posts than on the eternal Word, many experience spiritual anxiety or disillusionment. This fragility becomes apparent when influencers face personal failure or public scandal. Suddenly, their fan base must wrestle with questions about whether the truth they embraced was intact or compromised. While genuine online communities can foster encouragement, believers must discern whether their primary engagement is with Scripture or with personalities. The apostle Paul warned against placing confidence in human agency rather than in the power of God (2 Cor 3:5). In guiding the church through this digital landscape, leaders must emphasize that online platforms are tools to point people to Christ, not substitutes for face-to-face community and personal transformation. As we transition to the question of metrics that mislead, we will explore how numbers-driven thinking can further entangle fandom with faith at the expense of discipleship.

1.1.d Metrics That Mislead: Likes, Views, and Attendance Counts In contemporary church culture, it is common to equate success with numerical growth. Sunday attendance figures, social-media analytics, conference ticket sales, and podcast downloads are often presented as evidence of God's blessing. While there is nothing inherently wrong with measuring tangible outcomes, the danger arises when these metrics become the primary barometer of spiritual health. When pastors and ministry teams focus primarily on filling seats or increasing followers, they can inadvertently tailor programming to suit popular tastes rather than submitting to biblical convictions. Messages shift from convicting calls to radical obedience toward feel-good testimonials and tips for nominal Christian living. In this environment, people become accustomed to opting out if a teaching doesn't "fit their style," treating church as an audience-driven production. The church becomes analogous to a business, with leadership constantly asking, "What do people want to hear?" rather than "What does God's Word compel us to say?" As a result, the most meaningful gospel challenges—calls to surrender, repentance, self-denial—risk being downplayed or avoided. The fruit of this approach is shallow discipleship, in which attendees may gauge their faith by how they feel or by how many events they attend rather than by evidence of Christlike transformation (Col 2:6-7). Furthermore, social-media platforms inflate the illusion of connection. A thousand "likes" on a sermon clip can feel validating, yet true discipleship is measured in how one lives out Christ's commands in everyday contexts. Authentic spiritual growth often goes unseen by analytics, occurring in private moments of prayer, confession, and obedience. Church leaders who grow preoccupied with chasing numbers can lose sight of their calling to shepherd souls toward maturity (1 Pet 5:2–3). Discipleship thrives best in environments where genuine accountability, transparent relationships, and theological depth are prioritized over metrics. As we conclude our examination of fan culture's markers, we prepare to shift our focus toward understanding how followers are described in Scripture and how ancient discipleship models differ radically from modern fanhood.

Together, these explorations of celebrity fascination, transferred fandom, social-media amplification, and deceptive metrics set the stage for a deeper look into how the New Testament unfolds genuine following. With that context established, we now turn to the biblical background for the language of following.

1.2 Biblical Background for the Language of Following

1.2.a Ancient Rabbinic Discipleship Models In first-century Judaism, aspiring disciples sought out rabbis whose teaching resonated with them. A disciple would identify a rabbi, observe his character, inquire of his reputation among peers, and then make a solemn choice to leave all and attach himself to that rabbinic teacher. This relational model involved shared meals, traveling together, and intensive immersion in the rabbi's interpretation of the Law (Torah). Disciples did not merely receive information; they lived under the rabbi's roof, watched his manner of life, and learned through observation and imitation. The rabbinic chain of transmission emphasized fidelity to the tradition handed down from Moses, with careful attention to oral and written interpretation. In many cases, disciples repeated the rabbi's words verbatim, seeking to preserve the purity of the teaching. Such commitment required leaving family and economic security—social costs that created a razor-sharp distinction between true apprentices and casual observers. The rhetorical question "From where will a person gain wisdom?" implied that wisdom was not simply acquired from books but was imparted through close, lived association with a teacher. Jesus adopted and subverted this model by calling individuals to forsake their rabbinic allegiances and follow Him. While He affirmed the centrality of Scripture, His teaching frequently challenged prevailing rabbinic interpretations, insisting that true righteousness transcended mere external compliance (Matt 5:20). Jesus' discipleship model still relied on intimate proximity—"Come, follow me"—but it offered more than legal exegesis; it presented Himself as the embodiment of the Law (John 1:14). The rabbinic model thus provides crucial context for understanding the gravity of Jesus' call, as well as the costliness of discipleship in His framework. Rather than mere admiration for a teacher's eloquence, Jesus demanded a heart-level commitment to His person and mission (Mark 10:21). This ancient backdrop helps clarify why Jesus' call to "deny oneself, take up one's cross, and follow" (Luke 9:23) had radical implications that went beyond typical rabbinic apprenticeship.

1.2.b Old-Testament Precursors of Covenant Following (Deut 10:12-13) Long before the rabbinic era, the Old Testament pointed to an understanding of following that encompassed heart, soul, and strength. In Deuteronomy, Moses exhorted Israel to "fear the Lord your God, walk in all his ways, love him, serve the Lord your God with all your heart and with all your soul" (Deut 10:12). This call to covenant fidelity involved putting away foreign gods, keeping the commandments, and stewarding obedience in everyday life. The cultural context of ancient Israel anticipated that following Yahweh required holiness in social structures, personal ethics, and communal worship. Prophets like Micah emphasized that true devotion was not limited to ritual but included doing justice, loving kindness, and walking humbly with God (Mic 6:8). In this way, the Old Testament laid a foundation for a comprehensive understanding of following that addressed both inward transformation and outward action. Conventional Old-Testament faithfulness went beyond following a set of rules; it invited participation in a redemptive story that shaped all of life. When Israel embraced foreign gods, prophets warned that their hearts had drifted into "fanhood"—honoring God in word but not in deed (Isa 29:13). In contrast, the Psalms paint the picture of a soul that delights in the Law day and night (Ps 1:2), reflecting an intimate, personal affection for God's ways. These precedents informed the Jewish imagination as they awaited the Messiah who would fulfill the Law and the Prophets (Matt 5:17). By looking back to Israel's story, readers of this book can see that Jesus' invitation to follow was steeped in ancient imagery of allegiance, loyalty, and covenant identity. The Old-Testament narrative thus bridges the gap between mere appreciation of God's deeds and a wholehearted commitment to His character.

1.2.c Jesus' Distinctive Call: "Follow Me" (Matt 4:19; John 1:43) When Jesus walked the shores of Galilee and uttered the words "Follow me," He was issuing an invitation that reverberated through contemporary Jewish expectations (Matt 4:19). Unlike the rabbinic custom of a disciple seeking out a teacher, Jesus actively sought followers—fishermen, tax collectors, and strangers—calling them to leave nets and occupations behind to learn from Him. His summons was both shockingly simple and profoundly demanding. Those who followed saw Him heal, preach, cast out demons, and confront religious authorities. These formative experiences were not casual field trips; they were transformative encounters designed to reshape belief and lifestyle. As Jesus moved from village to village, entire crowds pressed in, hoping for signs and wonders. Yet He reserved the language of true "following" only for those ready to commit their lives. Peter and Andrew dropped their nets without hesitation; James and John left their father's boat behind. These inaugural moments of response illustrate that Jesus' call was not contingent on charisma alone but on divine authority and purpose (John 1:43–51). Followers learned that to truly follow Jesus was to identify with His mission: preaching the kingdom, serving the poor, and ultimately laying down life itself. His teaching "take up your cross" (Matt 10:38) underscored the paradox that true discipleship required the willingness to die. Such a call contrasted sharply with crowds that desired only miraculous bread (John 6:26). Jesus' use of the imperative "follow" indicated an ongoing, continuous action—an intentional posture that shaped every aspect of life. The examples of Matthew (Matt 9:9), Zacchaeus (Luke 19:5), and the rich young ruler (Matt 19:21) reveal varied responses: only those willing to relinquish possessions and status truly joined His band of followers. By focusing on Jesus' direct call, we recognize that genuine following involves a decisive turning away from former allegiances. This realization sets the stage for understanding how New-Testament followers differed fundamentally from modern fans who merely admire from a distance.

1.2.d Post-Resurrection Expansion of the Call (Acts 1:8) The resurrection narrative magnifies the scope of Jesus' invitation to follow. After His resurrection, Jesus appeared to His disciples in various locations, reaffirming His call and commissioning them to be witnesses "to the ends of the earth" (Acts 1:8). This expansion of "following" moved beyond physical proximity to Christ during His earthly ministry; it included participation in His mission after His ascension. The early church's understanding of following now encompassed risking persecution, crossing cultural barriers, and sacrificing comfort for the sake of the gospel. In Jerusalem, believers devoted themselves to teaching, prayer, and fellowship (Acts 2:42), demonstrating that following Christ meant building community shaped by Spirit-empowered devotion. As Peter and the other apostles stood before hostile authorities, they insisted that obedience to God took precedence over human authority (Acts 5:29), revealing that following Christ could lead to suffering rather than safety. The ministry of Paul further exemplifies this expanded call: he traveled thousands of miles, enduring shipwrecks, prison, and beatings to spread the message (2 Cor 11:23–27). In each context, followers were called not merely to admire Jesus' power but to embody it through sacrificial service. The book of Acts illustrates that true discipleship transcends geographical and cultural boundaries, linking believers across nations in a single body (Eph 2:19–22). When Jesus promises that His followers will receive power from the Holy Spirit, He signals that following Him involves living under divine guidance rather than relying solely on human leadership (Acts 1:8). This ethos distinguishes genuine disciples from fans, who seek proximity to a figure simply for inspiration or identity. The post-resurrection call invites believers into a shared journey that continues to this day: to follow Christ by advancing His kingdom, whether that means bold proclamation, compassionate service, or steadfast witness in adversity (Phil 3:10). As we conclude this section, we stand ready to examine diagnostic markers that help clarify whether one has truly crossed from fan to follower, recognizing that the biblical narrative sets a high bar for genuine allegiance.

1.3 Diagnostic Markers: Am I a Fan or a Follower?

1.3.a External Enthusiasm vs. Inner Allegiance In many congregations, it is easy to identify those whose faith consists largely of outward expressions: applauding emotive worship songs, taking selfies with charismatic speakers, or framing social media posts around church attendance. While such visible displays can signal genuine joy, they often coexist with superficial understanding of biblical truth. True inner allegiance, by contrast, reflects an ongoing commitment to Christ even when external accolades or positive feelings wane. A fan may be energized by a compelling preacher, but a follower remains steadfast when that preacher moves on or when the message ceases to stir emotions. Enthusiasm that revolves around special events—revival meetings, conferences, or concerts—can leave people spiritually restless once the lights dim and the crowds disperse. Genuine allegiance to Jesus, however, is evidenced by a soul that clings to Him in ordinary, everyday circumstances. A disciple's devotion does not hinge on the quality of the presentation or the volume of the praise band; it flows from a heart surrendered to Christ's lordship (Romans 12:1–2). When a person's faith is anchored in external affirmation—likes, shares, or attendance counts—they risk building on shaky foundations. Conversely, those who ground their identity in Christ's unchanging character display a resilience that survives seasons of doubt or remote wilderness experiences (Psalm 42:5–7). Inner allegiance also becomes visible in the way believers handle criticism, disappointment, or theological tension. Instead of abandoning church when a favorite teacher fall short or when doctrinal nuances become challenging, true followers press into Scripture and community to gain clarity. They do not look primarily to human approval but to God's commendation (Galatians 1:10). This inward disposition manifests in consistency: regular prayer, Bible study, and obedience reinforced by spiritual disciplines, even if no one is watching. The distinction between outside excitement and inside devotion is not a legalistic judgment of emotion itself but an invitation to examine the wellspring of our joy. As Jesus reminded the crowds, those who love only the illumination of the moment and reject deeper truth will wither like seed sown on rocky ground (Matthew 13:20–21). Thus, moving from external enthusiasm to inner allegiance requires shifting focus from what crowds find entertaining to what God finds precious. As readers reflect on this contrast, they should ask: does my heart still sing when no one else notices? Such self-examination leads naturally into understanding the difference between fleeting emotion and enduring covenant.

1.3.b Temporary Emotion vs. Lifelong Covenant Emotional experiences in worship—tears, laughter, or palpable spiritual "highs"—can foster a sense of connection to God. These moments can be valuable as reminders of God's love, but they can also become ends in themselves if unanchored from covenantal commitment. A fan often seeks the next "spiritual rush," hopping from one uplifting event to another to capture the same thrill. Yet Jesus warned that entry into His kingdom is not guaranteed by transient exhilaration but by abiding in His word and keeping His commandments (John 8:31–32). Festivals, revivals, and large-scale gatherings can stir powerful emotions, but they do not automatically solidify a disciple's lifelong allegiance. Covenant faithfulness involves persevering even when the senses detect little. Moses urged Israel to remember the covenant during both times of plenty and times of famine, emphasizing that the Lord's faithfulness does not depend on external circumstances (Deuteronomy 8:18). In the New Testament, believers are described as being sealed by the Holy Spirit as a guarantee of the inheritance to come (Ephesians 1:13–14). This sealing is not conditional on feelings but on God's promise. As a result, followers of Jesus are invited into an ever-deepening relationship that transcends fluctuating emotional states. When hardship arises, covenant-minded believers recall God's prior faithfulness and press into prayer rather than abandon ship. Those who build their lives on the rock of covenantal devotion withstand the storms of trials (Matthew 7:24–27). In contrast, believers who chase each emotional high can find themselves disoriented when life's pressures suppress their feelings. A covenantal framework calls for regular recommitment—through practices like baptismal reflection, communion, and corporate confession—to remind hearts that God's love is steadfast, even when feelings ebb. Covenant keeping also entails accountability: inviting others to speak truth into moments of discouragement or distraction. When a community upholds a lifelong covenant over momentary excitement, followers learn that faithfulness is measured by perseverance rather than performance. This understanding naturally transitions to the sobering reality that confession without cross-bearing cannot sustain true discipleship.

1.3.c Confession without Cross-Bearing (Luke 9:23) It is not uncommon for individuals to profess faith in Jesus without fully embracing the cost associated with that confession. Many are quick to affirm Jesus as Savior but hesitate when challenged to surrender personal agendas, comfort zones, or cherished ambitions. Jesus' call "If anyone would come after me, let him deny himself, take up his cross daily, and follow me" (Luke 9:23) exposes the depth of commitment required. Confession that fails to include cross-bearing can resemble a shallow overlay of piety rather than a profound reorientation of life. A fan might use religious language—"I'm a Christian," "I believe in Jesus"—but balk at relinquishing control over time, finances, relationships, or ethical decisions. Genuine followers recognize that discipleship entails a cruciform existence: living in submission to God's will, even when it contradicts personal desires or cultural expectations. Cross-bearing means welcoming suffering for Christ's sake, knowing that trials refine character and forge resilience (1 Peter 4:12–13). It involves daily choices to live counterculturally, whether that means extending forgiveness to an enemy, refusing to compromise integrity in the workplace, or caring sacrificially for the marginalized. Mere verbal allegiance does not necessarily produce these qualities; only embodied obedience undergirds true transformation. When confession is not coupled with cross-bearing, believers risk developing a form of godliness that denies its power (2 Timothy 3:5). In contrast, when followers embrace their crosses, they find that Jesus' yoke is light because it is laden with grace (Matthew 11:28–30). The process of taking up one's cross demands intentional self-examination, often catalyzed by circumstances that force a choice between comfort and obedience. For a parent, it may mean prioritizing spiritual health of the family over societal approval. For an entrepreneur, it could entail choosing ethical practices over maximum profit. Cross-bearing thus permeates every sphere of life. As the gospel advances, followers discover that true confession morphs into radical action, reshaping identities from consumers of faith to agents of change. Recognizing the indispensability of cross-bearing leads directly into the theme of perseverance under fire, highlighting that faith must be proven over time rather than declared at a moment.

1.3.d Faith under Fire: Perseverance Indicators (Hebrews 10:36-39) Enduring faith is seldom proven in times of ease; rather, it is forged in the crucible of adversity. The writer of Hebrews exhorts believers to perseverance, reminding them that those who shrink back are not pleasing to God (Hebrews 10:36–39). When trials pressure believers to compromise beliefs or question God's goodness, fans often retreat, seeking comfort in less demanding environments. A follower, by contrast, clings to God's promises, trusting that suffering serves a redemptive purpose (Romans 5:3–5). Endurance indicators surface when circumstances threaten to derail faith—loss of employment, health crises, relational betrayals, or societal hostility to biblical convictions. During such seasons, perseverance takes the form of unceasing prayer, patient trust in God's timing, and unwavering commitment to Christ's lordship. True followers use Scripture as a lamp to their feet when darkness looms, recalling stories of saints who triumphed through faith (Psalm 119:105; James 1:2–4). In contrast, a fan's devotion often unravels when the marquee lights fade. Historical examples from the early church show that believers who faced persecution did not flee but rallied around the cross, finding strength in communal solidarity and in the knowledge that Christ had overcome the world (John 16:33). This countercultural posture illustrates that perseverance is both an individual and corporate endeavor—followers encourage one another to press on (Hebrews 3:13). As faith endures through hardships, disillusionment gives way to deeper intimacy with Christ, as Philippians 3:10 describes: knowing Christ in the fellowship of His sufferings. Rather than viewing adversity as abandonment, steadfast followers interpret it as evidence of participating in Christ's sufferings, which ultimately yields greater glory (Romans 8:17). Perseverance indicators also appear in small, everyday choices: choosing forgiveness over bitterness, generosity over fear, joy over despair. These faithful patterns accumulate over months and years, painting a portrait of discipleship far more robust than any fan's fleeting enthusiasm. As believers recognize these perseverance indicators, they prepare to face the reality that the cost of following Jesus extends beyond personal comfort, leading naturally to considering what that cost entails in concrete terms.

1.4 The Cost of Discipleship

1.4.a Personal Renunciation and Self-Denial (Luke 14:27)
Discipleship demands a decisive turning away from self-centred ambitions and desires. Jesus made this clear when He said that anyone who does not carry his cross and follow Him cannot be His disciple (Luke 14:27). Carrying one's cross implies active renunciation of self-will; it means saying no to personal dreams or agendas when they conflict with God's purposes. Renunciation is not merely giving up bad behaviors but relinquishing any allegiance that competes with devotion to Christ. In the first-century context, carrying a cross signaled impending death; Jesus used this imagery to convey that following Him might require a similar willingness to sacrifice. Such self-denial extends to every aspect of life—time, resources, reputation, even relationships—when these threaten to eclipse ultimate loyalty to Christ. The apostle Paul echoed this call, affirming that he considered all things loss compared to knowing Christ and being found in Him (Philippians 3:8–9). This posture of renunciation frees followers to live with a singular focus: glorifying God rather than seeking their own advancement. Self-denial also shapes attitudes toward material goods; instead of hoarding for comfort, disciples steward resources for kingdom purposes. By denying the impulse to constantly accumulate, believers make room to serve the poor, support missions, and invest in eternal outcomes (1 John 3:17–18). Those who embrace personal renunciation discover that God's pleasure is found not in ease but in holy surrender. As the next section will show, self-denial often requires reordering relationships so that Christ reigns supreme over all other connections.

1.4.b Relational Reordering: Christ before Kin (Luke 14:26)
Jesus' statement that anyone who comes to Him must "hate" father, mother, wife, children, brothers, and sisters—and even their own life—can jar modern ears (Luke 14:26). This language of "hate" is a Semitic hyperbole indicating a preference order: loyalty to Christ must supersede all familial ties. For first-century Jews, family was the bedrock of identity and social security. To place Christ above

kinship meant risking ostracism, loss of inheritance, and severed relationships. In the same way, contemporary disciples confront scenarios where following Jesus draws sharp lines between biblical ethics and cultural norms—choices that can cost friendships, marriages, or even career prospects. Relational reordering does not mean neglecting family responsibilities but refusing to prioritize them over Christ's commands. For instance, if a spouse opposes a believer's conviction to evangelize in a dangerous region, the disciple must weigh obedience to Christ above domestic harmony. Similarly, when kin pressure a believer to compromise moral convictions for the sake of family approval, disciples affirm that God's authority transcends any earthly tie (Matthew 10:37). This solemn reordering liberates followers to invest in the global family of God, forging bonds of fellowship that can be deeper than biological connections (1 John 3:14). Throughout redemptive history, God's covenant family has been distinct from earthly lineages—Abraham left his native land, and Ruth adopted Naomi's God as her own (Ruth 1:16–17). These models illustrate that following Christ often requires radical allegiance, even at the expense of cultural or familial comfort. As believers reorder relationships, they discover new dimensions of God's relational intimacy, as Christ becomes their true brother, sister, and parent (Matthew 12:49–50). Recognizing the weight of this relational reordering leads naturally to the next cost: sacrificial stewardship of material possessions.

1.4.c Material Stewardship and Sacrifice (Mark 10:21) When the rich young ruler approached Jesus, he asked what he must do to inherit eternal life. Jesus told him to sell everything he had, give to the poor, and follow Him (Mark 10:21). This radical instruction highlights that material possessions can become idols, hindering wholehearted devotion. While not every believer is called to literal poverty, each is called to evaluate relationships with wealth and to remain open to sacrificial giving. True disciples understand that "where your treasure is, there your heart will be also" (Matthew 6:21). When resources are viewed as God-given tools to advance His kingdom, believers can joyfully sacrifice personal comforts to alleviate suffering, support missionaries, or invest in church planting. Sacrificial stewardship also appears in generosity toward those in need, reflecting the early church's example in Acts, where believers sold property and possessions to distribute to anyone who had need (Acts 2:44–45). This praxis exemplifies how material sacrifice flows from genuine love for neighbors. Conversely, a fan-like follower may view giving as an optional line item in a budget rather than a spiritual imperative. True disciples must guard against hoarding or becoming entangled with consumerist impulses that distract from eternal priorities. Material stewardship also involves making daily choices—walking away from extravagant lifestyles, resisting the urge to upgrade to the latest gadgets, or choosing fair-trade options that honor ethical production. In each case, followers live out faith through tangible decisions, acknowledging that "you cannot serve God and money" (Matthew 6:24). As believers embrace sacrificial stewardship, they experience deeper trust in God's provision (Philippians 4:19). This reorientation of resources prepares them for the final dimension of cost: embracing suffering as a normal part of the Christian journey.

1.4.d Suffering as Normal Christian Experience (2 Timothy 3:12) The New Testament does not sugarcoat the reality that following Christ often entails suffering. Paul candidly declared to Timothy, "Indeed, all who desire to live a godly life in Christ Jesus will be persecuted" (2 Timothy 3:12). Genuine discipleship thus involves expecting hardship rather than guaranteed success or comfort. This expectation contrasts sharply with the worldview of a fan, who assumes that aligning with Jesus brings prosperity or status. Instead, followers learn that suffering refines their character, shapes dependence on God, and fosters solidarity with Christ, who Himself suffered for our sake (1 Peter 2:21–23). Persecution can take many forms—social ostracism, loss of employment, violence, or simply enduring ridicule from peers for upholding biblical convictions. Believers are not called to suffer for its own sake, but when trials come, they draw near to God, finding grace to persevere (James 1:2–4). Suffering also opens doors for witness, as outsiders observe how Christian faith anchors hope amid difficulty (1 Peter 3:15). The early church's growth amid intense persecution underscores that suffering can serve as fertile soil for gospel advancement (Acts 8:1–4). Furthermore, when disciples share in Christ's sufferings, they discover a depth of joy that transcends circumstances (Romans 5:3–5). The paradox is that embracing suffering does not diminish life but enriches it with eternal significance (Philippians 1:21). This posture requires rejecting the notion that comfort is the ultimate sign of God's blessing. As readers internalize suffering's place in the Christian journey, they stand ready to identify cultural pressures that dilute discipleship.

We will now examine how cultural narratives and church dynamics can subtly undermine true following.

1.5 Cultural Pressures and False Metrics

1.5.a Consumer Christianity and the Spectator Mind-Set In many contemporary churches, worship services resemble entertainment events where high production values, dynamic emcees, and impressive stagecraft draw crowds. While excellence in production is not inherently sinful, it can foster a consumer mentality that treats worship as a transaction—attend this service, feel uplifted, then rate the experience on social media. When congregants become spectators rather than active participants, the body of Christ cannot function as intended. Scripture portrays the church as a living organism (1 Corinthians 12:12–27), where each member contributes to the health of the whole. Consumer Christianity, however, reduces involvement to passive reception: choosing services based on style preferences or relocating to the "coolest" church in town rather than seeking opportunities to serve and build relationships. This spectator posture mirrors the behavior of fans in secular arenas who pay for a ticket, watch the performance, then leave without further investment. In contrast, followers of Jesus are called to steward their gifts for the edification of others (Ephesians 4:11–13). When church leaders cater primarily to consumer tastes—avoiding challenging sermons or difficult theological issues—the result is a "church lite" phenomenon that offers little resistance to cultural drift. Over time, congregants grow accustomed to being served rather than serving, undermining the biblical vision of mutual care (Hebrews 10:24–25). Recognizing the dangers of consumer Christianity prompts a reorientation toward active participation: serving on teams, discipling others, and engaging in intercessory prayer. As believers shift from spectator to participant, they begin to experience the joy of sacrificial love, rooted in Christ's example (John 13:34–35). This new posture naturally leads into the question of whether worship experiences prioritize emotion over spiritual formation.

1.5.b Experience-Driven Worship vs. Word-Driven Formation
The explosion of mega-churches and non-denominational movements has often accompanied a shift toward worship experiences designed to elicit strong emotional responses. Flashy lighting, contemporary music, and multimedia presentations aim to create atmosphere, yet they can inadvertently reposition the Word of God as secondary to ambiance. When worship becomes primarily about "feeling something," attendees may leave with an emotional buzz but lack a deeper engagement with Scripture that transforms mind and character. The prophets and apostles consistently underscored that God desires truth spoken in love (Ephesians 4:15), and that Scripture is living and active (Hebrews 4:12). Tangible experiences can point hearts to God, but without a robust emphasis on the Word, believers risk floating on a sea of sentimentality. True disciples are formed by the Word, as Jesus Himself modeled when He combatted temptation by quoting Scripture (Matthew 4:1–11). The Reformation's rallying cry of Sola Scriptura reminds us that the Bible, not experiential hype, must steer the church's direction. When church leadership prioritizes experiences over exegesis, congregations may become adept at feeling inspired yet remain ill-equipped to apply biblical truth to daily challenges. For instance, someone might feel emotionally moved by a song about God's love but struggle to apply forgiveness in a fractured marriage. In contrast, Word-driven formation addresses the whole person: doctrine that informs ethics, narratives that shape identity, and precepts that govern action (2 Timothy 3:16–17). As believers internalize Scripture's authority, they develop discernment to evaluate cultural

trends, worship styles, and popular teaching through a biblical lens. Transitioning from experience-driven worship to Word-driven formation requires church leaders to balance creativity with theological depth, ensuring that emotive elements serve rather than supplant the centrality of Scripture. As readers reflect on this balance, they will see how metrics of success—attendance and spectacle—can distort the church's mission, leading into the next discussion on numerical growth versus spiritual depth.

1.5.c Numerical Growth vs. Spiritual Depth Churches often trumpet impressive attendance numbers, multi-site campuses, and social-media followings as indicators of health and vitality. While growth in reach can testify to the gospel's power, it is possible to expand numerically while simultaneously stagnating spiritually. The apostle Paul's letters encourage congregations to grow not only in numbers but in grace and knowledge of Christ (2 Peter 3:18). Spiritual depth manifests in transformed hearts, ethical conduct, sacrificial generosity, and perseverance under trial—markers that do not always attract headlines or viral posts. A rapid influx of new attendees may bring diversity and fresh energy, but without intentional discipleship pathways, newcomers can remain ungrounded, drifting without roots (Colossians 2:6–7). Churches focused solely on generating buzz may invest heavily in marketing budgets while neglecting pastoral care, small-group formation, and theological training. In this environment, spiritual depth is sacrificed at the altar of expansion. In contrast, a disciple-making church invests in mentoring relationships, equipping believers to interpret Scripture, understand theology, and apply God's Word to complex life situations (Ephesians 4:12–13). Growth measured by spiritual depth looks like families serving together in local outreach, converts being baptized and immediately connected to accountability groups, and mature believers modeling godly leadership. Such growth often flies under the radar because it prioritizes long-term transformation over short-term applause. Jesus warned that "the gate is narrow and the way is hard that leads to life, and those who find it are few" (Matthew 7:14). This sobering reality reminds us that true growth is costly and often contrary to public opinion. Recognizing the contrast between superficial expansion and deep formation prompts churches to re-evaluate their metrics—shifting from counting seats filled to counting lives changed. As this section closes, we turn to a final cultural influence that quietly reshapes modern faith: the rise of Moralistic Therapeutic Deism.

1.5.d Moralistic Therapeutic Deism: The Quiet Drift Sociologists have identified Moralistic Therapeutic Deism (MTD) as a prevalent religious framework among many who identify as Christians today. MTD holds that God exists to help people be nice, happy, and comfortable—viewing faith primarily as a means to personal fulfillment rather than a call to sacrificial obedience. Within this paradigm, moral behavior is valued but detached from the transformative power of the cross. Instead of seeing sin as rebellion requiring repentance and new birth, MTD emphasizes vague spirituality and individual happiness. When faith is reduced to a therapeutic tool, the radical demands of Scripture—holiness, sacrificial love, humility—are overlooked or softened. This quiet drift toward a feel-good faith blunts the church's prophetic voice in culture, as believers become unwilling to take unpopular stands on moral issues. Jesus' call to "deny oneself, take up one's cross" (Luke 9:23) contradicts MTD's focus on comfort and self-esteem. Similarly, the warning in Revelation 3:16—that being lukewarm displeases the Lord—underscores the danger of halfhearted religion that neither chills nor burns with genuine devotion. MTD's prevalence reveals how easily Christians can drift from robust discipleship to a religion that affirms whatever feels good, so long as it does not disturb personal or social comfort. Over time, this drift can result in congregations that are amiable but anemic, friendly but ineffective at advancing God's kingdom. Recognizing MTD's influence motivates believers to reclaim biblical distinctives—embracing conviction, confession, and communal accountability. When churches resist MTD's seductions, they cultivate environments where truth is spoken in love (Ephesians 4:15), sinners are confronted with grace (Romans 5:8), and believers are equipped for every good work (2 Timothy 3:17). As readers contemplate these cultural pressures and false metrics, they stand poised to enter the next chapter, where we will examine how crowds in the Gospels often exhibited fan tendencies that contrasted sharply with the call to costly discipleship.

1.6 Case Studies: Fans Who Became Followers

1.6.a Zacchaeus—From Curiosity to Costly Restoration (Luke 19:1–10) Zacchaeus was a wealthy tax collector in Jericho whose curiosity about Jesus drove him into the crowd and ultimately up a sycamore tree. His initial motivation resembled that of many fans—an eagerness to catch a glimpse of the celebrated teacher whose reputation for preaching and healing had spread rapidly. Despite his social stigma as a collaborator with the Roman authorities, his desire to see Jesus overcame any concern for public perception. When Jesus paused beneath the tree and called him by name, Zacchaeus experienced the shock of personal invitation: "Hurry and come down, for I must stay at your house today." This moment marked the shift from distant admiration to direct engagement. As a fan might cheer from the sidelines, Zacchaeus had watched from a safe remove, but Jesus beckoned him into a closer encounter. Relinquishing any pretense of propriety, Zacchaeus immediately welcomed Jesus into his home. That hospitality was not merely a cultural formality but a tangible expression of gratitude and openness to transformation. Whereas his life had been characterized by extortion and greed, the presence of Jesus confronted him with the stark reality of God's mercy. Under that roof, Zacchaeus acknowledged his sin, pledging to restore fourfold to those he had defrauded and to give half his possessions to the poor. This dramatic turn exemplifies how a fan's initial intrigue can become the catalyst for repentance and life change. The crowd grumbled at Jesus' association with a sinner, but Jesus declared that salvation had come to Zacchaeus' house, for he too was a "son of Abraham." This statement reveals that lineage and religious pedigree meant nothing without the inward reality of faith. Zacchaeus' restoration plan did not stem from obligation but from a heart captivated by grace. He moved from simply observing Jesus' ministry to embodying its fruit through tangible acts of justice. His pledge to give away wealth indicated that following Jesus requires more than moral improvement—it demands a reorientation of priorities and possessions. In this encounter, curiosity evolved into covenantal allegiance, illustrating that the difference between a fan and a follower lies in the willingness to risk tangible sacrifice for the sake of righteousness. Zacchaeus' story naturally leads to another example of a curious soul whose life was transformed when Jesus unveiled her deepest need.

1.6.b The Samaritan Woman—From Outsider to Evangelist (John 4:1–42) The Samaritan woman approached the well at midday, a time when most suited couples or women in her village would draw water, revealing her social isolation and perhaps the shame she carried. She had likely heard rumors about Jesus crossing Samaria from Judea, but it was her need for water that brought her face to face with the Messiah. At first, their conversation revolved around the practical offer of water, and she may have thought of Jesus only as an itinerant Jewish rabbi. Yet her curiosity deepened as Jesus asked her to fetch water for Him, breaking social norms by speaking publicly to a Samaritan woman. As any fan might treasure a brief moment with a renowned figure, she lingered, intrigued that He would offer her "living water"—a metaphor for the spiritual satisfaction only He could provide. When Jesus revealed that He knew details of her personal history, including multiple marriages, the woman recognized that He was no ordinary teacher. This revelation moved her from mere intrigue to a dawning realization that He could address her deepest longings and hidden shame. She left her water jar behind, a symbolic act signaling that her old preoccupations would no longer define her. Rushing to her village, she invited others to come and see a man who told her everything she had done. In that invitation, the Samaritan woman became the first evangelist to her community, exemplifying that once a fan encounters Jesus authentically, she emerges eager to share the transformative message. Many Samaritans believed in Jesus because of her testimony, and when they met Him for themselves, they encouraged Him to stay, and He remained for two days. During this time, He spoke to them about worshiping "in spirit and truth," challenging both Jews and Samaritans to transcend inherited prejudices. The shift from drawing water for daily sustenance to drawing spiritual sustenance for a community illustrates that true following generates missional impulse. Unlike a fan who might harbor admiration privately, the Samaritan woman publicly proclaimed her encounter, catalyzing collective faith. Her transformation underscores that Jesus' offer of "living water" quenches thirst for belonging, identity, and forgiveness—needs that mere fandom cannot satisfy. Because of her, many Samaritans came to believe, testifying that "He really is the Savior of the world." In their literal thirst for water, they found spiritual thirst satisfied. From being marginalized in society, the woman became a vital link between Jesus and an entire community, showing that following Jesus can recast social standing in terms of divine purpose rather than human consensus. Her story sets the stage for observing two other secretive admirers—Joseph of Arimathea and Nicodemus—whose journeys demonstrate how private wonder can blossom into courageous discipleship.

1.6.c Joseph of Arimathea & Nicodemus—Secret Admirers Turned Public Disciples (John 19:38–42) Joseph of Arimathea and Nicodemus both began as influential figures in Jewish society who admired Jesus from a distance but feared the repercussions of publicly aligning with Him. Nicodemus, a Pharisee and member of the ruling council, first encountered Jesus under the cover of darkness, signifying his fear of political backlash (John 3:1–2). He listened to Jesus' teaching on being born again and silently absorbed the radical truth that spiritual rebirth transcends religious pedigree. Although Nicodemus continued attending council meetings skeptical of Jesus, his heart was evidently stirred by the Savior's words. Similarly, Joseph of Arimathea, a wealthy and respected member of the council, had quietly provided a burial site for Jesus, demonstrating both reverence and courage. By night, they had supported Jesus through covert means—Nicodemus by offering counsel and Joseph by preparing for His burial. Their initial motivations were like those of fans who quietly collect memorabilia or anecdotes about a beloved figure without risking open allegiance.

Yet as they witnessed Jesus' crucifixion, their hidden admiration transformed into a public act of devotion. Nicodemus brought a mixture of myrrh and aloes, a prescription for embalming, to anoint Jesus' body—an act that flagrantly defied the council's collective silence. Joseph, having secured permission from Pilate, wrapped Jesus in linen cloths and laid Him in his own new tomb. Together, they stepped out of shadows into the glaring light of public scrutiny. By handling Jesus' body with honor, they joined Mary Magdalene and the other women in demonstrating that true following demands courageous, even sacrificial, demonstration in solidarity with Christ's suffering and death. Their public identification with Jesus functions as a powerful rebuke to fans who remain content with superficial admiration. Instead of remaining silent when truth demands boldness, Joseph and Nicodemus risked social and political standing to honor their Lord. The reverberation of their actions extended beyond that Friday afternoon—Nicodemus later appears in Acts presenting a defense for his fellow Jewish believers, and Joseph's tomb became the very place where the disciples found an empty grave, confirming the resurrection. Their journeys from secret admiration to public discipleship model how even those entrenched in religious structures can be liberated by encountering the risen Christ. By transitioning from quiet interest to visible allegiance, they foreshadow the New Testament pattern in which followers of Jesus pay any cost rather than maintain hidden devotion. As Chapter 1 concludes these case studies, readers will be prepared to examine in Chapter 2 how crowds in the Gospels often demonstrated fan tendencies and what that means for distinguishing spectatorship from authentic following.

Conclusion

Having explored the tension between transient enthusiasm and steadfast allegiance, we recognize that modern fan culture can masquerade as genuine devotion. True discipleship, however, demands more than emotional resonance—it requires a willingness to renounce self, reorder relationships, steward resources sacrificially, and endure hardship with unwavering trust in God.

When we measure spiritual health by attendance figures or social-media engagement, we risk overlooking the quiet but powerful work of the Spirit in hearts committed to obedience over popularity. The biblical testimonies of Zacchaeus, the Samaritan woman, Joseph of Arimathea, and Nicodemus remind us that authentic encounters with Jesus lead to life-altering obedience and courageous witness. As we leave behind the culture of spectator faith and embrace a covenantal, cross-shaped journey, we prepare ourselves to respond to the Gospel's call with renewed seriousness. In the following chapter, we will examine how crowds in the Gospels often exhibited fan-like tendencies and contrast their reactions to Jesus with the unwavering devotion of true disciples. May this reflection propel each reader toward a faith marked not by sensational moments but by enduring transformation and steadfast love for Christ.

Chapter 2 — Fans in the Gospels: Crowd Enthusiasm without Commitment

Jesus' earthly ministry was marked by immense public fascination: multitudes gathered wherever He went, hungering for signs, wonders, and the promise of immediate relief from distress. Their enthusiastic pursuit of His presence—whether to witness a healing, receive a free meal, or marvel at His teachings—reflected genuine curiosity and hope amid political turmoil and religious rigidity. Yet beneath the surface of this fervor lay a pattern of fickleness. Many who cried "Hosanna" one day would shout "Crucify Him" the next, revealing that crowd enthusiasm often masked shallow allegiance. By examining these episodes in the Gospels, we see how the allure of miraculous provision and spectacle frequently eclipsed the deeper call to sacrifice, repentance, and radical faith. As Jesus warned, "Many are called, but few are chosen" (Matthew 22:14), underscoring that the path of true discipleship involves more than momentary excitement. This chapter invites readers to peer behind the waves of applause and pageantry to discern the ticking heartbeats of those who followed for signs rather than for substance. Through these narratives, we learn to identify where admiration ends and authentic commitment begins, and we are challenged to ask whether our own devotion rests on enduring truth or on transient thrills.

2.0 Setting the Scene: Crowds and Christ

2.0.a The Magnetic Pull of Jesus' Public Ministry The ministry of Jesus Christ drew throngs of people from various regions, ethnicities, and socioeconomic backgrounds because the reports of His healing and teaching spread rapidly. Crowds followed Him across dusty roads, seeking miraculous signs, physical restoration, or spiritual insight. The Gospel authors emphasize how Jesus' presence in towns like Capernaum, Bethsaida, and Chorazin ignited public fascination. Itinerant preachers were not uncommon in first-century Palestine, but Jesus' authority surpassed that of other rabbis; He spoke as One who possessed divine prerogative. When He taught on mountainsides or beside the Sea of Galilee, people leaned forward, eager to hear His words. His reputation for feeding the multitudes, calming storms, and raising the dead propelled pilgrimage-like journeys toward Him. As crowds amassed, Jesus often retreated to pray, indicating His awareness that public acclaim carried the risk of superficial devotion. Those in the crowds saw in Him a figure of hope amid Roman occupation, political unrest, and religious legalism. Pilgrims brought their sick, believing that touching the hem of His garment could effect healing (Luke 8:44). When He entered cities, the noise of the multitudes was likened to a rolling thunder, underscoring both excitement and confusion among the populace. This magnetism was fueled by reports of exorcisms that struck at the core fears of first-century folk, who viewed demonic oppression as an immediate spiritual threat. As word spread, even the elite scribes and Pharisees tracked His movements, suspecting that a challenge to their religious influence was underway. The raw energy of these gatherings sometimes escalated into near-riot conditions, forcing Jesus to dismiss crowds or travel to secluded places. Despite the disorderly excitement, He remained focused on His mission, warning that many who followed for free bread would later abandon the higher calling of abiding in His teaching (John 6:26–27). Throughout His travels, the juxtaposition of large crowds with His moments of solitude reveals a tension between public fascination and personal communion with the Father. As we consider the magnetism of Jesus' public ministry, we must ask whether our own attractions to charismatic leaders mirror this crowd mentality or point toward genuine devotion to Christ Himself. Reflecting on this dynamic naturally leads to the next consideration: the blessing that visibility brings and the burden of superficiality it carries.

2.0.b Blessing of Visibility, Burden of Superficiality Jesus' fame brought remarkable opportunities to preach the kingdom of God to wide audiences, offering healing, forgiveness, and guidance to those hungering for hope. His visibility functioned as a divine strategy to inform the multitudes about God's mercy and the inbreaking of His reign. Yet with increased exposure came the burden of superficial responses that often co-opted His message for agendas not aligned with the Father's will. While many came genuinely seekers, others were drawn by curiosity or desire for spectacle rather than repentance. Some were more interested in assessing His miraculous power than in hearing His call to radical transformation. For instance, when the Pharisees demanded signs from heaven (Matthew 16:1–4), their request was less a humble plea for truth and more a challenge aimed at discrediting Jesus under the guise of impartial inquiry. Similarly, the Herodians sought signs to confirm or refute Him based on political motivations, reflecting that visibility can attract insincere curiosity as much as authentic faith (Mark 8:15). In this light, Jesus' public ministry resembled a double-edged sword: it amplified the gospel but also amplified misunderstanding and resistance. When individuals expected Jesus to become a political king who would overthrow Rome, they missed His declaration that His kingdom was not of this world (John 18:36). As a result, crowds would hurl palms and acclamations one week and demand His crucifixion the next (John 12:13; 19:15). The blessing of mass attention thus risked degenerating into fickle fandom if hearts were not anchored in the truths He taught. Moreover, His visibility drew individuals who wished to test His power for selfish ends, as evidenced when people attempted to throw Him off a cliff in Nazareth after rejecting His message (Luke 4:28–30). In each instance, Jesus refused to pander to superficiality, instead prioritizing allegiance over applause. Through these repeated tensions, He modeled that genuine ministry cannot be reduced to popularity metrics or crowd size. As readers reflect on the burdens that accompany visibility, they will see echoes in contemporary ministries that grapple with balancing influence and integrity. This reflection sets the stage for examining how Galilean crowds, enthralled by miracles, often failed to grasp the substance behind the signs.

2.1 Galilean Spectators and Miracle Seekers

2.1.a Feeding of the Five Thousand (John 6:26) The narrative of the feeding of the five thousand stands as one of the most widely recognized miracles performed by Jesus, yet it also showcases the fine line between spectator fascination and genuine faith. As Jesus withdrew to a solitary place, crowds pursued Him across the Sea of Galilee's shores, drawn by the testimonies of healing and teaching. When He saw the vast multitude, He inquired of Philip, "Where shall we buy bread, so that these people may eat?" (John 6:5). Though Jesus knew the means by which He would feed the hungry crowd, He used Philip's hesitation to test the disciples' trust in divine provision. Then, having taken five barley loaves and two small fish from a boy, He gave thanks, distributed them, and satisfied all who were present, with twelve baskets of leftovers collected afterward. Initially, the people marveled, not at the spiritual teaching but at their physical need being met. They exclaimed, "This is indeed the Prophet who is to come into the world" (John 6:14), echoing Messianic expectations without fully revering Jesus' identity as the Son of God. By seeking Him for bread that perishes, they revealed a tendency to value instantaneous miracles over introspection. When Jesus later addressed them, urging them to labor not for perishable food but for the food that endures to eternal life, their enthusiasm waned (John 6:27). This reaction underscores how quickly crowds can shift from wonder at a sign to indifference toward the One who performed it. Their initial clamor to make Him king by force demonstrated that their loyalty was based less on the message He proclaimed and more on the deliverance they sought. In this scene, the feeding miracle serves as a litmus test: will individuals pursue Jesus for advancement of their own needs or follow Him to find true satisfaction? As we reflect on this episode, it becomes clear that seeking signs alone can divert hearts from the deeper substance of Jesus' identity and mission, paving the way for mass exodus when deeper demands arise. This realization leads to the next observation: crowds thirsting for signs often display a disinterest in the substance of discipleship.

2.1.b Thrill over Signs, Disinterest in Substance Crowds who witnessed miraculous signs often displayed fervent excitement but lacked the patience or willingness to engage with Jesus' teaching that would reshape their hearts forever. After being fed, many followed Him across the sea, hoping for another display of supernatural provision. Yet when Jesus began to speak about His flesh and blood as true food and drink—a concept that confounded even His closest companions—most turned away (John 6:53–66). Their enthusiasm for the spectacle of bread multiplication disintegrated when confronted with a teaching demanding a deeper, more personal commitment. Those who remained, like Andrew and Peter, recognized that Jesus possessed "the words of eternal life" (John 6:68), distinguishing themselves from spectators whose devotion was conditional upon continued miracles. This pattern of seeking impressive signs without embracing the rigorous demands of the kingdom reveals the precariousness of fan-like faith. Jesus lamented such fickleness, stating, "Do you want to go away as well?" (John 6:67), challenging even His disciples to examine whether they truly believed or merely craved sensational experiences. The fickle nature of a crowd's devotion becomes evident when circumstances shift or when their expectations remain unmet. In Gennesaret, after Jesus healed many, He withdrew, prompting the crowd to threaten violence, but when He left, they dispersed, seeking Him elsewhere (Mark 6:53–56). Their fixation on physical healing eclipsed their grasp of His identity as the Bread of

Life. When Jesus mulled over feeding them spiritually, some concluded His words were "a hard saying" and found them intolerable (John 6:60). The momentary thrill of miraculous provision dissipated into disappointment when deeper substance was required. This phenomenon warns believers not to conflate spiritual depth with entertainment value, as healthy faith prioritizes truth over spectacle. As we transition from Galilean spectators to political aspirants, note how crowd enthusiasm for deliverance often confuses political aspirations with genuine kingdom allegiance.

2.2 Political Aspirants Hoping for a Revolt Leader

2.2.a Palm Sunday Expectations of Liberation (Luke 19:37–38)
On the day we now celebrate as Palm Sunday, Jesus approached Jerusalem amid a cacophony of praise, riding on a donkey's colt in fulfillment of Zechariah's prophecy (Zechariah 9:9). The crowds laid down cloaks and palm branches, shouting "Blessed is the King who comes in the name of the Lord!" (Luke 19:38). Their shouts echoed David's coronation psalm (Psalm 118:26), yet many in that multitude misunderstood Jesus' kingship. Instead of recognizing Him as the suffering Messiah who would redeem humanity from sin, they expected a political liberator who would overthrow Roman rule and restore Davidic sovereignty. This expectation ignited fervor among zealots who saw in Jesus a rallying figure for nationalist aspirations. The praises were heartfelt but misdirected, as the crowd's understanding of God's kingdom remained largely earthly and temporal. Though Jesus wept over Jerusalem, lamenting that the city did not know the things that make for peace (Luke 19:41–42), the people clamored for deliverance from Rome more than deliverance from sin. Their enthusiasm represented a fleeting convergence of religious hope and political ambition, reflecting years of Messianic prophecies that promised a conquering King. As Jesus entered the temple courts, He overturned tables, challenging that very politicized vision by emphasizing justice and mercy over rebellion. Yet the crowd's initial adoration overshadowed this corrective. In their revelry, they failed to perceive that His kingdom was not established through swords but through sacrificial love.

Their misunderstanding encapsulates how crowds can conflate miraculous acts with political clout, thereby reducing Jesus' mission to an earthly agenda. As we ponder their shouts of "Hosanna," meaning "Save us now," we must ask whether our own cries for deliverance are rooted in a narrow self-interest that overlooks Jesus' broader redemptive purpose. This reflection prepares us to consider how these same crowd expectations collapsed under the weight of a crucifixion they misunderstood.

2.2.b Hosanna vs. Barabbas — Misreading the Kingdom Agenda
Just days after the Palm Sunday procession, the same crowd that hailed Jesus as King would cry out for His crucifixion, demanding the release of Barabbas, a known insurrectionist (Luke 23:18). Their voices swelled from acclaim to accusation, revealing how swiftly political hopes can devolve into mob mentality. Pilate offered to release Jesus as part of a Passover custom, but when the crowd persisted in choosing Barabbas, they demonstrated that their allegiance was opportunistic rather than rooted in understanding Jesus' identity. Barabbas represented armed rebellion against Rome; his release symbolized the crowd's preference for violent nationalism over the peaceful sovereignty Jesus embodied. This tragic reversal underscores the fickleness of masses that pursue Jesus for temporal gain but reject Him when He does not align with their political agenda. In choosing Barabbas, the crowd unknowingly condemned themselves to the very bondage they sought to escape, for the kingdom Jesus offered transcended military might and worldly liberation. The irony of shouts of "Hosanna" transforming into "Crucify Him!" (Luke 23:21) reveals the danger of aligning faith with shifting political winds. Their mistake lay in a superficial desire for a Messiah who would conform to their preconceptions of power. Yet Jesus' kingdom was not of this world, a reality they struggled to accept until the veil was torn and the new covenant inaugurated through His death and resurrection (John 18:36; Matthew 27:51). Viewing this transition invites modern readers to examine whether their own support for religious leaders is contingent on those leaders fulfilling personal or political desires. Just as the crowd misread Jesus' agenda, contemporary believers can

be lured into supporting causes that use Christ's name for convenience rather than advancing His kingdom purposes. As we move to examine how disciples like Peter violently resisted arrest in Gethsemane, we continue to see how political zeal can clash with divine restraint, challenging followers to recalibrate their understanding of Jesus' mission.

2.2.c Swords in the Garden: Militant Zeal Meets Divine Restraint (Matthew 26:51–54) In the Garden of Gethsemane, Peter drew a sword and cut off the ear of the high priest's servant, attempting to defend Jesus with violence (Matthew 26:51). This rash act emerged from a misunderstanding of Jesus' role as the Messiah: Peter believed that Jesus would establish God's kingdom through force, so he was prepared to fight for that cause. Yet Jesus rebuked Peter, declaring that those who live by the sword will die by the sword (Matthew 26:52). His rebuke underscored that His kingdom would be advanced not through military tactics but through sacrificial surrender. By touching Peter's ear to heal it (Luke 22:51), Jesus demonstrated that love and restoration, not aggression, define the kingdom's values. This scene reveals how even close disciples could harbor fan-like zeal that looked for political or forceful triumph rather than the humility and suffering that Jesus embraced. The divine restraint Jesus exhibited in Gethsemane contrasts sharply with the militants who sought insurrection, reminding us that God's agenda often subverts human expectations. As Jesus allowed Himself to be arrested without resistance, He modeled that submission to the Father's will—culminating in the cross—was the pathway to true victory. The crowd that would later praise Him with palms had little comprehension of this ethos; they sought a conqueror who would impose earthly liberation rather than a servant-Leader who would liberate souls. Peter's actions and Jesus' response invite readers to examine their own temptations to force outcomes or impose God's will by human means. Genuine discipleship, as modeled here, requires trusting God's sovereignty even when it seems to contradict our deepest desires for justice or vindication. This trust in divine strategy prepares us for the next moment of collapse: the dispersal of the twelve when fear overtook them.

2.2.d Disillusionment at Gethsemane and the Scatter of the Twelve (Mark 14:50) As Jesus faced betrayal and arrest in the Garden of Gethsemane, His disciples, who had once eagerly followed Him, fled in fear and confusion (Mark 14:50). Their earlier confidence, fueled by miraculous signs and hopes of a triumphant Messiah, evaporated when confronted with the grim reality of suffering and humiliation. The disciples' swift abandonment exposes how shallow enthusiasm can shutter when trials intensify. Peter, who had once professed unwavering loyalty, succumbed to fear and denied Jesus three times, revealing that his allegiance was more contingent than covenantal (Luke 22:54–62). The other disciples scattered, seeking self-preservation rather than solidarity with their Teacher. This abandonment illustrates that fan-like devotion offers little fortitude when adversity arises. In contrast, Jesus endured the isolation of betrayal and the agony of crucifixion, epitomizing the cost of true discipleship. His solitary path through suffering underscores that following Him may lead to rejection and loneliness rather than earthly acclaim. The disciples' flight also sets up the narrative of restoration in John 21, where Peter's brokenness becomes the soil for renewed purpose and vision. Their failure in Gethsemane is not the final word; instead, it underscores that genuine faith must mature beyond initial excitement. The disciples' experience invites modern readers to ask whether their own loyalties shift when pressures mount or if they remain anchored in the promises of God. As we transition from political aspirants to private seekers like Nicodemus, we see how individuals in the crowd moved from curiosity to deeper, though still incomplete, understanding of Jesus' mission.

2.3 Curious Nicodemus under Cover of Night

2.3.a Intellectual Fascination with the Teacher from God (John 3:1–2) Nicodemus approached Jesus under the cover of night, his footsteps cautious yet determined because he recognized Jesus as an extraordinary teacher whose signs attested to divine authority. Despite Nicodemus's status as a Pharisee and member of the Jewish ruling council, he was willing to set aside concerns about reputation to explore the claims surrounding Jesus. His inquiry, "Rabbi, we know that you are a teacher come from God, for no one can do these signs that you do unless God is with him" (John 3:2), reflected a mind eager to reconcile empirical evidence—miracles witnessed—with theological convictions. Nicodemus's fascination was fueled by genuine respect for the miraculous healings and authoritative teaching he had observed in public synagogues and open-air gatherings. As a Pharisee, he had been trained to prioritize Scripture and tradition, yet Jesus's power pushed him to consider that God's kingdom could be breaking through in ways he had never contemplated. While other religious leaders remained skeptical or hostile, Nicodemus demonstrated openness to new revelation. His nocturnal visit highlights the tension between intellectual curiosity and doctrinal caution; he sought to learn without risking open allegiance. In this initial exchange, Jesus unfolded truths about rebirth and the Spirit, revealing that entrance into God's kingdom required more than scholarly attainment—it demanded spiritual transformation (John 3:3–8). Nicodemus listened with rapt attention as Jesus explained that what is born of the flesh is flesh, and what is born of the Spirit is spirit. He wrestled inwardly with the paradoxical notion of being "born again," evidencing that his fascination extended beyond mere interest in healing miracles to the very heart of God's redemptive work. Yet even as he probed these mysteries, Nicodemus's approach remained intellectual; he asked how these things could possibly happen. He exemplified the type of spectator who admires divine signs but hesitates when confronted with demands that challenge theological presuppositions. His status and training gave him access to debate, but it also limited him from full-hearted reception. This dynamic raises questions for modern readers about whether admiration for spiritual phenomena substitutes for a willingness to embrace the transforming Word of God. Nicodemus's first visit, rooted in respect and fascination, sets the stage for his ongoing journey from hidden inquiry to visible action, underscoring that early fascination does not guarantee final commitment.

Nicodemus's nighttime audience with Jesus illustrates how intellectual intrigue can draw individuals toward truth while still keeping them partially hidden in the shadows. His fascination with Jesus as a divinely endorsed teacher propelled him to risk social standing, yet his fear of communal backlash kept him from confessing faith openly. The account concludes with Nicodemus silent after hearing Jesus's words, but his heart was stirred. He likely spent that night pondering the Lamb of God imagery and the necessity of new birth, wrestling with the dissonance between his religious identity and the call of Christ. He returned to the night again after the feeding of the five thousand, defending Jesus to skeptical Pharisees (John 7:50–52), an action suggesting that his intellectual fascination was maturing into protective solidarity. These developments reveal that true discipleship often begins with a mind awakened by evidence but must progress through stages of illuminated conscience and courageous witness. As Nicodemus's story unfolds, it reminds readers that intellectual fascination, while necessary, must be accompanied by trust and obedience to move from fan-like intrigue to authentic following.

2.3.b Risk Aversion and Secret Inquiry Nicodemus's decision to meet Jesus at night speaks volumes about his risk aversion, born from a position of both power and peril within Jewish society. As a member of the Sanhedrin, Nicodemus risked jeopardizing his social capital and invitation to important council meetings by associating with a controversial figure like Jesus (John 19:38). The cover of darkness provided a shield that allowed him to glean truth without the public scrutiny he feared during daylight. This nocturnal approach mirrors the actions of many who privately admire spiritual leaders yet hesitate to pledge open loyalty, revealing how protective instincts can restrict spiritual growth. Nicodemus's secret inquiry underscores the tension between the desire for truth and fear of social repercussions. In one sense, his status afforded him the means to investigate Jesus; in another sense, it bound him to institutional allegiances that discouraged open acceptance of a radical teacher. His initial request for secret conversation demonstrates that even those closest to power structures can be gravely curious about alternate visions of God's kingdom, though hesitant to break ranks. As Nicodemus probed deeper, Jesus gently challenged him to display open faith—stating that no one can see the kingdom of God unless they are born again (John 3:3). This insistence on public transformation clashed with Nicodemus's cautious nature, illustrating how risk aversion can hinder genuine commitment. Nicodemus had to weigh the potential loss of honor among peers against the prospect of gaining eternal life through surrender to Jesus. His hesitancy serves as a cautionary example for readers today who admire Christian teachers but hesitate to integrate their convictions into public life. Hidden curiosity risks settling for partial truth; full allegiance demands transparency. The humanity of Nicodemus comes alive in his reluctance to invite others into his spiritual journey, showing that moving from fan to follower requires moving from secrecy to fellowship.

This motif of risk aversion transitions into a larger theme: the gradual illumination of Nicodemus's faith as he steps from the shadows. While his initial foray into Jesus's presence was clandestine, his subsequent actions reveal that genuine intrigue can evolve into increasingly bold engagement. As Jesus later spoke openly in the temple courts, Nicodemus faced choices about whether to remain silent or speak truth to power. The contrast between his sheltered stance in John 3 and his courage in John 7 underscores the trajectory from private inquiry to public witness. By reflecting on Nicodemus's early risk aversion, readers can examine their own reluctance to take spiritual risks—whether that means challenging cultural norms, advocating justice, or stepping out of comfort zones for the sake of Christ. Recognizing that true discipleship often involves stepping into the light, even when the way forward looks perilous, sets the stage for Nicodemus's emergence as a lone voice in the council and eventual public solidarity at the tomb.

2.3.c A Lone Voice in the Council—Gradual Illumination (John 7:50–52) During the Feast of Tabernacles, Jesus's discourse in the temple stirred significant debate among the Jewish leaders. The Pharisees and chief priests grappled with the implications of His bold claims, questioning the legitimacy of His teaching and miracles. Though many in the council were eager to condemn Jesus, Nicodemus rose to defend due process, asking, "Does our law judge a man without first giving him a hearing and learning what he does?" (John 7:51). His intervention, though brief, marked a pivotal moment in his gradual illumination—transitioning from private curiosity to public defense of Jesus's right to be heard. In that charged atmosphere, Nicodemus risked ridicule from his peers by standing up for fair treatment. His reference to Mosaic law demonstrated his deep familiarity with Scripture and his willingness to apply legal principles even when they favored a controversial figure. Though the council rebuked him, Nicodemus persisted, embodying the emerging conviction that justice must be pursued over institutional consensus. His lone voice exposed the hypocrisy among leaders who sought to silence Jesus without due inquiry. This act of moral courage provided a small but significant crack in the wall of institutional resistance, showcasing how one individual's integrity can challenge a collective rush to judgment. Nicodemus's defense of Jesus operates as a signpost for readers to consider: do we stand up for truth when it conflicts with popular opinion? His gradual illumination reflects the reality that faith often unfolds through incremental steps—from hearing the Word in private to speaking on its behalf in public forums.

Nicodemus's shift from risk-averse secret seeker to lone defender in the council invites readers to emulate his posture of principled advocacy. Even though the council ultimately rejected his plea, Nicodemus's action signaled that his heart was aligning with Jesus's mission rather than the entrenched power structures. His willingness to invoke the law for a man labeled a heretic marked progress from his nighttime visit; it revealed that his prioritization of truth over tradition was deepening. This transition also demonstrates that illumination need not arrive in one dramatic moment; often, it emerges through successive steps of courage, obedience, and faithfulness. As Nicodemus continued to observe Jesus's ministry, his conviction grew, preparing him for the ultimate act of solidarity—joining Joseph of Arimathea at the cross. His witness in the council teaches modern followers that authentic discipleship may involve lonely stands for justice, even when one's voice trembles among peers. This point leads naturally into the culmination of Nicodemus's journey, where his public solidarity at the tomb seals his transformation from covert admirer to sacrificial ally.

2.3.d Public Solidarity at the Tomb—From Shadow to Sacrifice (John 19:39–40) In the aftermath of Jesus's crucifixion, the body lay exposed on Golgotha, its dignity seemingly lost to the elements. Nicodemus, no longer content to remain in anonymity, brought nearly one hundred pounds of myrrh and aloes—an expensive perfume mixture—to assist in Jesus's burial (John 19:39–40). This act of devotion transcended silent admiration; it required significant expenditure of personal resources and risked public backlash. In an era when lying with crucified criminals invited defilement concerns and social ostracism, Nicodemus embraced solidarity with a man condemned as a blasphemer. His decision to step out of the shadows into the public eye symbolized the culmination of his journey from curious observer to cost-bearing follower. By anointing Jesus's body, Nicodemus performed a priestly function, honoring Jesus as the Messiah he believed Him to be. This demonstration also signaled allegiance to God above human authority, as he joined Joseph of Arimathea in burying Jesus in a new tomb. Theologically, his action foreshadowed the significance of Jesus's body as a sacrificial offering, and his choice to counter cultural taboo by touching a corpse highlights the depth of his devotion. Nicodemus's presence at the tomb offered a counter-narrative to the crowd that once chanted "Crucify Him"; it testified to a radical shift in his allegiance. By choosing to honor Jesus publicly when doing so carried social stigma, Nicodemus embodied the essence of costly following— eschewing personal safety for the sake of worship. His solidarity stands as an enduring example that genuine faith often demands visible, sacrificial acts, even when they elicit disdain from former peers.

Nicodemus's transformation from secret inquirer to public ally illustrates how the process of following Christ often moves from hidden curiosity to open sacrifice. His bold act at the tomb contrasts sharply with earlier tendencies to avoid risk, demonstrating that true disciples emerge from shadows when love and conviction converge. In leaving behind the safety of anonymity, Nicodemus aligned himself with Jesus's death and participated in the early community's redemptive work, preparing a tomb that would soon boast an empty victory. His journey from darkness into the light underscores the principle that God's kingdom invites all who dare to follow beyond the comfort zone into arenas of cost and consequence. As Nicodemus returned from that tomb, carrying sweet-smelling spices, his heart likely burned with new understanding of the resurrection hope. His example challenges readers to reflect on whether they, too, are willing to step into public spaces of risk for the sake of honoring Christ, even when it means alienation or sacrifice.

2.4 Sign-Demanders and Spectacle Seekers

2.4.a Pharisees Ask for a Sign from Heaven (Matthew 16:1–4)

The Pharisees and Sadducees approached Jesus, requesting that He show them a sign from heaven to prove His authority. Their demand was not born of genuine curiosity or humble seeking, but from a position of presumption and spiritual hardness. They had witnessed numerous miracles—healing the blind, calming storms, raising the dead—yet remained unconvinced, demanding a celestial spectacle to satisfy their skepticism (Matthew 16:1). Jesus, perceiving their demand rooted in unbelief, rebuked them, stating, "An evil and adulterous generation seeks for a sign, but no sign will be given to it except the sign of the prophet Jonah" (Matthew 16:4). By referencing Jonah's three days in the belly of the fish as a foreshadowing of His own death and resurrection, Jesus highlighted that their fixation on sensationalism blinded them to the deeper redemptive work unfolding before them. The Pharisees' request for a heavenly sign reflected their preference for tangible proof over the call to faith that requires trust in the unseen (Hebrews 11:1). Their demand also exemplified how fan-like insistence on spectacle can mask spiritual arrogance and refusal to submit to God's revealed will. Rather than humbly acknowledging Jesus's miraculous works, they insisted on a personalized guarantee, thus insulting the Spirit's work among them. Their encounter with Jesus reminds modern readers that craving continuous entertainment or validation can erode genuine faith, as the heart grows cold when God's prior works are not enough. The rebuke Jesus delivered exposed their unwillingness to accept the sign already given—His sacrificial death and triumphant resurrection. As this episode draws to a close, readers must consider whether they, too, require constant reassurance rather than resting in God's past faithfulness. This point sets the stage to explore how even political figures like Herod Antipas sought sensational signs for mere curiosity, a pattern that similarly reveals hearts more attracted to spectacle than substance.

2.4.b Herod Antipas' Craving for a Miracle Show (Luke 23:8–9)
Herod Antipas, the tetrarch of Galilee, heard of Jesus's exploits and was both curious and expectant of a demonstration that would confirm royal claims. When Jesus was sent to Herod by Pilate, he hoped to witness a miraculous sign that would validate Jesus's reputation and possibly provide political leverage (Luke 23:8). Instead, Jesus remained silent, refusing to perform or engage in the pageantry of Herod's court. Herod and his soldiers dressed Jesus in a magnificent robe and mocked Him as "the king of the Jews," transforming His presence into a caricature rather than a testament to divine authority (Luke 23:11). The episode underscores how craving spectacle can distort the perception of truth, as Herod's fascination with wonder overshadowed any genuine desire for repentance or spiritual insight. Having seen no miraculous sign, Herod sent Jesus back to Pilate with derision, demonstrating that his interest in Christ was superficial, rooted in entertainment rather than genuine recognition of God's work. Unlike the grieving Nicodemus, Herod's curiosity dissipated when Jesus refused to cater to his expectations. Through this encounter, Luke depicts Herod as emblematic of those who treat Jesus like an on-stage performer, hoping for displays that amuse rather than confront. Herod's treatment of Jesus as a novelty rather than the Messiah contrasts sharply with the deeply devotional acts of those who followed at personal cost. This behavior warns readers that political or social

curiosity about Jesus often lacks the humility to bow before His sovereign will. Herod's response also foreshadows the fickleness of audience interests when spectacle fades, prompting us to reflect on how easily modern admirers can skip from one viral sensation to another without genuine engagement.

Herod's encounter with Jesus illustrates a deeper spiritual lethargy, where even a ruler's curiosity fails to translate into authentic worship. His demand for a show reveals a heart uninterested in truth unless it affirm his own agendas or pique idle fascination. Modern parallels abound in audiences that flock to conferences or online events to see spiritual celebrities perform, yet rarely allow such encounters to transform the inner life or stir sacrificial obedience. The brief, anticlimactic meeting in Herod's court highlights that rejecting the humble humility of Christ—who came not to be served but to serve (Mark 10:45)—leads to spiritual emptiness, regardless of the exposure one receives. Herod's craving for a miracle show, unmet, led only to mockery, not to awe or repentance. Reflecting on this passage encourages readers to examine their own desires for signs and wonders rather than solid Food that endures to eternal life (John 6:27). This reflection points forward to how Jesus refused to entertain those who demanded signs, resisting the pressure to turn divine truth into mere spectacle.

2.4.c Refusal to Entertain: Jesus Leaves Them Wanting (Mark 8:11–13) When the Pharisees came seeking a sign to test Jesus, He sighed deeply and expressed frustration with their demand, refusing to perform a spectacle merely to satisfy their skepticism (Mark 8:11–12). His refusal was not a denial of power but a rebuke of their unbelieving hearts. Jesus understood that those who crave signs often do so to confirm biases rather than to be transformed by truth. He reiterated that no sign would be given except the sign of Jonah, pointing toward the ultimate display of His resurrection (Matthew 12:39–40). After His silence, the Pharisees departed, but Jesus, perceiving their hardness of heart, cautioned His disciples against the "leaven of the Pharisees," referring to their corrupting influence and insincere faith (Mark 8:15). This confrontation reveals how

Jesus consistently turned away from demands that reduced His mission to entertainment, instead channeling focus toward His redemptive work on the cross and the resurrection that would validate His identity. Despite the Pharisees' persistence, Jesus refused to deliver shallow proofs; He called for deeper faith rooted in His word. Their reaction—leaving without pressing further—demonstrates how easily people can give up on the search for truth when it demands more than spectacle. It also underscores that Jesus valued genuine transformation over superficial fascination. The disciples' silence in response to Jesus's stern rebuke indicates their growing awareness that faith requires more than witnessing miracles; it demands trust in the unseen purposes of God (Hebrews 11:1). Moreover, by rejecting the Pharisees' pressure, Jesus set a pattern for believers to resist cultural demands that reduce faith to a commodity. He showed that living water, not spectacle, sustains the soul, challenging modern readers to evaluate the sources from which they derive spiritual nourishment.

Jesus' departure from the crowd hungry for signs leaves modern audiences with a stark reminder: the quest for entertainment can stifle the reception of life-giving truth. Those who demand more wonders than provided often drift away, having failed to grasp the deeper significance of even the signs given. As Scripture records, many who followed Jesus for miraculous bread stopped following when He turned their focus to the bread of life (John 6:66). This narrative serves as a prophetic caution: when faith is built on sensationalism rather than substance, it lacks the depth to endure. By refusing to entertain shallow demands, Jesus revealed the radical nature of His kingdom—one that does not pander to popular expectations but summons hearts into sacrificial discipleship. This posture of refusal invites readers to examine whether their spiritual journeys gravitate toward experiences or toward encountering the living Word, pointing directly to the larger dynamics of crowd manipulation that emerge under Pilate's governance.

2.5 From Adoration to Rejection: The Crowd before Pilate

2.5.a Manipulated Masses Cry "Crucify Him" (Mark 15:11-14) As Pilate stood before the crowd, he offered the customary release of a prisoner to the people during Passover. Instead of advocating for Jesus, the chief priests stirred the crowd to demand Barabbas's release and to insist on Jesus's crucifixion (Mark 15:11-12). Having observed Jesus heal the sick, cast out demons, and proclaim truth, the crowds now shouted for His death, manipulated by religious leaders who twisted public opinion to protect their own status. The majoritarian voice, amplified by priests and scribes, morphs into a baying mob that equates Jesus with insurrection, even though He explicitly taught love for enemies and humility (Matthew 5:44; Matthew 11:29). Their cries of "Crucify him!" (Mark 15:13) reveal how easily crowds can be swayed from one extreme to another—praising one day only to demand execution the next. Pilate, though hesitant and finding no guilt in Jesus, succumbed to political pressure, washing his hands as though to absolve himself of responsibility while granting the mob's will (Matthew 27:24). This scene captures the fragility of popular piety: what began as genuine marvel at miracles and teaching devolved into a collective demand for bloodshed, fueled by fear and self-interest. The crowd's transformation from spectators to executioners demonstrates how public opinion can be weaponized, blinding individuals to truth and justice. Their fickleness served as a stark contrast to the unwavering devotion of those who remained steadfast at the foot of the cross, underscoring that crowds often seek immediate gratification or safety rather than enduring commitment. As readers consider this tragic reversal, they must ask whether their own loyalties shift with cultural winds or stand firm when confronted with unpopular obedience. This reflection prepares us to examine how the choice of Barabbas over Jesus reveals the crowd's final betrayal.

2.5.b Choosing Barabbas: The Fan's Final Betrayal Pilate presented two figures to the people: Jesus, the itinerant Rabbi heralded for compassion, and Barabbas, a notorious prisoner guilty of insurrection and murder (Mark 15:7). The crowd, biased by the religious elite, demanded Barabbas's release and Jesus's crucifixion, swallowing the distorted portrait of Jesus as a dangerous revolutionary. Their decision to free Barabbas—a figure who had led violent rebellion against Roman rule—reveals that their priorities were political expediency and preservation of the status quo rather than truth and justice. In choosing a convict over the sinless Son of God, the crowd embodied the tragic irony that often accompanies fan-like devotion: they preferred a familiar mode of rebellion to the radical redefinition of rebellion Jesus embodied, which was rooted in peace and humility (Matthew 5:9). Their choice underscores the hollowness of a faith based on emotional fervor rather than grounded in discernment. Barabbas, as a symbol of misguided zeal, highlights how crowds can confuse signs of strength—violent uprising—with genuine strength, which Christ demonstrated through sacrificial love (John 13:1–17). The crowd's final betrayal fulfilled Isaiah's prophecy that the Messiah would be "despised and rejected by men" (Isaiah 53:3), though they did so unwittingly. Their clamor for Barabbas instead of Jesus suggests that many were not seeking divine deliverance but a chance to maintain control within an oppressive system. This moment crystallizes the theme that fan-like allegiance provides no safeguard when loyalty demands self-sacrificial alignment with truth. By choosing Barabbas, the crowd sealed its fate, illustrating that popularity and momentum can lead to moral catastrophe when unmoored from the Word of God. As we transition to explore the broader psychology of mass movements, the choosing of Barabbas stands as a cautionary example of how collective choice can trump individual conscience.

2.5.c Mob Psychology and the Fragility of Popular Piety The willingness of the crowd to pivot from adoration to condemnation reveals how mob psychology can distort moral judgment. Individuals caught in a group dynamic often prioritize conformity over conscience, amplifying calls for action without fully understanding the reality of the choices before them. In Pilate's courtyard, what began as an interest in the man who performed miracles became a collective rage for blood, fed by echoing cries that drowned out voices of reason. The anonymity granted by the masses emboldened participants who might have resisted in private, underscoring the way crowds enable behavior that individuals would reject on their own. The chief priests manipulated this dynamic, exploiting fear of Roman reprisal to stoke the fires of hatred. As Christians reflect on the fragility of popular piety, they must acknowledge how easily admiration can turn to vilification when public pressure overrides individual discernment. The transformation of a crowd from spectators enthralled by miracles to executioners demanding death highlights the peril of a faith built on transient emotions. Popular piety, while seemingly powerful, can dissipate as quickly as it arises when underlying convictions are absent. The same crowds who greeted Jesus with palm branches one day turned their backs and demanded His agony the next, demonstrating that communal sentiment is fickle when not grounded in solid conviction. This sobering reality challenges readers to examine whether their own allegiances withstand scrutiny or are susceptible to prevailing winds of opinion. The lessons of mob psychology remind us that true discipleship requires standing firm in convictions even when the majority sways against truth. As we leave behind the spectacle of Pilate's courtyard, we prepare to turn our attention to those who refused to follow the crowd—individuals whose steadfast devotion contrasts sharply with the fickle throngs and who point us toward the pathway of authentic discipleship.

Having detailed the various ways crowds in the Gospels exhibited fan-like enthusiasm without committed loyalty, we move next to explore individuals who, though initially drawn by curiosity or compelled by circumstances, embody the depth of authentic following.

Conclusion

The Gospels present a stark portrait of crowds whose allegiance wavered when the demands of discipleship became clear. The same masses that flocked to Jesus for healing bread balked when called to embrace Him as the "Bread of Life" (John 6:35), and the crowds that anointed Him king could not endure the scandal of a Savior who would lay down His life. Their pattern reminds us that mere attraction to miracles or popular acclaim cannot withstand the trials that true following requires. Yet amid this tapestry of fickle faith, we also glimpse individuals who reject superficial spectacle in favor of costly surrender—signals that genuine devotion waits in the wings. As we move forward, the challenge is not simply to avoid the pitfalls of crowd mentality but to cultivate hearts that seek the enduring presence of Christ above all else. May these lessons sharpen our awareness of where we stand—whether on the shifting sands of fan enthusiasm or on the solid rock of heartfelt, sacrificial discipleship (Matthew 7:24–25).

Chapter 3 — Old-Testament Typology: Spectators of God's Works

From the moment Israel emerged from Egyptian bondage, the pattern of marveling at divine intervention without fully embracing God's ways recurred with disheartening frequency. At Sinai, the people eagerly affirmed covenant vows, only to fashion a golden calf when their leader tarried on the mountain (Exod 24:3; 32:1–4). In the wilderness, daily manna proved insufficient to sustain thankful hearts, as complaints about food revealed deeper issues of trust and ingratitude (Exod 16:2–3). Even prophetic pronouncements meant to jolt the nation toward genuine devotion—Isaiah's condemnation of empty worship (Isa 29:13) and Amos's plea for justice instead of hollow festivals (Amos 5:21–24)—often fell on deaf ears, demonstrating that ritual alone could not transform hardened hearts. As the judges arose, Israel's recurring cycles of victory and idolatry highlighted how fleeting zeal, once flickering, extinguished the very hope it had kindled (Judg 21:25). Solomon's majestic temple, intended as a tangible sign of God's presence, became a backdrop for syncretistic worship the moment his heart divided (1 Kgs 8; 11:1–8). These narratives, culminating in exile, paint a vivid portrait of a people prone to witness God's wonders yet reluctant to embody His righteousness. Yet woven through every failure and restoration promise is the thread of a greater design: each episode points forward to the fulfillment in Christ, where shadows give way to substance and divine presence dwells within transformed hearts. By examining Israel's journey from Sinai to exile and beyond, we grasp enduring lessons about the allure of spectacle, the peril of empty ritual, and the necessity of inward renewal that sets the stage for the New Covenant's realization.

3.0 Setting the Stage: Typology and Testimony

3.0.a Thematic Bridge from Gospel Crowds to Israel's Story The Gospels reveal crowds who flocked to Jesus for signs and wonders yet often failed to follow Him when deeper demands were made. This pattern echoes back to the Exodus narrative, where Israel witnessed divine interventions yet repeatedly drifted away from wholehearted devotion. By tracing these parallels, we see that human hearts are prone to admire God's works without truly embracing His ways. The Exodus generation heard God's voice at Sinai and saw the cloud and fire that led them, yet they still solicited the worship of a golden calf (Exod 32:1–6). Just as many in Jesus' day celebrated the feeding of the five thousand but walked away when teaching became difficult (John 6:60–66), so Israel accepted bread from heaven but complained when manna ceased to be a new novelty (Exod 16:2). Understanding these linkages helps us discern how superficial fascination can mask a deeper spiritual lethargy. Typology invites readers to recognize that the patterns of wandering and worship in Israel shed light on the choices faced by New-Testament crowds. This thematic bridge underscores that the call to genuine discipleship transcends covenant eras; both Israel and the church stand under God's unchanging call to obedience. By connecting Gospel crowds to Old-Testament participants, we prepare our hearts to learn from ancient testimony and to guard against repeating their failures. This awareness compels us to examine whether we, like Israel, are spectators of God's grace or participants in His covenant mission.

The juxtaposition of Sinai and Galilee compels a sober recognition: visible displays of divine power do not guarantee transformed lives. As we transition from examining gospel crowds to exploring Israel's wilderness journey, it becomes clear that the same yearning for spectacle drives both. While Jesus offered Himself as the Bread of Life (John 6:35), Israel consumed manna but soon found it mundane. This shift from wonder to weariness illuminates how quickly hearts can harden when experiences replace enduring faith. As we move into the narrative of Sinai, we will explore how Israel's acclamation of God's covenant at Sinai (Exod 24:3) was followed by swift regression to idolatry (Exod 32:1–6), revealing the precarious balance between worship and willful rebellion.

3.0.b Corporate Memory, Covenant Mercy, and the Anatomy of Drift The Exodus account is steeped in moments where Israel's corporate memory both fortified and failed them. As Moses ascended Sinai to receive the Law, the people below declared, "All that the Lord has spoken we will do" (Exod 24:3). This collective vow signaled an acute awareness of God's covenant mercy, for they had witnessed plagues, deliverance, and provision. Yet within days, that same community fractured under pressure, fashioning a golden calf to worship—an act of willful amnesia toward the Red Sea deliverance and Sinai theophany (Exod 32:1–6). The anatomy of this drift reveals that corporate memory, unaccompanied by personal, heart-level commitment, is insufficient to withstand trials. When hardships surfaced, their remembrance of mercy was overshadowed by the lure of false security in tangible idols. Centuries later, prophets would lament Israel's failure to remember God's acts (Isa 63:11–14), diagnosing a widespread phenomenon of ritualistic remembrance devoid of inward devotion. This pattern of spectacular deliverance followed by moral failure demonstrates that covenant mercy does not negate the human tendency to drift. As we move from the initial covenant moments at Sinai to the challenges in the wilderness, we will observe how daily dependence on God's provision—manna—was quickly supplanted by grumbling and unbelief (Num 14:1–4). In doing so, we will discern how corporate memory must be reinforced by active faith lest the anatomy of drift repeat in our own hearts.

The prophetic literature further underscores that Israel's drift was not merely historical happenstance but a theological pattern anticipated by God's messengers. Isaiah's critique of empty worship (Isa 29:13) and Amos's condemnation of religious festivals devoid of justice (Amos 5:21–24) reveal that the combination of corporate memory and covenant mercy can paradoxically breed complacency when genuine obedience is lacking. Thus, our exploration of Sinai leads seamlessly into the wilderness, where Israel's struggles with manna and disbelief exemplify the enduring challenge of turning divine experiences into lasting faith. As we proceed to the next section, we carry this insight: remembering God's mercy must lead to repentance and renewed covenantal allegiance rather than serve as a mere historical footnote.

3.1 Israel at Sinai: Acclaim without Obedience

3.1.a The Shout of Covenant Consent (Exod 24:3) At Sinai, Moses assembled Israel at the foot of the mountain and read to them all the words of the Lord, prompting an emphatic response: "All that the Lord has spoken we will do and be willing to obey" (Exod 24:3). Their unified shout underscores the communal dimension of covenant consent, reflecting both gratitude for deliverance and hope for divine guidance. In that moment, the people recognized God as their sovereign Redeemer, entrusted to lead them into new life. Their readiness to obey indicated a promising beginning for a nascent nation freshly liberated from Egyptian bondage. The significance of this collective vow extended beyond mere verbal affirmation; it signaled the formation of a corporate identity bound by divine law. Moses sprinkled the blood of sacrificial offerings on the altar and on the people, ceremonially sealing the covenant (Exod 24:8). As they beheld the divine glory on the mountain, they saw a preview of God's holiness and understood that their accession to the covenant came at the price of life itself. Yet beneath the surface of this jubilant moment dwelt an unspoken question: would this people heart remain as steadfast as their declaration? The grandeur of theophany, with thunder, lightning, and trumpet blast, stamped the seriousness of divine commitment on their memory (Exod 19:16–19). However, such dramatic encounters can mask inward frailty if not followed by deep-rooted worship and obedience. As the Israelite camp buzzed with excitement, Moses lingered on the mountain, absorbing both instruction and glory—a foreshadowing of the mediator's role in bridging divine holiness and human frailty. This scene invites reflection on how moments of spiritual high can easily be accompanied by blind spots that surface later in the narrative.

The covenant meal that followed, where Moses, Aaron, Nadab, Abihu, and seventy elders ate and drank in the presence of God (Exod 24:9–11), served to dramatize the intimacy intended in this relationship. The invitation to feast in God's presence signified that obedience was never meant to be a burdensome task but a pathway to ongoing communion. Yet Israel's consent, though fervent, had not yet endured the testing of practical obedience. As we transition to examine the subsequent golden-calf regression, we see that verbal vows can quickly dissipate when trials and temptations arise. The reality of obedience would be tested not in the shadow of Sinai but in the day-to-day challenges that awaited them beyond the mountain.

3.1.b Golden-Calf Regression (Exod 32:1–6) While Moses remained on Sinai to receive the tablets of stone, the people grew impatient, fearing prolonged absence of their mediator (Exod 32:1). Their eagerness devolved into frantic demand: "Come, make us gods who shall go before us" (Exod 32:1). Under Aaron's reluctant leadership, they demanded gold from their own jewelry to craft a calf, declaring, "These are your gods, O Israel, who brought you up out of the land of Egypt" (Exod 32:4). This idolatrous act constituted a brutal betrayal of the covenant they had just affirmed. The calf, a symbol reminiscent of Egyptian worship (Exod 32:4), starkly contradicted the command against graven images (Exod 20:4–5). Their regression reveals how quickly acclaim at Sinai shifted to apostasy when faced with the absence of visible leadership. The revelry that followed, with burnt offerings and dancing, masqueraded as worship but was fundamentally a denial of the true God. Moses's descent from the mountain, tablets in hand, confronted this scene of debauchery, thrusting into sharp relief the gravity of their betrayal (Exod 32:15–19). The idolaters' inability to wait for divine instruction speaks to a deeper craving for tangible affirmation rather than trust in unseen promises. This lapse occurred despite the ear-splitting trumpet and cloud that had stamped Sinai as God's holy domain. Their worship of a golden idol laid bare the superficial layer of devotion, demonstrating that external proclamations of faith can mask an inner hardness. As we reflect on Israel's swift backslide, we must ask whether our own devotional declarations are equally fragile when routine gives way to impatience.

The narrative of the golden calf also underscores Aaron's compromised leadership: though he protested the people's demands, he ultimately capitulated, fashioning the image they craved (Exod 32:2–5). This failure of leadership illustrates that fan-like obedience to popular demand can erode even those entrusted with guiding the community. While Moses embodies the ideal of intercession— pleading for mercy and seeking restoration (Exod 32:11–14)— Aaron's accommodation of the crowd's idolatry demonstrates how compliance with public pressure can lead to collective sin. The catastrophic fallout, where thousands perished from the plague (Exod 32:35), serves as a stark warning that a moment of idolatrous revelry can exact devastating consequences. As this section draws to a close, we see how Israel's acclaim at Sinai was swiftly inverted into outright rebellion, highlighting the urgent need for sustained obedience rather than intermittent enthusiasm. This sets the tone for reflecting on how the initial covenant encounter failed to permeate their wilderness journey, where daily provision from heaven would be met with daily complaints.

3.1.c Ratification Meal and Shared Vision (Exod 24:9–11) Before the golden-calf episode, Moses, Aaron, Nadab, Abihu, and seventy elders of Israel ascended partway up Mount Sinai and beheld divine glory (Exod 24:9–11). In this sacred tableau, they encountered a vision of God that transcended human experience: beneath His feet lay a pavement of sapphire, clear as the sky itself. The invitation to "see the God of Israel" offered an intimacy reserved for spiritual leaders, testifying to the seriousness of the covenant. There, in the rarefied atmosphere of divine presence, they celebrated a sacrificial meal, eating bread and drinking wine in communion with the Lord. This ratification meal symbolized not just consent to divine law but the establishment of a shared vision oriented toward God's holiness and justice. Their participation in the feast signaled inclusion in obedience, as each participant became a covenant representative for the wider community. This moment underscores that worship involves both encounter and embodiment—witnessing God's glory and internalizing His instructions. The communal aspect of the meal modeled that obedience is not a solitary endeavor but a shared pilgrimage with mutual accountability. Yet, this profound shared vision was not destined to endure, for the later events at the golden calf demonstrate that even privileged access to God's presence could not prevent apostasy. The meal's symbolism, akin to a foretaste of the eschatological banquet, would later be echoed in prophetic promises of a renewed covenant (Isa 25:6;Jer 31:12). As readers contemplate this scene, they are invited to consider how moments of deep worship should imprint our communal memory, forging resilience in the face of future temptations. However, as Israel's story unfolds, we will see how the contrast between this sacred meal and subsequent rebellion highlights the peril of fleeting devotion.

The shared vision at Sinai also underscores the role of mediated leadership. While Moses and the elders communed directly with God, they bore the weighty responsibility of translating that encounter to the people. Their return to the camp, tasked with transmitting divine decrees, exemplified how vision must be accompanied by faithful teaching. Yet the inevitable failure to sustain this vision reveals that prophetic insight, without continuous reinforcement, can dissipate amid the everyday grind. As the ratification meal fades into memory, Israel's inability to cling to that glimpse of divine glory—opting instead for a golden idol—exposes the fragility of human commitment. This dynamic primes us to understand why, in the wilderness, daily dependence on God's provision did not produce lasting gratitude, but instead provoked repeated complaining.

3.1.d Tabernacle Blueprints and Delayed Discipleship (Exod 25–31) Following their dramatic covenant ratification, God provided Moses with detailed instructions for constructing the Tabernacle, a portable sanctuary that would house His presence among the people (Exod 25–31). The blueprint encompassed intricate designs for the ark of testimony, the table of showbread, the golden lampstand, and the altar—all signifying the holiness and accessibility of God's presence. Though these instructions were intended to shape Israel's worship and daily rhythms, the people's commitment to execute them faithfully was tested by subsequent events. The Tabernacle's design required skilled artisans—Bezaleel and Aholiab—endowed with wisdom and creativity by the Spirit (Exod 31:1–6). Their appointment signals that God invests His people with gifts to facilitate genuine worship, yet the provision of talented leaders does not guarantee communal obedience. As we consider these tabernacle blueprints, we recognize that God sought to dwell among His people, not as a distant deity but as an engaged, communal God. The meticulous nature of the instructions points to a theology that intertwines ritual with relationship: every cloth, rod, and oil had spiritual significance. However, the delay in constructing the Tabernacle—interrupted by Israel's idolatry at the golden calf—reveals that even divine provision and meticulous guidance can be sidelined when hearts drift. The thwarted discipleship of Israel in this period teaches that God's provision of resources and leadership must be met with willing obedience to yield lasting transformation. As we reflect on the Tabernacle's intended role, we discern that its ultimate fulfillment in Christ—a living Temple (1 Pet 2:4–5; John 2:19–21)—would eclipse the portable structure. Yet Israel's delayed commitment to build the Tabernacle highlights how necessary it is to move from hearing divine instruction to embodying it consistently.

The Tabernacle blueprints also function as a teaching tool, illustrating how God's presence and holiness govern communal life. As Israel journeyed through the wilderness, the Tabernacle served as a constant reminder that genuine worship requires care, intention, and reverence. However, the people's failure to prioritize its construction reflects a failure to internalize its theological import. This delayed discipleship parallels their later reluctance to enter the Promised Land, signifying that hearing and seeing God's provision does not automatically yield courageous obedience. As we transition to the next section on the wilderness generation, we will see that the same hearts that struggled to build a sanctuary to God also struggled to trust Him for daily manna, revealing the depth of their spiritual drift.

3.2 Wilderness Generation: Manna Fans, Mission Failures

3.2.a Daily Provision Yet Daily Complaints (Exod 16) As Israel embarked on their desert trek from Sinai toward Canaan, they quickly faced the harsh reality of life in the wilderness. In response to their murmurings about hunger, God promised to rain bread from heaven—manna—each morning (Exod 16:4). This daily provision, described as white like coriander seed and tasting like wafers with honey (Exod 16:31), exemplified God's faithfulness to care for His people's needs. Despite this generous miracle, the Israelites frequently complained of their circumstances, longing for the varied diet of Egypt rather than content with the miraculous sustenance provided by God (Exod 16:3). Their grumbling reveals a deeper spiritual malaise: they valued the memory of earthly comfort more than the present reality of divine provision. Each day's supply of manna came with an invitation to trust in God's consistency, yet their hearts craved autonomy over their circumstances. The requirement to gather only enough for each day (Exod 16:4–5) was intended to teach reliance on God rather than hoarding security. Yet some disobeyed, storing leftover manna that bred worms and stank (Exod 16:20), a stark demonstration that greed can corrupt even God's blessings. As Joshua and Caleb would later exhort the people to trust God for Canaanite provision, the pattern of distrust set here in the wilderness undermined their confidence (Num 14:6–9). Their fixation on material comfort served as a barrier to shaping a resilient faith that could endure trials. In this way, the manna narrative foreshadowed the deeper lesson that miraculous provision, when misused or taken for granted, can become a catalyst for spiritual decline. This daily cycle of miracle and murmur reminds us that consistency in God's care should lead to gratitude rather than grumbling.

As we reflect on these episodes, we recognize that the wilderness journey was designed to graduate Israel from dependence on Egyptian bondage to mature trust in Yahweh. Yet their agitation over food expectations reveals that the transition was far from seamless. The Israelites' inability to appreciate manna as a gift, rather than a right, demonstrates how quickly divine generosity can be overshadowed by consumerist impulses. This dynamic sets the stage for their more consequential failure at Kadesh-barnea, where distrust of God's promises would bar an entire generation from entering the Promised Land. As we move to examine their unbelief, we see that the daily manna, while miraculous, was insufficient to renew hearts that clung to past securities.

3.2.b Unbelief at Kadesh-barnea (Num 14:1–4) When Israel reached Kadesh-barnea, the people sent twelve spies to survey the land of Canaan, seeking assurances of victory (Num 13:2, 17–20). Though they returned with evidence of fruitful land and fortified cities, ten spies decried it as insurmountable, declaring, "We seemed to ourselves like grasshoppers, and so we seemed to them" (Num 13:33). Their report fueled widespread fear, leading the congregation to complain and long to return to Egypt rather than trust God's promise (Num 14:2–4). The palpable despair among the people reflected a deep-seated unbelief that overshadowed God's prior acts: deliverance from Egypt, parting of the Red Sea, and daily manna. Their murmuring, which they repeated with vehemence, revealed that hope rooted in God's word had been eclipsed by a fixation on perceived obstacles. This collective refusal to trust God's sovereign plan triggered severe consequences: God vowed that none of that generation, except Joshua and Caleb, would see the Promised Land (Num 14:22–23). Their unbelief at Kadesh-barnea illustrates a crucial lesson: proximity to God's provision does not guarantee trust in His promises. The very people who had tasted manna and witnessed countless signs faltered when confronted with the prospect of conquest. Their self-perception as weak undercut a posture of faith, demonstrating that worldview, not outward experience, governs how we respond to divine directives. This episode underscores that God's call to enter the inheritance requires a posture of trust that embraces God's perspective over human assessment. As we transition to the story of fiery serpents, we see how God's discipline sought to awaken a hardened generation to the perils of unbelief.

3.2.c Fiery Serpents and Bronze Remedy (Num 21:4–9) As Israel journeyed from Mount Hor toward Edom, they again spoke against God and Moses, lamenting the lack of food and water as they hated the "miserable food" of manna (Num 21:4–5). In response to their grumbling, God sent fiery serpents among the people, whose bites inflicted painful death (Num 21:6). When the people repented and begged Moses to intercede, God commanded Moses to make a bronze serpent and lift it on a pole; those bitten would live if they looked at it (Num 21:8–9). This provision of a remedy through an unlikely medium—gazing on a hiss-producing idol—challenged Israel's faith to move from complaining to trusting God's instruction for healing. The bronze serpent, later called "Nehushtan" in David's time (2 Kgs 18:4), symbolized both judgment for sin and the means of divine grace. It echoed the principle that looking to God's appointed means would bring life, foreshadowing Christ's crucifixion, where looking in faith brings spiritual healing (John 3:14–15). Yet the ease with which Israel shifted from repentance to subsequent complaisance reveals that even miraculous rescue can be fleeting if hearts remain prone to distrust. Their failure to internalize the significance of God's mercy resulted in repeated cycles of sin and deliverance. This incident underscores that, while God's grace is available in times of peril, genuine transformation requires an enduring posture of faith that transcends immediate relief. As the wilderness narrative unfolds, this pattern of judgment and provision anticipates future murmuring, reminding us that repeated exposure to grace does not insure spiritual maturity.

3.2.d Balaam's Oracles vs. Israel's Fear (Num 22–24) In parallel to the physical journey through the wilderness, Balaam, a pagan prophet, was summoned by Balak, king of Moab, to curse Israel. Despite Balak's enticement with rewards, God commanded Balaam not to curse the people, for they were blessed (Num 22:12). As Balaam attempted to proceed, God thwarted him by using the mouth of Balaam's donkey to warn him of angelic opposition (Num 22:28–30). Eventually, Balaam, under compulsion, pronounced blessings over Israel instead of curses, declaring that "those who bless you are blessed, and those who curse you are cursed" (Num 24:9). The potency of these oracles highlighted Israel's divine election and the futility of opposing God's purposes. Yet despite such unambiguous supernatural interventions, Israel's fear would later lead them astray, succumbing to Moabite temptation and Baal worship (Num 25:1–3). Their capitulation to fear and pagan influence demonstrates how even prophetic assurances cannot override a heart that clings to worldly security. The contrast between Balaam's God-directed utterances and Israel's subsequent compromise underscores that hearing God's Word does not suffice unless it is embraced wholeheartedly. Moreover, the narrative reveals that God can use controversial figures to affirm His covenant even when His own people falter. As we reflect on Balaam's oracles, we see that Israel's fear at Kadesh-barnea reemerges here in a different form: a willingness to compromise holiness for perceived peace. This dynamic illustrates that consistent faith requires a resilient trust that withstands both external threats and internal yearnings for comfort. As this section closes, we anticipate how these wilderness episodes light the path toward understanding prophetic critiques of superficial worship in the ensuing chapters.

We will next explore how the prophets later condemned the lingering spectatorial tendencies that undercut genuine devotion, calling the people back to the heart of covenant faith rather than lip-service religion.

3.3 Prophetic Warnings against Lip-Service Religion

3.3.a Isaiah on Empty Worship (Isa 29:13) Isaiah's critique in chapter 29 sharply condemns the disconnect between Israel's external religious practices and their internal spiritual condition. The Lord declares, "These people draw near with their mouth and honor me with their lips, while their hearts are far from me" (Isa 29:13), exposing a performative piety that values ritual over relationship. The prophet's words underscore that God is not impressed by aesthetic displays of devotion when genuine obedience is absent. In the context of Jerusalem's temple-centric worship, the people had perfected their liturgical expressions—sacrifices, festivals, and temple sacrifices—yet they neglected justice, mercy, and humility in daily life. Isaiah's warning highlights that worship reduced to script and spectacle breeds complacency, fostering an illusion that ritual alone suffices. This chasm between mouth and heart had begun in the wilderness, where outward consent at Sinai (Exod 24:3–8) gave way to idolatrous regression (Exod 32:1–6). Isaiah's indictment reminds us that divine presence cannot be contained by external forms when hearts remain unchanged. His pronouncements call Israel to recognize that God's revelation demands a transformed inner life rather than adherence to mechanical religious routines.

The prophet's language is intentionally provocative, describing worshipers as those who "assemble as if they were bringing acceptable offerings" but whose "hands are full of blood" (Isa 1:11–15, cf. Isa 29:13). Isaiah exposes the hypocrisy of a populace that can recite prayers with flawless diction yet engage in social oppression, bribery, and deception. This prophetic tension between ritual competency and ethical failure serves as a perennial warning: genuine devotion to God must begin with a heart aligned to His character. Isaiah's own experience—visions of God's glory in the temple (Isa 6:1–5)—instructs that intimacy with God inevitably convicts of sin. His message calls for a radical inversion of priorities: rather than seeking God on their own terms through muted lips and empty gestures, Israel must seek Him with contrite spirits, confessing sin and pursuing righteousness. This transition from hollow ceremony to wholehearted worship lays the groundwork for Amos's even fiercer rebuke of festival fatigue and social injustice, demonstrating that God's displeasure extends beyond individual hypocrisy to corporate indifference. As we move to examine Amos's lament, we see that empty worship leads to ethical erosion, threatening the very foundation of covenant faith.

3.3.b Amos on Festival Fatigue (Amos 5:21–24) In his uncompromising critique of Israel's religious life, Amos confronts a people wearied by ritual yet unmoved by righteousness. The prophet declares, "I hate, I despise your feasts, and I take no delight in your solemn assemblies" (Amos 5:21), an astonishing condemnation from a Lord who instituted festivals for joy and remembrance (Lev 23). Under the veneer of piety, Israel's elite clung to sacrifices, believing that offerings—game, grain, and wine—could mask systemic injustice. Amos counters this by demanding, "But let justice roll down like waters, and righteousness like an ever-flowing stream" (Amos 5:24), redirecting focus from performance to practical compassion. His words highlight that God's priorities transcend temple service; they encompass how people treat the widow, orphan, and sojourner. While Judah and Israel celebrated days of solemn assembly with music and sacrificial lambs, heinous acts went unaddressed: bribery corrupted courts, the rich exploited the poor, and the powerful oppressed the marginalized. Amos's indictment reveals that festival participation without ethical action aggravates divine disfavor. His call challenges Israel's complacent assumption that formal worship alone guarantees God's favor.

Amos's context in Bethel, a shrine-city prized for its golden calves (1 Kgs 12:28–29), emphasizes the ease with which superficial devotion can erode national integrity. When the people gathered for prescribed celebrations, they did so with hearts unmoved by the God they claimed to honor. Amos's metaphor of water pouring away illustrates how rituals can seem vital but become empty when divorced from righteous living. The prophet's words also foreshadow New-Testament cautions: Jesus would later condemn similar patterns of religiosity devoid of love (Matt 23:23–28). Amos insists that God demands more than lip service; He calls for a social transformation that manifests love of neighbor in tangible ways. This prophetic appeal exposes how the Exodus generation's eagerness for manna (Exod 16) and their readiness to query heaven for signs (Num 21:4–9) paralleled Israel's subsequent disinterest in alleviating human suffering. With Amos's clarion call echoing in our ears, we move to Micah's succinct summary of what God requires—underscoring that ritualistic fervor cannot substitute for justice, mercy, and humility.

3.3.c Micah on Justice, Mercy, Humility (Micah 6:6–8) Micah, contemporary with Isaiah, distills God's demands into a concise ethical imperative that challenges both individual hearts and corporate structures. When Israel ponders what offerings might please the Lord—thousands of rams, rivers of oil, or even the life of one's firstborn—Micah rebukes these sacrificial extremes, declaring that what truly pleases God is this: "to do justice, to love kindness, and to walk humbly with your God" (Mic 6:8). This threefold summons underscores that worship is not primarily about extravagant offerings but about living out divine character in everyday choices. Justice in Micah's vision entails equitable treatment for the marginalized, ensuring that courts, markets, and policies reflect God's impartiality. Loving-kindness (hesed) goes beyond random acts of charity; it embodies covenantal loyalty, compassion that endures despite injustice or harm. Walking humbly involves recognizing one's dependence on God rather than exalting oneself through religious performance or social status. Micah juxtaposes these values against Israel's systemic corruption—oppressive farmers, cheating merchants, and negligent priests—revealing that ritual without reform perpetuates exploitation.

Micah's prophetic voice addresses a society rich in temple activity yet impoverished in moral integrity. His emphasis on ethical lifestyle over elaborate sacrificial systems resonates with earlier Sinai warnings: communal consent at Sinai (Exod 24:3) meant little when replaced by idolatry at the golden calf (Exod 32:1–6). Micah's words anticipate New-Testament affirmations that true worship is expressed in love (Rom 12:1–2) and that faith without works is dead (James 2:26). By centering justice, mercy, and humility, Micah reveals that God's covenant transcends cultic forms and anchors itself in kingdom ethics. His prophetic wisdom sets a clear standard: true worship cannot be compartmentalized into occasional religious observance; it must infuse every dimension of life with God's justice and compassion. As we transition to Hosea's critique of ritualized religion, we carry forward this understanding that covenant fidelity demands sincerity of heart, not merely the repetition of religious acts.

3.3.d Hosea on Covenant Love over Ritual (Hos 6:4–6) Hosea's ministry unfolds in northern Israel, where rampant idolatry and moral decline prompt God to speak of marital betrayal—Israel as the unfaithful spouse. In Hosea 6:4–6, the Lord laments, "What shall I do with you, O Ephraim? What shall I do with you, O Judah? Your love is like a morning cloud, like the dew that goes away early." This imagery portrays fleeting devotion—affection that vanishes before the heat of the day—illustrating Israel's tendency to renounce God's ways when pressures rise. Hosea contrasts their insincere displays of love for God, disguised as ritual compliance, with the enduring commitment He seeks. Crowds might assemble at altars, sprinkle sacrifices on groves, and present offerings, yet their hearts remain distant (Hos 5:15). Hosea insists, "For I desire steadfast love and not sacrifice, the knowledge of God rather than burnt offerings" (Hos 6:6), echoing earlier prophetic themes about authentic devotion. His critique targets a religious system that reduced covenant to a series of mechanical obligations while sidelining compassion, faithfulness, and intimate communion with God. In Hosea's context, the worship of Baal idols, political alliances with pagan nations, and tolerance of injustice all flow from this shallow religiosity. The prophet's call to "let us know; let us press on to know the LORD" (Hos 6:3) beckons Israel to genuine conversion—a wholehearted return to the covenant. Hosea's message reminds us that ritual observance without transforming love is an affront to God's very nature, as He embodies steadfast love (hesed) toward His people even amid their waywardness.

Hosea's personal life—marrying unfaithful Gomer, whose infidelity mirrors Israel's spiritual adultery—lends poignant force to his message. His relentless pursuit of Gomer, redeeming her from slavery, symbolizes God's covenantal love that rescues despite betrayal. This passionate portrayal of divine love contrasts sharply against Israel's cold adherence to sacrificial schedules and festival customs. Hosea warns that when rituals become ends in themselves, they betray the relational core of covenant. His imagery of morning dew dissolving as the sun rises underscores the transience of worship that lacks depth. As we end our exploration of prophetic warnings, Hosea's plea for experiential knowledge of God prepares us to consider subsequent historical cycles—Judges' era patterns of retreat and revival—where Israel's compromise and fleeting zeal will manifest in new contexts. Through Hosea's eyes, we see that genuine faith demands constant movement toward God, not mere participation in religious rites.

3.4 Judges' Cycle: Short-Lived Zeal and Deepening Apostasy

3.4.a Gideon's Fleece and Faltering Faith (Judges 6–8) Gideon's narrative begins with Israel's cry for deliverance from Midianite oppression, highlighting how the people's cycles of sin and repentance created a vacuum exploited by adversaries (Judg 6:1–6). When the angel of the Lord visited him in Ophrah, Gideon, who was threshing wheat in a winepress to hide from raiders, responded skeptically to the divine call to deliver Israel (Judg 6:11–15). Seeking signs to confirm God's promise, Gideon asked for a fleece: dew on the fleece while the ground remained dry, and then dew on the ground while the fleece stayed dry (Judg 6:36–40). These conditional tests reflect Gideon's wavering faith—a desire for divine validation tempered by lingering doubt. Yet God graciously accommodated his hesitancy, granting the signs and affirming Gideon's call. Armed with a small army of 300 men, Gideon executed a daring nighttime assault, routing the Midianites with torches and trumpets (Judg 7:19–22). His victory exemplified how God's strength is made perfect in human weakness (Judg 7:2; cf. 2 Cor 12:9). However, after the triumph, Gideon failed to dismantle the ephod he fashioned from the spoils of war; this ephod became an object of idolatry, leading Israel astray (Judg 8:27). Gideon's wavering faith and eventual lapse into idolatry serve as a cautionary tale: even those who experience clear manifestations of God's power can drift into disobedience. His story underscores that faith tested by divine signs must mature into unwavering trust, lest initial zeal give way to spiritual compromise. As Israel rejoiced under his judgeship, they still struggled to wholeheartedly abandon the idols they had manufactured, revealing communal susceptibility to return to broken patterns.

Gideon's post-victory failure transitioned seamlessly into Israel's repeating spiral of rebellion, oppression, and deliverance, prompting the next judge to rise when they again "did what was evil in the sight of the LORD" (Judg 9:1; cf. 2:19). Gideon's personal journey from insecurity to courage, followed by residual spiritual weakness, exemplifies the broader national dynamic where fleeting triumphs seldom produced lasting devotion. His hesitancy and subsequent lapse also prefigure the dangers of entangling divine purpose with personal ambition—a tendency that would plague the Israelite monarchy. As we shift from Gideon's story to Samson's narrative, we will see how another judge, empowered by God to deliver Israel, repeatedly succumbed to personal passions, further illustrating the tenuousness of godly zeal divorced from consistent obedience.

3.4.b Samson's Strength Squandered (Judges 13–16) Samson's life began with divine promise: an angelic announcement to his barren parents that he would be a Nazirite from birth, set apart to begin delivering Israel from Philistine oppression (Judg 13:2–5). Yet as he came of age, Samson's personal choices frequently contradicted his divine calling. Though endowed with supernatural strength, he pursued Philistine women—first marrying a Timnite woman and later involving himself with Delilah—actions that repeatedly entangled him with the very nation oppressing Israel (Judg 14:1–3; 16:4–5). Each lapse demonstrated a misalignment between his identity as God's deliverer and his cravings for personal gratification. His victories—tearing a lion apart (Judg 14:5), slaying a thousand Philistines with a jawbone (Judg 15:14–15), and toppling the temple pillars in his final act (Judg 16:27–30)—revealed God's enabling presence. Yet these exploits did not translate into lasting spiritual renewal for Samson or the nation. When Delilah coaxed him into revealing the source of his strength—his uncut hair as part of a Nazirite vow—Samson paid the ultimate price for failing to guard his consecrated identity (Judg 16:17). The Philistines blinded and imprisoned him, forcing him to grind grain in a prison house (Judg 16:21). His final act of bringing down the temple on the assembled Philistines at Gaza's temple stands as a potent illustration of God's redeeming might, yet it also tragically closes Samson's story with personal ruin.

Samson's trajectory underscores how divine gifting, when coupled with moral compromise, can produce spectacular outcomes that nevertheless fail to secure long-term faithfulness. His life reveals that natural talent or even supernatural empowerment cannot compensate for a compromised heart. Even as he fulfilled his role in delivering Israel—judging for twenty years (Judg 16:31)—he remained captive to selfish impulses and unchecked desires. His story teaches that departing from God's standards, even in minor ways, can precipitate devastating consequences, both personally and communally. As the reader absorbs Samson's legacy of squandered strength, they are prepared to grapple with the broader pattern of Judges: a people whose cycles of fervor and failure culminate in the haunting refrain, "In those days there was no king in Israel; everyone did what was right in his own eyes" (Judg 21:25). This refrain sets the stage for reflecting on how cultural relativism corroded Israel's moral fabric, inviting the establishment of monarchy as a remedy.

3.4.c "Everyone Did What Was Right" — Cultural Relativism (Judges 21:25) The Book of Judges concludes with a sobering declaration: "In those days there was no king in Israel; everyone did what was right in his own eyes" (Judg 21:25). This refrain encapsulates the chaotic moral landscape that emerged when covenantal fidelity eroded. Israel's repeated cycles of oppression and deliverance left a spiritual vacuum exploited by tribal alliances and personal agendas. Without a centralized authority or unifying theology, tribal loyalties often superseded divine directives, leading to internecine violence such as the atrocity at Gibeah (Judg 19–20), where an entire clan nearly annihilated the tribe of Benjamin (Judg 20:47). The result of this moral anarchy manifested in horrific acts, revealing how cultural relativism thrives when collective memory of God's covenant fades. This refrain strikes a stark contrast to the earlier Sinai moment, where Israel approached God with reverent awe (Exod 19:16–18), pledging to obey His statutes. Over time, drifting hearts treated God's commands as optional suggestions, shaping an ethos where personal preference reigned. This moral landscape highlights the necessity of prophetic and judicial interventions, yet even these could only provide temporary remedy. As a result, the stage was set for Israel's cry for a king—a human solution to a spiritual crisis (1 Sam 8:5). The Judges' conclusion thus functions as a candid appraisal of the perils of subjective morality, warning that without a transcendent standard anchored in God's revealed will, nations descend into self-willed chaos. As readers reflect on this sobering legacy, they recognize how easily patterns of compromise can become entrenched, paving the way for the next epoch—Israel's monarchy, with its own tensions between royal pageantry and covenant fidelity.

3.5 Royal Pageantry vs. Covenant Fidelity

3.5.a Solomon's Temple Dedication Glory (1 Kings 8) Solomon's reign began with a theocratic promise: God appeared to him twice, granting wisdom and affirming the Davidic covenant (1 Kgs 3:5–14; 1 Kgs 9:4–5). His crowning accomplishment was the construction of the Temple in Jerusalem, a structure whose grandeur rivaled the world's greatest edifices. After seven years of labor (1 Kgs 6:38), the Temple stood as an architectural and theological marvel, designed according to the divine blueprint revealed to his father, David (1 Chron 28:11–19). When the Ark of the Covenant was brought into the Holy of Holies, "the glory of the Lord filled the house of the Lord" (1 Kgs 8:11), manifesting God's acceptance of the Temple as His dwelling place. Solomon's prayer of dedication poured forth in evocative language that acknowledged God's greatness, confessed national sin, and solicited divine mercy (1 Kgs 8:22–53). He asked that God's name be honored when prayers ascended from the Temple (1 Kgs 8:29), linking worship with heartfelt devotion. The ceremony also included peace offerings, reigning as a communal act of thanksgiving and consecration (1 Kgs 8:62–64). Solomon's words captured both gratitude for the past and hope for the future: if Israel would gather at the Temple to pray when afflicted, God would hear from heaven (1 Kgs 8:34–36). This monument of royal pageantry signified the zenith of Israel's union of monarchy and worship. Yet beneath the splendor lay nascent cracks—a latent tension between institutional ritual and authentic covenant faith that would soon widen.

Despite the magnificent dedication, Solomon's later actions revealed a growing drift from covenant fidelity. As he aged, he amassed foreign wives and concubines who introduced idolatrous practices into the royal court (1 Kgs 11:1–8). His heart, once singularly devoted, turned to worship at high places built for Ashtoreth and Milcom (1 Kgs 11:5–7). This disregard for the exclusivity of Yahweh's worship starkly contrasted with the unity and holiness celebrated during the Temple's dedication. Solomon's fall underscores how even grand religious achievements cannot substitute for ongoing covenant loyalty. His story teaches that pageantry and architectural magnificence can cloak a heart prone to compromise. As readers consider Solomon's trajectory, they see that devotion genuine in one season can erode when no longer rooted in consistent obedience. This realization transitions naturally into examining how the Kingdom's division and the proliferation of high places further fractured Israel's covenant relationship.

3.5.b High Places, Split Kingdom, and Idolatry (1 Kings 11–12)
Following Solomon's death, the kingdom split under Rehoboam's reign, fracturing into northern Israel and southern Judah (1 Kgs 12:16–20). Jeroboam, an Ephraimite leader, feared that pilgrimages to Jerusalem would erode his political power, so he established golden calves at Bethel and Dan (1 Kgs 12:28–29). In urging Israel to worship these images, he proclaimed, "Here are your gods, O Israel, who brought you up out of the land of Egypt" (1 Kgs 12:28), a blunt echo of the golden calf at Sinai (Exod 32:4). These high places, sanctified by calves rather than the Ark, institutionalized idolatry and entrenched ritualistic patterns outside the true Temple. This move solidified political division by exploiting religious nationalism, transforming sincere longing for divine presence into state-sponsored paganism. As elders and common folk assembled at these sites three times yearly (1 Kgs 12:32–33), their worship devolved into a toxic mix of tradition and idolatry. Rituals persisted—burnt offerings, feast days, festivals—yet the core of covenant fidelity crumbled. Prophetic voices, later from Elijah to Hosea, would fiercely rebuke these high places (1 Kgs 18:20–40; Hos 4:13), but for many, the appeal of localized worship overshadowed the call to centralized, undivided devotion. Israel's identity became entangled with sacred sites that contradicted God's command, accelerating spiritual decline.

This proliferation of high places and the formal split of the kingdom fractured Israel's collective memory, leaving each half vulnerable to idolatrous innovations. While Judah maintained a semblance of Temple worship in Jerusalem, even there high places became entrenched (2 Kgs 21:3–4). The fracturing undermined prophetic ministry by scattering voices and diluting theological coherence. Religious syncretism—melding Yahwist elements with Canaanite worship—became normative, denying the exclusivity Yahweh demanded (Deut 6:4–5). The schism also foreshadowed successive exiles: Assyria would deport northern Israel (2 Kgs 17:23–24), and Babylon would later exile Judah (2 Kgs 25:12–21). Their fall stands as a sobering testament to the dangers of conflating political expediency with religious expression. As we turn to Elijah's dramatic confrontation at Carmel, we see how prophetic fervor sought to rekindle authentic devotion, challenging the superficial worship entrenched by high places.

3.5.c Elijah's Showdown on Carmel: Fire without Follow-Through (1 Kings 18)

Amid Israel's deepest idolatrous mire, Elijah emerges as a lone prophet confronting King Ahab and Queen Jezebel's Baalist agenda. Challenging 450 prophets of Baal and 400 prophets of Asherah, he calls Israel to decide, "How long will you go limping between two different opinions?" (1 Kgs 18:21). The dramatic contest on Mount Carmel pits Yahweh against Baal: the prophets of Baal frantically invoke their god, cutting themselves to elicit a response, yet nothing happens (1 Kgs 18:26–29). Elijah, by contrast, prays quietly and methodically, dousing his altar with water thrice that it might be evident this is no mere parlor trick (1 Kgs 18:33–35). God answers with consuming fire that charred the offering, wood, stones, dust, and even licked up the water in the trench (1 Kgs 18:38). At that moment, the people fall prostrate, confessing, "The Lord, he is God; the Lord, he is God" (1 Kgs 18:39). Elijah's victory manifests divine supremacy, yet his triumph is short-lived. As Jezebel threatens to kill him, he flees to Mount Horeb, slipping into despair rather than consolidating the spiritual renewal he had sparked (1 Kgs 19:1–4). His encounter with God in a still, small voice (1 Kgs 19:12–13) redirects him to appoint new prophets, foreshadowing the Elisha succession.

Despite this stunning vindication of Yahweh's power and Israel's momentary confession, the nation soon returns to Baal worship. The fleeting devotion stirred on Carmel dissipates when Jezebel's threats loom large. Ahab's half-hearted repentance (1 Kgs 21:27–29) does little to stem the tide of apostasy, and soon the kingdom speeds toward collapse. Elijah's showdown demonstrates how divine interventions, however spectacular, cannot guarantee lasting spiritual awakening when hearts are unprepared for the sustained discipline of covenant living. Mount Carmel's blaze of glory invites us to consider how mimicking such fervor without integrating it into daily obedience risks returning to complacency. As we move beyond these royal narratives, we are reminded that the pattern of initial zeal followed by regression, seen here and throughout Israel's history, finds its ultimate resolution in Christ, who invites us to genuine, enduring discipleship that transcends fleeting spectacles.

3.6 Exile and Return: Echoes of Spectator Spirituality

3.6.a Lament by the Rivers of Babylon (Psalm 137; Jeremiah 29:4–14) Psalm 137 captures the raw anguish of exiled Israelites "sitting by the waters of Babylon," their harps hung on the willows because they could not sing the Lord's songs in a foreign land (Psalm 137:1–2). The physical dislocation became the backdrop for spiritual despair: as captives, the exiles felt their identity and worship outlawed, draped in the humiliating irony of forced Babylonian service. Their lament—"How shall we sing the Lord's song in a foreign land?" (Psalm 137:4)—reveals that even sacred memory, once vivid, can become a source of bitter pain when lived out under duress. They pledged to remember Zion, promising "If I forget you, O Jerusalem, let my right hand forget its skill" (Psalm 137:5–6), invoking a covenantal oath to preserve their corporate memory despite physical displacement. Yet in their frustration, some voiced imprecatory prayers ("Happy shall they be who take your little ones and dash them against the rock!"; Psalm 137:9), exposing how captivity can warp the heart into bloodlust rather than mercy. This chilling fervor illustrates how spectator faith—remembering only what was lost—can devolve into vindictive impulses when hope is suspended. Jeremiah, in parallel, addressed the exiles in Babylon with a surprising word: "Thus says the Lord of hosts, the God of Israel, … build houses and live in them; plant gardens and eat their fruit" (Jeremiah 29:4–5). He instructed them to seek the welfare of the city where they were taken and to pray for its peace (Jeremiah 29:7). This counsel countered the temptation to remain stuck in nostalgic passivity; rather than merely lamenting, they were to engage structurally with their context. Jeremiah's famous promise—"For I know the plans I have for you … to give you a future and a hope" (Jeremiah 29:11)—reinforced that God's redemptive purpose transcended immediate suffering. The exiles' initial reaction, however, mirrored Israel's earlier tendencies: disheartened seeking of miraculous rescue rather than trusting in incremental restoration. Their role shifted from passive spectators of Jerusalem's fall to active participants in Babylonian society—tentmakers and planters—yet maintaining spiritual fidelity. This tension between lament and engagement exemplifies the challenge of preserving covenant identity amid dislocation. As the exiles navigated foreign influences, their struggle illustrates how memory without mission can devolve into morbid nostalgia. Jeremiah's letters remind readers that true return must begin with present obedience rather than mere longing for past glories. Their experience anticipates how, even when God's people physically return to the land, the deeper work of heart renewal remains essential to avoid repeating old patterns.

The exilic community's efforts to preserve worship—assembling in local dwellings to recite Torah passages—laid the groundwork for synagogue life (Nehemiah 8:1–3). Yet the lingering question remained: would they, once back in Jerusalem, maintain the theological and ethical shifts they embraced in Babylon? The next prophetic voices—Haggai and Malachi—would challenge the postexilic generation precisely on that point: returning physically without genuine renewal of heart equated to mere spectator worship. As we turn to Haggai's rebuke of paneled houses versus the house of God, we see how the early returnees struggled to prioritize spiritual formation over personal comfort.

3.6.b Haggai's Rebuke of Paneled Houses vs. House of God (Haggai 1) Upon the initial wave of return under Zerubbabel and Joshua, the returned exiles faced hardships: fields remained untilled, houses lay unfinished, and the new temple stood as a modest shell compared to Solomon's glory (Haggai 1:3–4). While personal homes received new cedar paneling and luxurious touches, God's dwelling lay in ruins, reflecting a skewed set of priorities. Haggai confronted this disparity with divine urgency: "Is it a time for you yourselves to dwell in your paneled houses, while this house lies in ruins?" (Haggai 1:4). His indictment exposed how comfortable living had lulled the people into neglecting communal worship and covenant renewal. Despite the grand promises Jeremiah proclaimed, the exiles' focus on private prosperity blinded them to the need for covenantal presence. Instead of prioritizing the house of God, they sought to enhance their own dwellings, betraying an inward turn that replayed Sinai-era spectator tendencies: they admired past glories but failed to invest in present obedience. Haggai's message called the community to reflect on how their "multiplied possessions" had become evidence of disobedience rather than blessing (Haggai 1:10–11). He urged them to "Consider your ways" (Haggai 1:5) and to "rise, get to the hills, bring wood, and rebuild the house" (Haggai 1:8). This call demanded practical sacrifice and redirected their affections from personal comfort to communal covenant. Their fear of economic hardship—"The heavens have withheld the dew, and the earth has withheld its crops" (Haggai 1:10)—underscored that true blessing hinges on obedience to God's priorities. Thus, Haggai linked material well-being with spiritual fidelity, reminding the people that God's presence, when restored, ushers in abundant life beyond mere survival.

The response to Haggai's rebuke proved swift; Zerubbabel and Joshua rose to lead the remnant, defying threats and beginning reconstruction (Haggai 1:14–15). Their obedience demonstrates that prophetic challenge can pierce the veneer of comfortable religion and reorient hearts toward divine purpose. As the foundation of the temple took shape under adverse conditions, the people witnessed miraculous provision—"I will shake the heavens and the earth and overthrow the throne of kingdoms" (Haggai 2:6)—a promise whose fullness awaited the coming of Christ. Yet this renewed zeal also highlighted how easily initial enthusiasm can ebb once construction pressures ease. The pattern of starting well but risking future neglect parallels Joshua's commissioning of leaders to guard God's law (Joshua 1:7–8). Their experience serves as a caution: building God's house demands ongoing vigilance lest zeal transform into a new form of personal aggrandizement. As Haggai's remnant labored with trembling hands (Haggai 2:4), they embodied a renewed covenant posture—one that would soon be tested again under Malachi's scrutiny for half-hearted offerings.

3.6.c Malachi's Oracle on Half-Hearted Offerings (Malachi 1:6–14; 3:8–10) Several decades after Haggai and Zechariah, Malachi confronted a postexilic community whose initial zeal for temple reconstruction had waned. He observed a priesthood offering polluted sacrifices—"a lame sheep and a blind" (Malachi 1:8)—displaying contempt for the Lord's name. The priests' negligence contradicted God's demand for reverence and purity: "If you will not hear, if you will not lay it to heart to give honor to my name, says the Lord of hosts, then I will send a curse upon you" (Malachi 1:9). This rebuke parallels Sinai's command against offering defective animals (Leviticus 22:20–25) and reveals that ritual without regard for God's holiness devolves into hypocrisy. As worshipers continued bringing substandard offerings, they treated temple service as a hollow form rather than a means to cultivate reverence. Their failure to recognize God's worthiness of "firstfruits" (Malachi 2:1; 3:10) reflected a heart that had drifted from covenant love. In Malachi 3:8–10, God laments, "Will a man rob God? Yet you are robbing me. But you say, 'How have we robbed you?' … in tithes and offerings." This indictment reveals that true worship extends into daily stewardship, not confined to temple rituals. The people's failure to bring the full tithe hindered social welfare and the gleaning commands that sustained Levites and the poor (Deut 14:28–29). Malachi's warning underscores that neglect of material faithfulness undermines spiritual vibrancy, perpetuating spectator spirituality rather than active devotion.

Malachi's comical irony—"Bring the full tithe … and thereby put me to the test" (Malachi 3:10)—invites the community to experience God's abundant blessing when they embrace covenant obedience. The prophetic promise of overflowing provision ("I will rebuke the devourer for you, so that it will not destroy the fruits of your ground, and your vine in the field shall not fail to bear fruit"; Malachi 3:11) recalls the wilderness provision of manna but reorients the focus from passive consumption to faithful giving. Yet the risk of regression loomed large, as the pattern of initial reform under Haggai could easily give way to inertia once material needs were met. Malachi's final oracles, foretelling the coming of Elijah before the great and terrible day of the Lord (Malachi 4:5), pointed toward an eschatological renewal transcending external ritual. Their failure to heed Malachi's call reveals how returning from exile without deep heart transformation perpetuates spectator faith under the guise of restored temple rites. This realization bridges us to recognize how these Old-Testament shadows find substance in Christ, as typology converges in New-Testament fulfillment.

3.7 Typology Fulfilled: From Shadow to Substance in Christ

3.7.a Bread from Heaven to Bread of Life (John 6:32–35) In the wilderness, God provided manna—bread from heaven—to sustain Israel's physical needs daily (Exodus 16). This provision, while miraculous, served as a temporary solution to the deeper hunger of the heart. In John 6, Jesus seizes upon this typology when, after performing the feeding of the five thousand, He tells the crowd, "Truly, truly, I say to you, it was not Moses who gave you the bread from heaven, but my Father gives you the true bread from heaven" (John 6:32). He clarifies that the manna sustained physical life temporarily, but He offers Himself as the true Bread of Life, promising that "whoever comes to me shall not hunger, and whoever believes in me shall never thirst" (John 6:35). This declaration reframes the wilderness provision as a shadow pointing beyond itself to the incarnate Word, who embodies God's provision in human flesh (John 1:14). Whereas the Exodus generation consumed manna and died, Jesus invites the crowd to partake of living bread—His own body and blood—to obtain eternal life (John 6:53–58). His teaching confounds many, as the demand to "eat my flesh" and "drink my blood" surpasses mere physical hunger, requiring faith in sacrificial substitution. In this way, the pattern of daily dependence on miraculous bread finds its fulfillment in communion, as Jesus becomes the sustaining presence once and for all. Those who embrace Him as the Bread of Life experience a fulfillment of covenant promises that transcends temporary sustenance, signifying a transformation from spectator consumption to participatory communion.

Jesus's identification as the Bread of Life also links to the prophetic promise in Isaiah 55:1–2, where God bids the thirsty to "come, buy and eat" without money. In Jesus, the proffered invitation extends to all nations, fulfilling the eschatological vision of universal access to God's provision. As the crowds in Capernaum responded with grumbling—"This is a hard saying; who can listen to it?" (John 6:60)—Jesus contrasted their fleeting fascination with the demands of genuine discipleship. His words underscore that typological anticipation in the wilderness must lead to wholehearted embrace of the Messiah, not repeated cycles of seeking signs and drifting when substance arrives. This theological pivot prepares us to see how the Tabernacle and Temple, once central to Israel's identity, give way to a living Temple where believers are consecrated stones in Christ's body.

3.7.b Stone Temple to Living Temple (1 Peter 2:4–5) Israel's Tabernacle and Solomon's Temple functioned as God's earthly dwelling places—a meeting point between divine transcendence and human immanence (Exodus 25:8; 1 Kings 6:1–38). Yet these structures remained physical, subject to destruction, exile, and reconstruction. In 1 Peter 2:4–5, the Apostle Peter proclaims that Jesus, as the living Stone, replaces the old edifice: "As you come to him, a living stone rejected by men but in the sight of God chosen and precious, you yourselves like living stones are being built up as a spiritual house." Here, believers are invited to become living stones, collectively forming a spiritual house in which God dwells by His Spirit. This shift from stone temple to living temple underscores a fundamental reorientation: God's presence is no longer confined to bricks and mortar but resides within the community of faith. Believers, individually and corporately, embody the worship and service once enacted in the temple courts. As living stones, followers of Christ bear the responsibility of holiness (1 Peter 2:9)—a priesthood of all believers—rather than delegating spiritual functions to a separate caste. This democratization of sacred space fulfills Ezekiel's vision of God's Spirit descending among the exiles, making them a temple to inhabit (Ezekiel 37:26–28). The early church's gatherings in homes (Acts 2:46) reflect this new reality: every meeting becomes a locus of divine encounter. Moreover, Jesus's own declaration that He would build His church (Matthew 16:18) confirms that the ecclesial body, not a physical building, constitutes the locus of God's reign. This theological innovation challenges readers to consider whether their own worship practices cling to inherited structures at the expense of embracing the living community where God's Spirit dwells.

The living temple concept also addresses the Exodus generation's partial vision: they beheld God's presence above the mercy seat (Exodus 25:22) but failed to internalize His holiness in their daily lives. In contrast, first-century believers experienced the Spirit indwelling each person, effecting a transformation that surpasses any external sanctuary (Romans 8:9–11). This transition from stone to Spirit invites a reevaluation of how we understand sacred space: worship is not confined to a building but flows from hearts connected to the living Stone. As the living temple grows, it embodies God's redemptive purposes in the world, serving as a witness to the nations, much like the prophets envisioned (Isaiah 2:2–4; Zechariah 8:20–23). This reality sets the stage for the final typological fulfillment: the promise of a new covenant written on hearts rather than tablets.

3.7.c New-Covenant Heart Surgery Promised and Performed (Jeremiah 31:31–34; Hebrews 8:8–13) Jeremiah's prophecy announced a day when God would establish a new covenant distinct from the Mosaic arrangement: "I will put my law within them, and I will write it on their hearts. And I will be their God, and they shall be my people" (Jeremiah 31:33). This promise envisioned an intimacy where obedience flows from inward transformation—heart surgery—rather than external regulation. God declared that under this new covenant, "they shall all know me, from the least of them to the greatest" (Jeremiah 31:34), eliminating the priestly intermediaries of old. The prophecy highlighted that no longer would people need to teach one another to know the Lord, "for they shall all know me" (Jeremiah 31:34). In Hebrews 8:8–13, the author interprets Jeremiah's oracle as fulfilled in Christ, asserting that the old covenant has become obsolete and is soon to disappear. The sacrificial system foreshadowed two realities: Christ's one-time atoning sacrifice and the Spirit's indwelling presence effecting internal renewal (Hebrews 10:16–17). The emphasis shifts from inscribed tablets of stone to inscribed hearts, signaling that true righteousness arises when God empowers human will from within. This theological development addresses the Exodus generation's insufficiency: their initial consent at Sinai (Exodus 24:3–8) and reliance on external ordinances could not alter the heart's inclination toward rebellion (Romans 8:3–4). In the new covenant, Jesus becomes the ultimate mediator, offering not temporary provisions like manna but life-giving nourishment that regenerates the inner person. Believers, as recipients of this fulfillment, experience forgiveness of sins "for I will be merciful toward their iniquities" (Hebrews 8:12), marking a stark departure from sacrificial coverings that had to be repeated.

The new-covenant enactment culminates in Pentecost, when tongues of fire rest on the disciples (Acts 2:1–4), empowering them to live out God's written law in liberated, Spirit-led communities rather than stone-bound codes. This entails a transformation in ethical behavior—believers now love their enemies (Matthew 5:44), feed the hungry (Matthew 25:35), and embody the fruit of the Spirit (Galatians 5:22–23). As the Spirit writes God's decrees on hearts, genuine obedience arises from love (Romans 13:8–10) rather than fear of sanction. The new covenant thus realizes Jeremiah's vision: a people who truly know God, whose relational bond renders them active participants in His redemptive story. This typological fulfillment invites readers to examine whether they have embraced the internal work of the Spirit rather than remaining mere spectators of God's works.

Conclusion

The trajectory of Israel's history cautions us against settling for spiritual spectacle in place of wholehearted fidelity. Whether at Sinai, in the wilderness, under judges, or in monarchic grandeur, repeated patterns reveal that external signs cannot guarantee internal obedience. Prophets like Haggai and Malachi lamented the hollowing of worship when personal comfort or economic concerns eclipsed commitment to Yahweh (Hag 1; Mal 3:8–10). Yet even in the depths of exile, Jeremiah proclaimed a future where God would write His law on human hearts (Jer 31:31–34), offering hope beyond ritual reconstruction. In Christ, the manna typology finds its perfection in the Bread of Life, the temple shadow dissolves into the living fellowship of Spirit-wrought community, and the covenant promise of inner transformation arrives in fullness (John 6:35; 1 Pet 2:4–5; Heb 8:8–13). As modern readers reflect on these ancient testimonies, we are invited to examine whether our own devotion remains tethered to external forms or embraces the dynamic reality of a heart renewed by grace. May the echoes of Israel's triumphs and failures propel us toward genuine discipleship—where awe at God's works leads inevitably to obedience, justice, and steadfast love.

Chapter 4 — The Cost of Being Merely a Fan

In a world where spiritual engagement can be as fleeting as a social-media trend, many find themselves drawn to the surface-level thrills of faith without anchoring deeper. Like spectators at a sports game who cheer for a moment and then disappear when the rally fades, so "fans" of Jesus risk enjoying intermittent emotional highs—powerful worship gatherings, compelling sermons, or extraordinary testimonies—while sidestepping the everyday costs of surrender. Yet Jesus never offered a cheap spirituality; He repeatedly warned that following Him would demand self-denial, unwavering allegiance, and a willingness to bear the weight of the cross. When faith stops at applause and applause alone, it shrivels at the first sign of hardship or challenge. The danger is not merely momentary disillusionment but a faith so shallow it cannot weather life's storms, leading to moral compromises, fractured communities, and ultimately, the sobering reality of standing before Christ unprepared. This chapter explores the hidden price tag on a faith that stops at fervor—unpacking how superfical devotion undercuts true transformation, damages witness, and jeopardizes eternal life. As we examine the stakes and consequences of remaining a fan, we'll also begin to chart a path toward wholehearted discipleship—one marked not by occasional enthusiasm but by resilient roots, genuine community, and sacrificial love.

4.0 Counting the Hidden Price

4.0.a Illusion of Low-Risk Religion Many today draw near to Jesus with fan-like enthusiasm, treating faith as a low-risk, high-reward proposition. They attend a service or download a sermon podcast expecting inspiration without anticipating any personal cost. This mindset arises from a consumer mentality that views religion as a commodity—something one samples when convenient and sets aside when it challenges comfort. Unlike the early disciples who walked dusty roads to follow Jesus, modern "fans" often remain in the comfort of their homes or cars, never venturing beyond the edges of safe relevance. They applaud uplifting music and compelling stories but shy away when the message turns toward self-denial, moral integrity, or communal accountability. This approach echoes the wealthy young ruler who admired Jesus' teaching but went away sorrowful when told to sell all and give to the poor (Mark 10:21–22). When religion is perceived as low-risk, the cross is reduced to a symbol rather than an invitation to actual transformation. In this warped posture, God's call to "take up your cross" (Luke 9:23) sounds more like a quaint slogan than a decisive, life-altering commitment. The illusion of low-risk religion overlooks the reality that genuine discipleship often entails relational sacrifices, reputational costs, and the willingness to stand alone against prevailing cultural currents. Jesus never promised a life free of struggle; He foretold persecution, betrayal, and hardship for His followers (John 15:20; 2 Timothy 3:12). When believers treat faith as a safe hobby rather than a covenantal alliance, they forfeit the richness of intimacy with God that emerges in trials and steadfast obedience. The danger of this illusion lies not only in the absence of depth but in the damaging disillusionment that follows when circumstances inevitably become difficult. As we turn to consider Jesus' warning about calculating the cost, we see that the call to follow Him is meant to unsettle assumptions of minimal personal investment.

4.0.b Why Jesus Warned Would-Be Disciples to "Sit Down and Calculate" (Luke 14:28–30) Jesus did not sugarcoat the demands of following Him; rather, He urged seekers to "sit down and count the cost" before committing (Luke 14:28). This startling metaphor invites prospective disciples to deliberate over the sacrifices required, akin to a builder assessing whether he has sufficient resources before erecting a tower. Jesus illustrated that starting a project without adequate provision invites public shame if one cannot finish—drawing a parallel to the disciple who enthusiastically begins but abandons the journey under pressure. In first-century Palestine, large building projects were communal endeavors demanding not only materials but sustained labor, implying that discipleship requires consistent investment over time. Jesus's stark admonition stands in sharp contrast to a fan's fleeting enthusiasm, which collapses when emotional fervor fades or when personal inconvenience intrudes. Implicit in His words is the expectation that authentic disciples will embrace the totality of His lordship, even when the path leads to betrayal, rejection, or material loss (Luke 14:26–27). The builder's example also illuminates that discipleship requires foresight; there is no glorious spiritual construction without intentional planning, means for perseverance, and readiness for adversity. Those who fail to calculate the cost risk starting strong with much promise yet finish empty-handed when storms blow. This teaching shatters the illusion that faith can flourish without personal overhaul. Jesus further underscored His demand for radical allegiance by teaching that "anyone who does not carry his cross and follow me cannot be my disciple" (Luke 14:27). His call was not a casual invitation but a summons to a pathway mirroring His own—marked by suffering, humility, and sacrificial love. As fans wrestle with whether to measure costs, true followers recognize that the press of Christ's call assures eternal reward outweighs temporal sacrifice (Luke 14:28–33), setting the stage for exploring how shallow roots lead to spiritual superficiality when difficulties arise.

4.1 Spiritual Superficiality and Shallow Roots

4.1.a Parable of the Soils—Rocky Ground (Mark 4:16–17) In the Parable of the Soils, Jesus paints a vivid picture of people who receive His word with immediate joy but falter when trials or persecution surface (Mark 4:16–17). Those whose hearts resemble rocky ground spring up quickly, yielding what appears to be good fruit, yet their roots remain shallow. When discomfort or hardship arrives, such as social backlash for embracing unpopular teachings, these "shallow" individuals wither and fall away. Their initial excitement mirrors the "fan" mentality: uplifted by moving stories or miraculous signs, they eagerly proclaim allegiance but lack depth. Without anchoring beliefs in personal sacrifice or sustained obedience, their faith evaporates at the first hint of cost. Their reaction underscores that the soil of the heart must be prepared beyond mere initial reception; it requires intentional cultivation through spiritual disciplines and community. The rocky ground also represents hearts that look receptive but conceal hardness—like a thin layer of topsoil over unyielding stone, concealing true capacity for growth. In environments where faith seems fashionable, many rush to join the bandwagon, only to depart when that bandwagon hits bumps—criticism, theological challenge, or ethical demands that conflict with personal comfort. This superficiality reflects a desire for the benefits of faith—identity, community, well-being—without embracing its burdens. The parable warns that those who fail to deepen their roots before enthusiasm fades will not only lose joy but also risk public shame, as their collapse becomes visible to others. By transitioning from this image of rocky hearts, we recognize the urgent need to establish enduring spiritual habits that build depth, leading naturally into a discussion about distinguishing fleeting emotional highs from practices that foster resilience.

4.1.b Flash-in-the-Pan Enthusiasm vs. Enduring Spiritual Habits Flash-in-the-pan enthusiasm often ignites when believers encounter emotive worship songs, inspiring testimonies, or powerful prayer events. Yet without follow-through, this fervor fades like fireworks after a brief spectacle, leaving hearts drifting back to prior patterns of self-reliance. Enduring spiritual habits—daily prayer, regular Scripture engagement, and consistent fellowship—serve as the gentle rain that fosters deep roots, enabling faith to weather seasons of drought. The Hebrew writer encourages believers to look to Jesus, "the founder and perfecter of our faith," who endured the cross for the joy that was set before Him (Hebrews 12:2). Emulating His disciplines—early-morning prayer (Mark 1:35), corporate worship (Hebrews 10:25), and sacrificial service—cultivates depth far deeper than the highs of a one-time experience. Without these habits, even the most fervent declarations of love for Christ can dissolve when personal agendas collide with gospel demands. Flash enthusiasm neglects the gradual process of sanctification that unfolds in everyday choices: choosing Scripture over social media, objecting to gossip in the break room, and seeking forgiveness rather than just tolerance. These seemingly mundane practices accumulate into spiritual capital, so that when life's storms—loss, illness, persecution—arrive, believers stand on firm ground. Conversely, those who chase emotional peaks without establishing steady rhythms find their faith tethered to external stimuli rather than internal conviction. This reliance on peaks renders them vulnerable to every novelty and prone to abandon the journey when no longer entertained. Understanding the gulf between fleeting fervor and lasting formation prepares us to examine how the absence of disciplines imperils shallow roots, leading to spiritual fragility and inconsistent witness.

4.1.c Absence of Spiritual Disciplines: Prayer, Word, Community Without the anchor of regular prayer, believers risk drifting into reactive spirituality—seeking God only when needs intensify rather than maintaining ongoing communion. Jesus modeled early morning withdrawal to pray (Mark 1:35), showing that consistent solitude with the Father fuels strength and clarity. When prayer becomes intermittent, the heart shrinks from dependence to self-reliance, and quick fixes replace sustained trust. Similarly, immersion in Scripture provides nourishment and corrective perspective. Psalm 119 celebrates God's law as a lamp to our feet and a light to our path (Psalm 119:105), signaling that daily exposure to God's truth shapes character more than sporadic emotional encounters. Yet fans often consume Scripture like a buffet—skipping challenging portions and selecting only feel-good passages. This selective engagement overlooks the transformative power residing in every page, from Genesis to Revelation, which collectively teaches holiness, righteousness, and the fear of the Lord. The result is a patchwork faith that unravels when confronted with moral complexity or theological tension. Finally, community serves as both a greenhouse and a guardrail for growth. Acts 2:42 portrays the early church devoted to the apostles' teaching, fellowship, breaking of bread, and prayer. This communal environment created mutual accountability—encouraging perseverance, convicting sin, and celebrating progress. In contrast, isolated fans confuse individual inspiration for corporate edification, losing the benefit of shared wisdom and accountability. When struggles arise—confusion over doctrine, temptation toward sin, questions about calling—community provides perspective and restitution long after the stage lights fade. Without these disciplines, fans remain stranded on rocky ground, unprepared for struggles that inevitably come, paving the way to vulnerability to disillusionment and apostasy.

4.1.d Storm-Time Revelation—Trials that Expose Root Depth (James 1:2-4) Trials function as spiritual stress tests, revealing whether faith is anchored in superficial enthusiasm or rooted in unwavering trust. James exhorts believers to "consider it all joy" when encountering various trials, because testing produces steadfastness (James 1:2–3). This testing exposes the roots: superficial faith balks under pressure, while deep-rooted faith unfurls resilience. Like trees bracing against wind, believers with deep roots draw nourishment from God's promises and clinging prayer rather than succumbing to fear or despair. The storm-time revelation can come as illness, relational breakdown, or persecution—scenarios that eluded fans chasing emotional highs. When a crisis severs access to uplifting music or charismatic teaching, the shallow-rooted believer faces a collapse of faith, whereas the deeply rooted disciple leans into God's presence, even in the silence. The apostle Peter describes trials as brief and purposive, designed to refine faith "like gold that perishes though it is tested by fire" (1 Peter 1:7). This analogy underscores that genuine faith is proven under heat, not in the comfortable haze of emotional peaks. In the wilderness, Israel's roots were tested when manna ceased to suffice and unbelief reigned at Kadesh-barnea (Num 14:1–4). Those who trusted God inherited the Promised Land; those with shallow roots died in the desert. In the New Testament era, the early church's growth amidst persecution (Acts 8:1–3; 1 Thessalonians 2:14) illustrated how trials can cultivate profound endurance among true followers. As we reflect on storm-time revelation, we see that training for resilience involves embracing daily cross-bearing—choosing obedience precisely when comfort beckons or confusion clouds the path. This understanding leads us to the next section on emotional volatility and disillusionment, examining how unmet expectations drive many fans away from faith altogether.

4.2 Emotional Volatility and Disillusionment

4.2.a The Crowd Abandons Him (John 6:66) Jesus' Bread of Life discourse reveals the fickleness of crowds who follow for immediate benefits rather than deeper commitment. After feeding the five thousand, many gathered again at Capernaum, expecting more free sustenance. When Jesus explained that the true bread from heaven required them to "eat His flesh and drink His blood" for eternal life, many observers recoiled at the metaphor, though it pointed toward sacrificial union (John 6:53–56). Their hearts, unprepared for this radical demand, turned from Him at once: "After this many of His disciples turned back and no longer walked with Him" (John 6:66). This abandonment underscores how emotional volatility—seeking only what satisfies present desires—renders faith vulnerable to collapse when teachings become countercultural or demanding. The crowd's initial following, galvanized by miraculous provision, failed to transition into sustained obedience; once the feeding spectacle passed, their engagement evaporated. Their disillusionment stemmed not from inadequate evidence of Jesus' power but from the unpalatability of His deeper message. This episode highlights how fans often conflate faith with transient emotional uplift, interpreting difficulty and complexity as obstacles rather than pathways to spiritual maturity. When Jesus insisted on sacrificial commitment, the crowd's emotional investment in comfort and familiarity outweighed any desire to know Him more intimately. Their abandonment illustrates that religion grounded in personal gratification cannot endure the humble call to follow a suffering Savior. As these protean hearts found the Bread of Life too hard to swallow, their departure attests to the peril of tethering faith to emotional satisfaction rather than to the unchanging character of God's Word.

The scene at Capernaum functions as a litmus test for volatility: when the initial attraction to miracles subsides, many withdraw, revealing that their loyalties were neither secure nor rooted. In contrast, Peter's resolute response—"To whom shall we go? You have the words of eternal life" (John 6:68)—shows that true disciples anchor themselves in Christ's person and promise, not in momentary experiences. For modern readers, this incident invites self-examination: do we cling to the aspects of faith that affirm our desires, or do we embrace the full counsel of God, even when it challenges our preferences? By moving from this narrative of abandonment, we are prompted to analyze how unmet expectations breed disillusionment, preparing us to explore the dynamics by which fans become susceptible to apostasy when Jesus refuses to perform on cue.

4.2.b Unmet Expectations: When Jesus Refuses to Perform on Cue Fans of Jesus often approach Him with a transactional mentality—come, perform the miracle, and life will proceed on familiar terms. Yet the Gospels frequently depict Jesus refusing to comply with such demands, choosing instead to prioritize spiritual integrity over immediate applause. When a Syrophoenician woman begged Him to cast a demon out of her daughter, He initially remained silent and then stated that His mission was to the lost sheep of Israel (Matthew 15:22–24). This response did not concern discourtesy but underscored that timing and focus follow divine purpose, not human whims. Similarly, when crowds clamored for signs at various points—Pharisees demanding a sign from heaven (Matthew 16:1-4) or political leaders seeking sensational spectacles—Jesus refused to become an object of showmanship. He rebuked those who sought proof as evidence of stubborn unbelief, stating, "An evil and adulterous generation seeks for a sign" (Matthew 16:4). These refusals shattered the illusion that Jesus existed merely to fulfill human wish lists. Fans who thrived on constant supernatural affirmation found themselves disoriented when the Teacher remained quiet or redirected attention back to the Father's will. This dynamic of unmet expectations mirrors a deeper tension: faith built on experiential appeasement cannot sustain when divine priorities diverge from personal desires. Those disappointed by Jesus' refusal demonstrated that they loved the benefits of His power, not the profundity of His message. Their defection underlines how fans can drift into a faith of convenience and demand rather than commitment. Recognizing this pattern prepares us to understand how the offence of hard sayings—doctrines that unsettle shallow faith—often propels fans toward disillusionment or outright rejection.

4.2.c The Offence of Hard Sayings—"Eat My Flesh, Drink My Blood" When Jesus proclaimed that those who partake of His flesh and blood will have eternal life, many followers balked, declaring that such teaching was "hard" (John 6:60). This reaction exemplifies how hard sayings of Jesus—and indeed any gospel previously unvoiced expectations—can offend fans attached to a comfortable image of faith. His words did not fit within the prevailing paradigm of messianic deliverance they sought—another twist rather than a straightforward path to physical prosperity or national liberation. In response to their murmurings, Jesus did not dilute His message but reiterated the necessity of abiding in Him (John 6:51, 58), exposing that true discipleship demands the willingness to embrace what our reason or cultural template may find unacceptable. The offence of hard sayings also emerges in ethical teachings: loving enemies, forgiveness without limit, and renouncing possessions. Fans, acclimated to a friendlier gospel, recoil when these demands conflict with their comfort zones. The offence intensifies when this teaching challenges prevailing ideologies or cherished traditions, as the Samaritan woman discovered when Jesus spoke of worship "in spirit and truth" (John 4:23–24), confronting entrenched religious assumptions. Those who cling to fan-level faith treat deeper doctrines as dispensable, fleeing from the very source of spiritual nourishment and growth. Consequently, the offence of Jesus' harder teachings can lead to fragmentation—some following for a while, others departing entirely. Recognizing the pattern of offeased fans reminds us that embracing Christ's full revelation invariably triggers a divisive response among those unwilling to relinquish easy expectations. As we consider the offence of hard sayings, we also see how attachment to worldly securities, as exemplified by the rich young ruler, further isolates fans from authentic following.

4.2.d Case Study: Rich Young Ruler and the High Price of Attachment (Mark 10:21–22) The rich young ruler approached Jesus with earnest admiration, kneeling and addressing Him as "Good Teacher" (Mark 10:17–18). He promised to keep the commandments and asked what more he must do to achieve eternal life. When Jesus told him to sell all he possessed, give to the poor, and follow Him, the man's face fell, for he had great wealth (Mark 10:21–22). Despite tracking Jesus for a time, his attachment to riches trumped his longing for eternal life. His departure in sorrow underscores how fans—drawn by charisma or message—can crumble when genuine obedience requires relinquishing cherished securities. This case study illustrates that worship of material comfort or status often masquerades as devotion to God. Wealth itself was not the issue; rather, the young ruler's love for wealth eclipsed his love for God, revealing that fan-like devotion to transient blessings yields to refusal when asked to embrace true discipleship. His story flows naturally from the theme of false expectations: he expected a religious formula that accommodated his lifestyle, not a call to radical reorientation. When Jesus presented a kingdom agenda that threatened his temporal advantage, he chose the path of least resistance, demonstrating that fans frequently recoil from the high price of allegiance. This scenario reminds modern readers that cultural affluence and moral compromise can conspire to stifle authentic faith, highlighting how disillusionment is often the product of clinging to lesser joys rather than embracing the joy set before us in Christ (Hebrews 12:2). As we transition to the next chapter examining ethical inconsistency, we see that refusal to bear the cross inevitably leads to fractured witness and doctrinal dissonance.

4.3 Ethical Inconsistency and Witness Damage

4.3.a Hypocrisy as Stumbling Block (Matthew 23:13) Jesus delivered a scathing rebuke to religious leaders who meticulously observed external rituals while neglecting justice, mercy, and faithfulness (Matthew 23:23–24), highlighting that genuine worship must align with ethical integrity. In condemning the scribes and Pharisees, Jesus accused them of shutting the kingdom of heaven in people's faces, for they neither entered themselves nor allowed others to enter (Matthew 23:13). This hypocrisy functioned as a stumbling block, turning seekers away from truth rather than drawing them into deeper relationship with God. Hypocrisy often begins when individuals prioritize appearances over character, presenting a façade of righteousness while harboring unconfessed sin or actively neglecting the vulnerable. Such duplicity destroys credibility, for when a leader preaches kindness but practices exploitation, observers detect the disconnect between words and actions. The result is not simply private moral failure; it is a public discrediting of the gospel message. Hypocrisy cripples evangelistic witness, as onlookers assume that if a religious system tolerates duplicity among its leaders, then its teachings lack divine authority. In the early church, Paul reminded believers to "prove yourselves to be blameless and innocent, children of God without blemish in the midst of a crooked and twisted generation" (Philippians 2:15), underscoring the essential link between ethical consistency and effective witness. When fans of Jesus adopt superficial piety—attending services, posting Scriptures on social media, yet refusing to address injustice—they mirror the hypocrisy Jesus condemned, undermining the transformative power of the gospel. This pattern invites readers to examine their own lives: do our actions reinforce or contradict our confessions of faith? As we move to consider public scandals and their impact on credibility, the reality of how private hypocrisy ripples outward into communal damage becomes starkly evident.

4.3.b Public Scandals and the Credibility Gap When ethical failures among Christian leaders surface—embezzlement, sexual misconduct, or abuse of power—churches and faith communities suffer collective harm. These public scandals create a credibility gap, for outsiders often perceive that if spiritual leaders cannot practice what they profess, then the principles they espouse must be negotiable or insubstantial. Consider the fallout when a pastor known for preaching holiness is exposed for moral compromise: congregants wrestle not only with betrayal but also with the disillusionment that their spiritual guide might have been motivated by personal gain rather than divine call. News of hypocrisy spreads faster than truth, feeding cynicism about the integrity of the broader Christian witness. In the first century, when Peter denied Christ publicly (Luke 22:54–62), he later experienced repentance and restoration (John 21:15–19), but the damage to Jesus' movement was immediate: the friends who once followed fervently fled in fear (Mark 14:50). Similarly, modern scandals prompt people to abandon church attendance, rejecting faith not because of theology but because of discredited leadership. The ripple effect extends to subsequent generations, who may inherit skepticism about genuine Christianity. Organizations like Promise Keepers and emerging church movements often address these credibility gaps by emphasizing transparency, accountability structures, and restorative processes for leaders who fail. As readers reflect on these phenomena, they recognize that ethical consistency is indispensable for sustaining trust. Practical steps such as third-party financial audits, independent counseling, and robust church discipline demonstrate that communities take misconduct seriously, working to bridge the credibility gap. This vigilance prevents isolated incidents from undermining the faith of many. Transitioning from public scandals, we turn to the uniquely modern challenge of social-media Christianity, where curated images can mask hidden realities.

4.3.c Social-Media Christianity: Curated Image vs. Hidden Reality In the digital era, social media platforms offer Christians unprecedented opportunities to share Scripture, testimonies, and worship experiences. However, these same platforms can foster a culture of carefully curated spiritual personas that conceal underlying struggles, doubts, or compromises. A pastor might post daily devotionals and photos of community outreach, giving the impression of unflappable devotion, while privately battling financial stress or relational strife. This disparity between the public image and private reality erodes authenticity, as online admirers assume the doting facade equates to genuine spiritual maturity. Social-media Christianity turns faith into a performance art, where metrics—likes, shares, and comments—become substitutes for true community and accountability. Followers risk idolizing the digital persona rather than engaging with the real person behind the screen. When a spiritual influencer's curated identity unravels due to revealed flaws, followers experience disorientation akin to discovering a deceiving magician behind the curtain. The gap between image and reality also tempts "fans" to assume that spiritual growth requires only viewing polished content rather than doing the hard work of personal reflection and obedience. This dynamic can stunt discipleship, as individuals mistake passive consumption for active transformation. As the writer of Hebrews admonishes, "We desire each one of you to show the same earnestness to have the full assurance of hope until the end" (Hebrews 6:11), implying that passive spectatorship cannot yield sustained confidence. Moving from social-media Christianity's curated cheery veneer, we consider how confession and restitution become vital for healing the wounds inflicted by ethical inconsistency, paving the way to rebuilding trust and credibility.

4.3.d Healing the Reputation Wound—Repentance and Restitution When ethical failures fracture the credibility of a believer or faith community, genuine healing requires more than apologetic statements; it demands repentance and tangible restitution. Biblical precedent abounds: when David confronted his adultery and murder, he publicly confessed, "I have sinned against the Lord" (2 Samuel 12:13), yet his repentance also included accepting Nathan's proclamation that the child born to his illicit union would die (2 Samuel 12:13–14), reflecting concrete consequences. Similarly, Zacchaeus's encounter with Jesus led him to pledge fourfold restitution to those he had defrauded (Luke 19:8), demonstrating that genuine repentance must involve repairing harm whenever possible. In contemporary contexts, church leaders who misuse funds might repay embezzled amounts, step aside from leadership for a season, and commit to transparent oversight as part of rebuilding trust. When broken trust has inflicted emotional trauma—such as in cases of pastoral abuse—restoration can include counseling, financial assistance for victims, and public acknowledgment of wrongdoing. These steps demonstrate a sincere desire to reconcile relationships and uphold justice, addressing both the spiritual and emotional dimensions of the wound. The apostle Paul counsels that when a believer is overtaken in a trespass, "you who are spiritual restore him in a spirit of gentleness. Keep watch on yourself, lest you too be tempted" (Galatians 6:1). This restorative process demands humility from the offender and compassion from the community, creating a space where healing can occur. Over time, consistent repentance, demonstrated change, and ongoing accountability can bridge the credibility gap. As we transition to exploring isolation from transforming community, we see how the absence of genuine fellowship leaves fans vulnerable to ethical drift, underscoring that accountability and restoration are not optional but essential to sustained faithfulness.

4.4 Isolation from Transforming Community

4.4.a Consumer Church vs. Covenant Family (Acts 2:42–47) The New Testament depicts the early church as a covenant family wherein believers devoted themselves to apostolic teaching, fellowship, breaking of bread, and prayer (Acts 2:42). This holistic commitment made them more than spectators; they were active participants in a community of mutual care and spiritual formation. In contrast, consumer church attendees treat worship services as entertainment events—arriving, observing, and departing—without genuine engagement or investment in others' growth. Consumer church prioritizes personal preference over communal responsibility, offering a buffet of worship styles, classes, and programs for individuals to sample at leisure. Yet the New Testament model emphasizes sacrificial service: believers shared possessions, distributed to anyone in need, and praised God with glad and generous hearts, enjoying favor with all people (Acts 2:44–47). This covenantal posture fostered deep relationships, supported vulnerable members, and provided accountability when sin surfaced. The consumer approach, by contrast, fosters isolation; individuals opt for services that suit their preferences, avoiding the discomfort of deeper connection. This transactional mindset overlooks that spiritual growth flourishes in relationships where love, challenge, and correction coexist. Lacking true community, fans miss opportunities to develop the humility and empathy Jesus exemplified. As Christian author Dietrich Bonhoeffer observed, "Christianity without discipleship is always Christianity without Christ"—a warning that false comfort in consumer church obscures the cost of following. Transitioning from the early church's vibrant community, we explore how lone-ranger spirituality deepens isolation and erodes accountability.

4.4.b Lone-Ranger Spirituality and Accountability Drift A lone-ranger approach to faith treats the believer as an isolated hero—self-sufficient, free from oversight, and exempt from communal correction. This mentality often emerges when individuals, fearful of exposure or criticism, withdraw from small groups or accountability relationships, preferring solitary Bible study or online devotionals. While quiet reflection has its place, the absence of a tethered community creates an accountability drift where hidden sin festers unchecked. The apostle Paul exhorted believers to "consider how to stir up one another to love and good works, not neglecting to meet together" (Hebrews 10:24–25), underscoring that faith thrives in community. Lone-ranger spirituality, however, neglects this biblical prescription, resulting in moral blind spots that gradually widen. A person who refuses to share struggles or submit to counsel remains vulnerable to deceptive narratives about personal righteousness. Without trusted peers to speak truth in love, individuals can fall prey to rationalizations: "I'm just being real with God," ignoring the fact that God often uses fellow believers to reveal blind spots (Proverbs 27:17). This isolation births arrogance or despair: some imagine they are spiritually superior because no one witnesses their private life, while others feel alienated, believing no one cares to walk beside them in hardship. Ultimately, lack of accountability leaves fans stranded on rocky ground, where shallow roots cannot secure them when temptation or crisis arrives. As we transition to the next section, we see how replacing spectator seats with serving roles—the very antidote to lone-ranger isolation—reintegrates believers into transformative community.

4.4.c Spectator Seats or Serving Teams: Where Growth Actually Happens Spectator seats in a church environment offer a comfortable vantage point for observing spiritual activities but rarely compel personal transformation. Those who remain in spectator mode watch worship services, applaud emotionally stirring moments, and consume sermons without ever stepping into roles that require vulnerability or sacrifice. In contrast, serving on a team—whether children's ministry, hospitality, prayer ministry, or outreach—places believers in situations that test faith, cultivate humility, and foster reliance on the Spirit. The apostle Paul compares the church to a body in which each member has a role to play; when all serve, the body functions smoothly, and growth ensues (1 Corinthians 12:12–27). Serving not only advances ministry but also reveals gaps in knowledge, character flaws, and spiritual gifts, prompting deeper dependence on God and others. For instance, leading a small group requires not only biblical literacy but also empathy, patience, and the courage to address sin compassionately. These experiences forge resilient faith in ways that passive listening never can. Moreover, serving alongside others builds trust and mutual edification, illustrating that growth happens in the context of shared mission and accountability. Those who remain spectators risk stagnation, for sermons may inform but do not automatically transform. The early church's commitment to "breaking bread in their homes" exemplifies how shared meals and service to one another created an environment for continuous growth (Acts 2:46). By shifting from spectator seats to serving teams, fans embark on a journey through the crucible of ministry that refines character and deepens roots, setting the stage for mutual burden-bearing that counters isolation.

4.4.d Mutual Burden-Bearing as Antidote to Fanship (Galatians 6:2) Galatians 6:2 instructs believers to "bear one another's burdens, and so fulfill the law of Christ," highlighting that true community involves active engagement with others' struggles. Fans, disconnected from such mutual care, often perceive faith as a series of personal experiences rather than a shared journey. Burden-bearing requires vulnerability—confessing doubts, fears, and failures—and others willing to walk alongside without judgment. This shared vulnerability cultivates empathy and humility, two virtues antithetical to the self-centred posture of fandom. When a member stumbles, the community intervenes with grace and accountability, preventing sin from remaining hidden and festering. Likewise, in seasons of grief or despair, believers envelop one another in prayer and practical support, embodying Christ's compassion. This synergy of spiritual gifts—encouragement, exhortation, teaching, mercy—manifests most fully when mutual burden-bearing is prioritized over individual satisfaction. Without such relational depth, fans remain spiritually orphaned, lacking the lifelines that sustain faith under pressure. Moreover, mutual burden-bearing models the kingdom ethic that Jesus taught: "By this all people will know that you are my disciples, if you have love for one another" (John 13:35). This outward witness emerges not from finely choreographed services but from authentic community where burdens are shared and joys multiplied. As we transition to examining missed mission opportunities, we see that fans, detached from community, also wander away from the shared mission that defines genuine discipleship.

4.5 Missed Mission Opportunities

4.5.a Barren Fig Tree—Promise Without Produce (Luke 13:6–9) In the parable of the barren fig tree, a landowner seeks fruit from a tree that has failed to produce for three years (Luke 13:6–9). The gardener pleads for more time, promising to cultivate the soil and fertilize the tree; if it still bears no fruit, it will be cut down. This image reveals that superficial association with the owner—receiving shade and belonging to the vineyard—must translate into tangible fruit. Fans often identify with the vineyard, enjoying the blessings of God's provision and the community's reputation, yet offer little in return. They miss mission opportunities by clinging to personal benefit rather than bearing fruit destined for God's kingdom—compassion, evangelism, justice, and sacrificial service. The gardener's interventions—pruning, fertilizing, digging—symbolize intentional measures to spur growth; without these disciplines, the tree remains barren. Similarly, believers who neglect mission risk stagnation, for they may still enjoy spiritual privileges without participating in the vineyard's work. The warning is profound: unfruitful associations eventually lead to divine pruning or even removal from the community of faith. For modern readers, this parable challenges us to evaluate whether our engagement yields tangible impact: do we invest in sparking spiritual renewal, or do we passively absorb resources until inertia sets in? The landowner's patience extends only so far—reflecting God's longsuffering that seeks repentance but does not indefinitely tolerate stagnation. As we transition to consider buried talents, we see the cost of fearing risk and neglecting opportunities entrusted to us.

4.5.b Buried Talents and the Fear of Risk (Matthew 25:24–30) In Jesus' parable of the talents, a master entrusts servants with differing sums of money before departing on a journey. The servant who received one talent buried it in the ground out of fear, returning only what he had been given, to the master's condemnation (Matthew 25:24–30). This servant's decision exemplifies how fans, clinging to comfort and avoiding risk, bury their spiritual gifts rather than invest them in mission. Fear of failure or criticism leads to passivity, robbing the kingdom of potential growth and perpetuating the illusion that preservation of self outweighs faith-based generosity. The master's displeasure stems from the servant's refusal to align his heart with the master's vision; he valued safety over stewardship. In contrast, the servants who risked their resources doubled them, reflecting that successful ministry often requires stepping beyond comfort to confront spiritual and social challenges. The parable's warning resonates with any believer who hesitates to engage in missional initiatives—whether sharing the gospel in their neighborhood, mentoring younger Christians, or advocating for justice. By burying their talents in the ground, fans forfeit the joy of co-laboring with Christ, missing the opportunity to experience the "great joy" the master promised to the faithful (Matthew 25:21). This narrative compels readers to reconsider their posture toward risk: starching their portfolios in fear may safeguard reputation but stifles the flourishing God intends for His kingdom. As we move toward the image of salt losing its savour, we see how neglecting mission leads not only to wasted resources but to cultural irrelevance and spiritual decay.

4.5.c Salt That Loses Its Savour—Cultural Irrelevance (Matthew 5:13) Jesus likened His followers to salt, declaring, "You are the salt of the earth" (Matthew 5:13). Salt's primary functions include preserving, seasoning, and purifying. When salt loses its saltiness—through contamination or exposure to moisture—it becomes useless, cast out and trodden under foot. Similarly, fans who disengage from mission become spiritually bland, failing to preserve godly influence in society or to season conversations with the wisdom of Christ. Cultural irrelevance follows when Christians withdraw from public discourse, charities, or social justice efforts, believing that faith is a private affair. In a world shaped by secular narratives, this departure allows toxicity—corruption, injustice, apathy—to spread unchecked. By neglecting mission, believers forfeit their role as a moral compass, becoming bystanders to societal decay. Purifying influence evaporates when the church retreats behind its stained-glass windows, leaving the hungry and hurting without a demonstrable example of Christ's love. This irrelevance undermines the church's capacity to engage meaningfully with issues such as poverty, human trafficking, or moral confusion. In contrast, salt that retains its savour effectively collaborates in God's redemptive work, manifesting Christ's compassion and justice. As we shift from this image, we consider how redeeming the time—transforming passive attendance into active witness—reinvigorates salt that had grown tasteless.

4.5.d Redeeming the Time—From Passive Attendance to Active Witness To "redeem the time" (Ephesians 5:16) means to grasp every opportunity to live intentionally for Christ, converting passive attendance at church into dynamic engagement with God's mission. Passive attendance—showing up for a weekly service—can become a ritual that offers minimal spiritual return if unaccompanied by active participation in the kingdom's work. Redeeming the time involves identifying local needs—homelessness, educational gaps, mental-health crises—and mobilizing faith, gifts, and resources to address them. It requires asking hard questions: Do action and prayer intersect in our schedules? Have we shifted our focus from self-preservation to self-giving? Engaging in tangible outreach, such as mentoring at-risk youth or supporting refugee families, transforms believers into hands and feet of Jesus. This hands-on involvement resists the temptations of busyness and distraction that plague modern life, fostering a lifestyle that prioritizes kingdom impact over personal convenience. By tracking Jesus' example—welcoming children, touching lepers, table fellowship with outcasts—believers learn that redeeming the time often entails stepping into inconvenient spaces, risking discomfort for the sake of compassion. This posture also grounds faith in the reality of human need, reminding fans that Christianity extends beyond aesthetically pleasing sanctuaries into the messy realities of broken lives. As the apostle Paul exhorted, "I strive to present everyone mature in Christ" (Colossians 1:28), concluding this section underscores that maturity arises when faith shifts from mere observation to dynamic engagement, catalyzing the transformation of both witnesses and world.

4.6 Eternal Stakes of Fan-Level Faith

4.6.a "I Never Knew You"—Superficial Association vs. True Union (Matthew 7:21-23) Those who merely call Jesus "Lord" without living under His lordship will stand condemned when His return brings final judgment. Jesus warned that not everyone who addresses Him as "Lord" will enter the kingdom of heaven; only those who do the will of the Father will secure a place there (Matthew 7:21). This stark pronouncement underscores that superficial profession of faith—using His name without submitting to His authority—proves hollow when tested by eternity's demands. Many in Jesus' day admired His teaching or enjoyed being associated with a vibrant movement, yet when He called for genuine repentance, they drifted away. In the same way, modern fans who admire Jesus' miracles or moral teachings but refuse the call to daily cross-bearing find themselves in trouble when they discover He will expose every hidden motive. Those who worked deeds in His name—casting out demons or prophesying—will nonetheless hear the shocking words, "I never knew you; depart from me, you workers of lawlessness" (Matthew 7:23). Their labor, performed apart from heart-level allegiance, lacked the Spirit's life and proved useless for eternity. This scenario reveals that mere affiliation with Christ's ministry, without an ongoing, obedient relationship, leaves one vulnerable to final rejection. A fan who remains content to stand on the sidelines of authentic discipleship risks discovering that casual association is insufficient when faced with the reality of divine holiness. Neither good works nor passionate declarations can replace the intimate knowledge of Christ that arises from living in covenantal union. As Jesus' own words echo through history, they sever the complacent safety net of cultural Christianity, demanding that faith become more than a comfortable label. Recognizing the eternal stakes propels us to search our hearts: have we truly known Christ, or have we merely admired a distant figure?

Transitioning from the sobering reality that false profession cannot secure salvation, we turn next to the Parable of the Wheat and Tares, which illustrates how superficially similar appearances can hide fundamentally different realities, setting the stage for awareness of separation at the final judgment.

4.6.b Wheat and Tares: Indistinguishable Now, Separated Later (Matthew 13:24–30) Jesus told a parable in which a farmer sowed good seed, but an enemy came at night and sowed weeds among the wheat. At first glance, both grew side by side, indistinguishable until the harvest. This illustration conveys that in the present age, true disciples (the wheat) and false disciples (the tares) can appear remarkably alike—attending the same gatherings, professing the same beliefs, and performing similar spiritual activities. Outsiders cannot easily discern whose root runs deep in Christ or who merely mimics the outward form of faith. The farmer prohibited uprooting the weeds prematurely to avoid destroying the wheat, indicating that God allows both groups to coexist until the appointed end (Matthew 13:29–30). At that time, angels will separate the righteous from the lawless, casting the latter into the fiery furnace (Matthew 13:49–50). This separation underscores the urgency of distinguishing genuine faith from fan-level imitation. While fans might wear the same "garb" as believers—participating in worship, quoting Scripture, and performing religious rituals—their internal allegiance remains shallow. In contrast, those whose hearts are united with Christ's Spirit bear the fruit of righteousness even under pressure. The parable assures us that God alone judges the root, and He will bring to light every hidden thing at the final harvest. For modern Christians, this parable warns against complacency with surface-level spirituality; it calls us to examine whether our faith bears the fruit of genuine transformation. As long as wheat and tares look alike, human judgment stays suspended, but at the last day, the divine standard prevails. Understanding this principle compels followers to cultivate authenticity now, lest they awaken at the harvest to discover they were sown among the tares.

Turning from the inevitability of future separation, we examine the Parable of the Wedding Banquet to see how a prepared posture and appropriate garment become necessary for entrance into the King's celebration, further clarifying the eternal stakes of genuine discipleship.

4.6.c The Wedding Banquet and Garments of Righteousness (Matthew 22:11–14) In the Parable of the Wedding Feast, invited guests initially refuse to attend, so the king opens the banquet to anyone found on the streets—both good and bad (Matthew 22:8–10). Guests fill the hall, yet one man arrives without the wedding garment provided by the host. Though he manages to slip in among the others, the king confronts him and orders his removal, casting him into outer darkness (Matthew 22:11–13). This parable teaches that mere physical presence at the feast, or being counted among the invited, does not guarantee acceptance. The wedding garment symbolizes the righteousness required to enter the kingdom—imputed through faith in Christ and manifested in a life transformed by grace. Fans may attend potlucks, join Sunday services, and even participate in church-sponsored trips, yet without donning the righteousness of Christ, they cannot stand before the king. The provided garment underscores that salvation is not self-attained through works but gifted by God; guests must accept and wear it to enter the feast. While crowds might view themselves as "saved" by mere proximity to church culture, the banquet's scenario warns that without embracing Christ's robe of righteousness, they remain unprepared for the moment of reckoning. The invitation extends widely, yet heart-level transformation is the non-negotiable dress code. This parable transitions us from exploring general separation in the field to specific readiness for the master's table, illustrating that casual association with Christ's kingdom fails in the face of divine requirements. Recognizing this demand moves us to ask whether we have clothed ourselves in the garment provided by the Master or whether we stand exposed in our own unrighteousness.

4.6.d Perseverance of the Saints: Security for Followers, Warning for Fans (Hebrews 10:36–39) Hebrews warns believers to persevere, for enduring faith proves genuine and guarantees participation in God's promises. The author exhorts, "You need endurance, so that when you have done the will of God, you may receive what is promised" (Hebrews 10:36). This perseverance indicates that followers who remain steadfast under trial, holding fast to Christ, demonstrate the life-giving power of the Spirit within them. The contrast emerges with those who shrink back: "But we are not of those who shrink back and are destroyed, but of those who have faith and preserve their souls" (Hebrews 10:39). For fans, initial enthusiasm often fades when suffering comes—whether social ostracism, personal loss, or theological challenges—leading them to drift away. True disciples, strengthened by covenant assurance, press on because they know the One they have believed in is trustworthy. Their perseverance is not mere stubbornness but a reflection of divine work within, enabling them to endure hardship with hope. The church's historical martyrs exemplify this reality: they surrendered wealth, status, even life itself rather than renounce Christ, evidencing a faith that transcends temporal comforts. Their witness reassures modern believers that even in the absence of tangible success, perseverance affirms union with Christ. For fans, the warning to shrink back exposes the façade of shallow trust. The author of Hebrews encourages his readers to draw near with a sincere heart, confident that their perseverance fosters holiness and ushers in God's rest (Hebrews 10:22–25). As we transition from eternal stakes to practical pathways of moving from fan-level faith to authentic discipleship, this reminder of the necessity of perseverance underscores that the cost of being merely a fan is too great to bear when eternity hinges on endurance.

4.7 Crossing the Line: From Fan to Follower

4.7.a Honest Self-Inventory and Spirit-Led Conviction (Psalm 139:23–24) David's prayer, "Search me, O God, and know my heart; test me and know my anxious thoughts" (Psalm 139:23), models the posture of honest self-inventory necessary for transitioning from fan-level faith to authentic discipleship. Fans often avoid introspection, content to bask in the glow of occasional spiritual highs while neglecting areas of hidden complacency or unconfessed sin. But emerging followers invite the Spirit to reveal covert attitudes—pride, fear, greed—so they can be brought into the light of God's truth. Conviction then germinates, stirring a willingness to relinquish half-hearted devotion and pursue Christ wholeheartedly. This self-evaluation requires courage to face uncomfortable truths: perhaps a reluctance to serve, a tendency to judge, or resistant pockets of the heart. When the Spirit brings these to mind, as Psalm 139 indicates, the disciplined response is not defensiveness but humble confession: "See if there is any grievous way in me, and lead me in the way everlasting" (Psalm 139:24). Followers recognize that growth flows from God's refining work, so they submit their wills to His probing. This ongoing heart examination aligns with Jesus' promise that those who abide in His word will be truly His disciples (John 8:31), for abiding demands willingness to be corrected. As we move from conviction to action, we see that authentic faith blossoms when self-awareness sparks genuine repentance, paving the way for deeper roots and resilient witness.

Transitioning from honest self-inventory, we embrace the Spirit's call to embed our lives in practices that cultivate enduring devotion, leading into the next step of establishing root systems through the Word, prayer, and obedience.

4.7.b Establishing Root Systems—Scripture, Prayer, Obedience Rhythms To grow beyond fan-level enthusiasm, followers establish root systems—dedicated times for reading Scripture, praying, and obeying God's commands in daily life. Scripture informs the mind, setting the foundation for right belief and shaping desires; as Paul wrote, "All Scripture is breathed out by God and profitable for teaching, for reproof, for correction, and for training in righteousness" (2 Timothy 3:16). When believers immerse themselves in God's Word, they internalize truths that guard against deception and replace frivolous spiritual trends with enduring wisdom. Prayer, modeled by Jesus in the Garden of Gethsemane (Mark 14:35–36), becomes the lifeline that connects the heart to the Father amid daily challenges. Through prayer, followers articulate struggles, receive guidance, and cultivate intimacy, resisting the allure of fan-driven experiences. Obedience rhythms—small decisions like practicing gratitude, extending forgiveness, or choosing integrity—build spiritual muscle over time, forming habits that carry faith through adversity. This triad of disciplines—Word, prayer, obedience—operates like a deep root system that anchors believers during storms of doubt, criticism, or temptation. Just as a tree withers without water, a faith not nourished by these practices shrivels under pressure. Unlike fans who vanish when distractions or difficulties arise, rooted followers continue bearing fruit because their roots drink deeply of God's steadfast presence. Transitioning from establishing discipline to engaging in community, we see that roots multiply strength when intertwined with others who share the journey, moving toward re-embedding in missional community.

4.7.c Re-Embedding in Missional Community A vital step in crossing from fan to follower is re-embedding oneself in a missional community—a group oriented toward serving Christ and advancing His kingdom rather than merely meeting social or emotional needs. In such communities, believers practice "one-anothers" of Scripture: loving one another deeply, bearing one another's burdens, and spurring each other on toward love and good deeds (John 13:34–35; Galatians 6:2; Hebrews 10:24). This immersive relational context functions as both a greenhouse for spiritual growth and a guardrail against self-focused wandering. Followers engage in collective prayer, communal study of Scripture, and corporate action for justice and mercy, embodying the gospel's power to renew social structures. As members share testimonies of grace, they encourage one another to persevere, especially when trials tempt them to desert the journey. Missional community also provides a laboratory for practicing spiritual gifts—teaching, prophecy, service—equipping each person for kingdom engagement (Ephesians 4:11–13). By embedding in such a community, believers validate their identity as part of Christ's body rather than isolated fans seeking occasional inspiration. This re-embedding fosters accountability, enabling open discussion of doubts, temptations, and failures, ensuring that no one labors in silence or drifts into apathy. As followers participate in communal mission—feeding the hungry, visiting prisoners, advocating for the oppressed—they live out authentic faith that transcends personal piety. Transitioning from communal engagement, we turn to embracing daily cross-bearing and long-term joy as the final pathway to sustaining wholehearted following.

4.7.d Embracing Daily Cross-Bearing and Long-Term Joy (Luke 9:23; Philippians 3:8–10)

Jesus' invitation to "take up your cross daily and follow me" (Luke 9:23) beckons believers into a rhythm of self-denial and sacrificial love that permeates everyday life. This daily cross-bearing rejects self-centered ambitions—seeking status, comfort, or acclaim—in favor of Christ's priorities: love for the vulnerable, integrity in work, and unwavering loyalty to the gospel. When followers embrace specific opportunities to lay down personal agendas—choosing humility over honor, service over selfishness—they participate in Christ's redemptive suffering and discover a joy that transcends temporal circumstances. Paul exemplified this posture in Philippians, counting everything as loss compared to knowing Christ and the power of His resurrection (Philippians 3:8). His willingness to be "found in Him, not having a righteousness of my own" (Philippians 3:9) illustrates that true joy springs from identifying with Christ's suffering and triumph, not from worldly achievements or positive self-image. Through daily cross-bearing—confessing sin, forgiving offenses, championing justice—followers experience the paradoxical joy that emerges when surrendered lives align with divine purposes (Philippians 2:17–18). This long-term joy becomes a sustaining force, enabling perseverance amid trials and fueling passion for mission. Unlike fans whose fleeting enthusiasm dissolves when the moment passes, followers anchored in cross-centered delight cultivate a secure confidence in Christ's abiding presence (Philippians 4:4–7). As we draw this chapter to a close, we recognize that embracing Christ's call to daily cross-bearing not only secures personal transformation but also draws others into the radiant joy of authentic discipleship.

Conclusion

The allure of fan-level faith promises thrills without tribulation, yet beneath the surface lies a precarious façade destined to collapse under pressure. True discipleship, by contrast, requires more than admiration—it calls for a willing embrace of Jesus' call to self-denial, moral integrity, and active engagement in His mission. When faith is built on transient experiences rather than on the steady disciplines of prayer, Scripture, and community, it risks evaporating in the face of trials, ethical dilemmas, or unmet expectations. But the cost of following Jesus in earnest—the cross, the risk, the daily surrender—yields a joy and purpose that transcends any temporal discomfort. As fans turn to followers, they discover that enduring roots, honest accountability, and fruitful service create a faith capable of thriving through every season. In light of the eternal stakes at hand, the choice is clear: to remain a spectator or to step into the demanding, life-giving journey of genuine discipleship, confident that every sacrifice made for Christ is ultimately rewarded by an unshakeable hope.

Chapter 5 — Crisis Encounters That Separate Fans from Followers

Moments of rupture—when expectations collapse and familiar frameworks shatter—serve as spiritual litmus tests that reveal the depth of our allegiance. Across the Gospels and early church narratives, crises compelled would-be followers to confront what they truly treasured: comfort, certainty, or the living Christ. When hunger for free bread met a call to "eat My flesh," many drifted away; when fear of ridicule met the demand to "pick up your cross," entire groups scattered into the night. In the post-resurrection era, doubt and wonder intertwined as hardened hearts met the risen Lord, forcing questions about the nature of belief itself. These fractures in faith strike at the core of our identity, peeling back layers of fan-like enthusiasm to expose the raw material of genuine devotion. In every generation, pressures—whether theological challenges, moral collapse, or physical persecution—prompt a defining choice: remain a spectator of spiritual spectacle, or step into the cruciform trajectory of those who follow Jesus regardless of personal cost. By exploring encounters that test, torment, and transform, we uncover how true disciples emerge not in placid moments of agreement but in the furnace of trial, where trust in Christ alone proves resilient.

5.0 Threshold Moments: Why Crises Clarify Commitment

5.0.a Pressure Reveals the True Object of Trust When life's pressures intensify—be it financial hardship, relational conflict, or moral compromise—they act like a furnace, testing whether faith rests on Christ or on conveniences of culture. Most people are comfortable following Jesus when blessings abound: health is stable, relationships are intact, and financial abundance invites generous giving. Yet when storms arise—job loss, betrayal, or chronic illness—the veneer of cultural allegiance quickly dissolves. In those moments, fans of Jesus discover that their faith was tethered more to the benefits Christianity offered than to the Person of Christ. The psalmist reflects this dynamic vividly: "When I am afraid, I put my trust in you" (Psalm 56:3), acknowledging that true trust arises only when fear strips away all illusions of self-sufficiency. The trials of Job further illustrate that crises reveal whether one worships God for His gifts or for who He is (Job 1–2). Amid suffering, Job refused to curse God, demonstrating that his loyalty transcended temporal comfort. Fans, by contrast, often desert ship at the first sign of hardship, pursuing solace in more comfortable ideologies. The New Testament recounts Peter's confession of Jesus as the Christ (Matthew 16:16) followed by his thrice-denial under pressure (Luke 22:54–62), exposing how even a "rock" can crumble without tested trust. Conversely, Paul's response to his thorn in the flesh—asking the Lord for relief and then embracing God's grace in weakness (2 Corinthians 12:7–10)—models resilience that emerges when faith rests on God's sustaining presence rather than on favorable circumstances. As pressure reveals true objects of trust, we are forced to ask: do we trust Christ or the safety nets we've built? The crucible of crisis distinguishes mere admirers, who seek comfort, from devoted followers, who cling to Christ despite unmet expectations.

Recognizing this dynamic encourages believers to proactively build faith on enduring foundations rather than on shifting sands of prosperity or personal peace. By examining how crises unveil hidden allegiances, followers can identify areas where their trust remains superficial. As we transition to exploring how faith must evolve from comfort-based to covenantal resilience, we acknowledge that only genuine reliance on God's character sustains us when the storms of life threaten to overwhelm.

5.0.b From Comfort-Based Faith to Covenant Resilience
Comfort-based faith regards Christianity primarily as a means to secure physical well-being, emotional security, and social acceptance. This pragmatic approach interprets gospel promises in transactional terms: pray for healing, give generously, and expect prosperity in return. While Scripture affirms God's care for our needs (Matthew 6:31–33), the covenantal model calls believers to embrace a relationship marked by loyalty through thick and thin. Abraham's willingness to sacrifice Isaac (Genesis 22), despite the promise of descendants through his beloved son, exemplifies covenant resilience: he trusted God's character over immediate comfort. Jesus taught that following Him might lead to familial estrangement and societal scorn (Luke 14:26), yet covenant faithers endure these costs because they believe that God's redemptive purposes surpass temporal affliction. When Shadrach, Meshach, and Abednego faced the furnace for refusing to bow to Nebuchadnezzar's idol (Daniel 3:16–18), their confidence was not rooted in personal safety but in God's sovereignty, whether He chose to rescue or refine them. Their covenantal stance contrasts sharply with those who abandon faith when comfort disappears. New Testament believers, persecuted early on, embodied this covenantal ethos: Acts 5:41 records how apostles rejoiced to suffer for Christ's name rather than compromise ministry. The writer of Hebrews exhorts endurance by reminding readers that "discipline seems painful rather than pleasant at the moment" but later yields "peaceful fruit" (Hebrews 12:11). This shift from comfort-based to covenantal faith transforms suffering into a context for intimacy with God, forging resilience in our inner being. As we prepare to examine how

Jesus' hard sayings act as catalysts for this transformation, we see that only those willing to forsake comfort can truly follow Him beyond the superficial thrills of faith.

5.1 The Hard Sayings of Jesus

5.1.a "Eat My Flesh, Drink My Blood" (John 6:53–56) Jesus' declaration that followers must eat His flesh and drink His blood stood in stark contrast to the prevailing expectations of a political Messiah who would free Israel from Roman oppression. This hard saying, delivered after He fed five thousand (John 6:1–14), intensified confusion: people came seeking more bread, but Jesus offered Himself as sustenance for eternal life (John 6:27). His words transcended mere metaphor; they foreshadowed the sacramental reality of communion (John 6:53). Many who had witnessed miracles found this teaching "a hard saying" and turned away (John 6:60–66). Their departure revealed that they sought physical benefits rather than the deeper, mysterious union with Christ that demands total surrender. The twelve disciples themselves struggled: Peter's counter of "Lord, to whom shall we go?" (John 6:68) marked a decisive moment of commitment to the hard path. The Eucharistic language underscores that authentic following requires internalizing Christ's sacrifice—participating in His death and resurrection—rather than merely admiring external wonders. When hands clutch broken bread and lift a cup of wine, Christ's words become tangible: His life nourishes us, His death reconciles us. Fans, however, balk at such depth, desiring only the notion of Jesus as provider without embracing the scandal of a crucified Lord. By inviting listeners into this radical intimacy, Jesus separated those willing to embrace His full identity from those who sought a religion of convenience. As hearts wrestle with this teaching, they face a fork in the road: either move deeper into covenant union or drift away in disappointed disillusionment. This hard saying sets the stage for exploring other radical demands, such as the call to "hate father and mother," which further highlight the cost of discipleship.

5.1.b "Hate Father and Mother" (Luke 14:26–27) Jesus' command to "hate father and mother, wife and children, brothers and sisters, and even life itself" (Luke 14:26) uses Semitic hyperbole to convey the necessity of absolute devotion. In first-century Judea, family bonds formed the bedrock of identity and social security; to prefer Christ over one's own kin was culturally revolutionary. When Jesus uttered these words, many who admired His teaching recoiled, for they could not imagine severing or subordinating family loyalty. Yet this stark demand reveals that true discipleship requires prioritizing God's will above all human relationships (Matthew 10:37). To hate here means to love at a lesser degree, indicating that loyalty to Christ must eclipse even the most cherished attachments. When a son or daughter's faith choices conflict with family expectations, the disciple faces a crisis: obey the Father in heaven rather than human parents (Matthew 10:35–37). This teaching challenges the shallow allegiance of fans who profess loyalty to Jesus so long as it brings social harmony. Realizing that devotion to Christ may fracture household relationships causes many to retreat into nominal faith. Yet those who press on discover that placing Christ first does not destroy family bonds but reorders love so that all other relationships flow from a unified allegiance to the true head of the household. This realignment frees followers to love their families with healthy boundaries rather than conforming to cultural or familial pressures. The demand to take up the cross daily (Luke 9:23) intersects here: hating earthly ties shines light on the weight of the cross, revealing that loving Christ supremely requires ongoing relinquishment of lesser claimants on the heart. As we transition to the invitation to pick up one's cross, we see this statement of radical loyalty prepares believers for deeper sacrifices.

5.1.c "Take Up Your Cross Daily" (Luke 9:23) Jesus' directive to take up one's cross daily challenged His followers to embrace a posture of continuous sacrifice and self-denial. In Roman-occupied Judea, a cross symbolized agonizing execution reserved for criminals; to carry one publicly equated to anticipating death. By instructing disciples to carry their own crosses, Jesus reframed the image of execution as a daily lifestyle of dying to self-interests, pride, and comfort. This radical call demanded that followers willingly walk paths of suffering for His sake rather than pursuing safe, comfortable religious experiences. His earliest disciples witnessed through the Garden of Gethsemane that taking up a cross might lead to betrayal, arrest, and crucifixion (Mark 14:32–42). Yet Jesus' resurrection affirms that taking up one's cross leads to life—eternal life infused with divine power. When believers choose daily obedience over personal preference, they participate in Christ's own cruciform pattern, receiving contours of His character: compassion, humility, and joyful endurance. This pattern stands in stark contrast to fans who attend worship services seeking inspiration but balk when confronted with service-driven lifestyle demands. Scripture confirms that followers are called to share in Christ's sufferings (1 Peter 4:13) and to reap joy that thrice outweighs grief (James 1:2–4). As we transition to the lesson of the rich young ruler, we see how Jesus' cross-bearing call intersects with the invitation to sell all, demonstrating how ultimate allegiance manifests when we defy comfort for Christ.

5.1.d "Sell All You Have"—The Rich Ruler's Rubicon (Mark 10:20–22) The rich young ruler approached Jesus identifying himself as a devout adherent to the commandments, yet his heart's ultimate allegiance was revealed when Jesus instructs him to "sell all that you have, give to the poor, and follow me" (Mark 10:21). This demand touched a deep nerve: although the man sought eternal life, his amassed wealth foreshadowed a security blanket he refused to surrender. Many fans of Jesus embrace His teachings so long as personal possessions and status remain intact. Yet Jesus' instruction represented a Rubicon—crossing from fan-level admiration to sacrificial following that entangles material possessions with spiritual devotion. In first-century context, Jewish law did not require literal poverty; however, Jesus sought to expose the man's true king—his money. The man's sorrowful departure underscores how attachment to temporal assets can rival loyalty to Christ (Matthew 6:24). For modern readers, the challenge persists: to whom do we lend our hearts? Wealth, if unexamined, casts a spell of self-sufficiency that resists Christ's radical call. Yet the man's potential to follow Jesus was eclipsed by fear of loss, a powerful testimony that discipleship demands not just moral alignment but transformational reorientation of priorities. When followers willingly obey Christ's directive to place possessions under His lordship, they cross from fanship into the realm of covenant trust. This encounter bridges us to consider how crisis of interpretation occurs when metaphor demands surrender, preparing hearts to wrestle with Jesus' hardest sayings.

5.1.e Crisis of Interpretation: When Metaphor Demands Surrender Jesus often spoke in parables and metaphors that sounded safe until listeners recognized their radical implications. Fans accustomed to surface-level interpretation misunderstand metaphors as optional or symbolic suggestions rather than binding demands. When Jesus taught that unless a seed died, it remains alone (John 12:24), many failed to see their own call to self-sacrifice. This crisis of interpretation arises when conflating literal and figurative language without grasping Jesus' intent: metaphors extend beyond imagery into living reality. For instance, "salt of the earth" (Matthew 5:13) implies a lifestyle of preserving and seasoning culture, not merely wearing a Christian label. Followers who wrestle with metaphorical intensity experience cognitive dissonance: honoring father and mother may clash with reordering loyalties, and eating spiritual flesh conflicts with instinctive reverence for personal autonomy. This interpretive tension forces an existential decision: treat words as decorative adornments or as life-altering commands. The Bereans exemplify faithful interpreters, examining the Scriptures daily to verify Paul's teachings (Acts 17:11), showing that meticulous engagement resolves interpretive crises. In contrast, fans who skim scriptures for feel-good passages evade the transformative core. As followers embrace the full weight of Jesus' metaphors—dying to self, carrying the cross, living sacrificially—they separate from fans who prioritize comfort over obedience. By confronting and embracing the crisis of interpretation, believers open themselves to radical reorientation that reveals the chasm between mere admiration and authentic following.

5.2 Trials and Persecutions as Refining Fires

5.2.a Gethsemane Desertion and the Flight of the Twelve (Mark 14:43–50) The Garden of Gethsemane stands as a pivotal crisis encounter, revealing how closely even devoted followers cling to personal safety when trials intensify. Jesus withdrew with His inner circle to pray, modeling intimate dependence on the Father amid impending agony (Mark 14:32–36). Yet when Judas arrived with a mob and the soldiers laid hands on Him, the disciples faltered: Peter drew a sword, severing the ear of the high priest's servant, only to be rebuked by Jesus for resisting divine discipline (Mark 14:47–48). In the chaos, all twelve disciples fled (Mark 14:50), abandoning their Teacher to face suffering alone. This betrayal by those closest to Him starkly contrasts with fan-like admiration, which often collapses when the cost becomes too great. These men had fanned the movement with enthusiasm just days earlier, yet when obedience demanded loyalty beyond danger, their allegiance evaporated. In the aftermath, Peter's denial, though heartbreaking, transitions into repentance and restoration (John 21:15–19), demonstrating that crises, though exposing weakness, can also catalyze deeper devotion. The flight of the twelve reveals that trials function as refining fires: they strip away pretense and compel individuals to choose between self-preservation and Christ. Fans, unaccustomed to such pressure, often melt away; followers, humbled by failure, can be restored and strengthened. As we move from this episode to Pentecost boldness, we see that genuine discipleship emerges not in the absence of trials but through God's redemptive work amid them.

5.2.b Pentecost Boldness after Arrests (Acts 4:1–22) In the aftermath of Stephen's martyrdom (Acts 7), believers in Jerusalem faced escalating hostility. Peter and John, arrested for preaching the resurrection, stood before the Sanhedrin and boldly proclaimed Jesus as the only name under heaven given among men by which we must be saved (Acts 4:12–13). Despite threats to cease speaking in His name, they declared they must obey God rather than men (Acts 4:19–20). This confrontation illustrates how trials and persecutions ignite followers to articulate unwavering allegiance, contrasting sharply with fan-level faith that dissolves under scrutiny. The boldness of Peter and John emerged not from natural eloquence but from the filling of the Holy Spirit (Acts 4:8), demonstrating that genuine discipleship finds its strength in divine empowerment rather than personal courage. When faced with imprisonment, they refused to retreat into self-preservation, choosing instead to testify to Christ even at great risk. Their response encapsulates the shift from comfort-based following to covenantal resilience: they saw God's sovereign hand in persecution, leveraging it as a platform to proclaim the gospel rather than a call to capitulate. The Sanhedrin's threats only spurred the believers to pray for boldness (Acts 4:24–31), after which the place where they were gathered shook and they were all filled with the Holy Spirit, speaking the word of God with boldness (Acts 4:31). This supernatural boldness stands in stark contrast to the fearful flight in Gethsemane, illustrating that the same Spirit who reveals our weaknesses also empowers us to overcome them. As we transition to Stephen's martyrdom, we see how successive layers of persecution refine the church's commitment, forging a witness that transcends adversity.

5.2.c Stephen's Martyrdom—Fan Scattering, Follower Steadfastness (Acts 7:54–60) Stephen's public preaching, culminating in a scathing indictment of the Jewish leaders, triggered intense opposition that led to him being stoned to death (Acts 7:54–60). While fans of the law applauded his execution, Stephen's resolve to look to heaven and pray for his persecutors (Acts 7:55–60) revealed a spirit marked by Christlike mercy amid suffering. As stones rained down, he echoed Jesus' words from the cross: "Lord, do not hold this sin against them" (Acts 7:60), demonstrating that trials refine disciples into wrath-resistant vessels of grace. His martyrdom sparked terror among spectators, yet his faithful witness also moved witnesses like Saul to persecute more zealously (Acts 8:1–3). The scattering of believers following Stephen's death dispersed mission efforts beyond Jerusalem, fulfilling Jesus' command to be His witnesses to the ends of the earth (Acts 1:8). This tragic event underscores that persecution, while traumatic, can catalyze expansion of genuine faith communities rather than extinguishing them like fleeting flames. Stephen's courageous example brings into stark relief the contrast between those who follow Christ only when safe and those whose allegiance remains unshakeable even in the face of death. His martyrdom invites modern readers to consider whether fandom can endure under opposition or whether it evaporates, revealing the necessity of embedding faith in the promise of resurrection power (Romans 8:35–39). As the church transitions from Jerusalem's persecution to a wider mission, believers learn that hardship does not derail God's purposes but refines and redirects them toward greater fidelity.

5.2.d Early Church Under Nero—Costly Allegiance in the Arena
By the mid-first century, Christianity's exponential growth drew the suspicion and ire of Roman authorities. Emperor Nero, seeking a scapegoat for the Great Fire of Rome, blamed Christians, unleashing brutal persecutions around AD 64. Believers faced arrest, public flogging, and execution. Tactics included being sewn into animal skins and thrown before wild beasts, set aflame as staggered torches to light Nero's gardens, or crucified along roadsides. These gruesome punishments frequently took place in front of masses who cheered for the spectacle. Under such persecution, fan-level faith shattered; those whose allegiance had been superficial abandoned the faith quickly or recanted to avoid torture. Conversely, countless followers displayed unwavering fidelity—some pagan observers remarked that Christians sang praises to God even as they burned. These martyrdoms not only emboldened remaining believers but also drew pagans to question their own gods, as they witnessed Christians embracing death with hope rooted in resurrection (Acts 1:8). The church's perseverance under Nero's reign exemplifies how trials, far from destroying the movement, validated the power of the gospel. When superficial admiration gives way to persecution-fueled hostility, only covenantal faith that trusts in God's unbreakable commitment can endure. As we consider modern parallels where believers face digital harassment, censorship, or physical violence for their faith, we see that the heritage of Nero's church resonates in communities worldwide, reminding us that costly allegiance transcends cultural and temporal boundaries, compelling readers to

evaluate whether their faith can stand when pressured by contemporary forms of persecution.

5.2.e Modern Parallels: Underground Churches and Digital Doxxing In the twenty-first century, persecution takes myriad forms—physical oppression in some regions, legal restrictions in others, and digital harassment in nearly every context. Underground house churches in hostile nations meet in secret, risking arrest, torture, or execution for gathering to worship. Their unshakable commitment contrasts sharply with Western fans who readily disengage at the slightest discomfort, such as theological disagreement or cancellation on social media. Digital doxxing campaigns target outspoken believers, exposing personal information, inciting harassment, and threatening livelihoods. These modern crises test whether Christianity is merely a cultural badge or a covenant identity worth defending at great cost. Some believers lose jobs for refusing to compromise on biblical convictions, akin to Shadrach, Meshach, and Abednego facing the fiery furnace (Daniel 3:16–18). When families are ostracized or children bullied for attending church, many fans retreat into the safety of lukewarm faith, abandoning public witness to avoid conflict. In contrast, resolute followers embrace Jesus' promise that "whoever loses his life for my sake will find it" (Matthew 10:39), choosing integrity over comfort. The digital age's amplification of conflict underscores how crisis encounters continually separate fans from followers: while fans may ignore offensive posts, followers craft thoughtful, prayerful responses that reflect Christ's love under fire (1 Peter 3:15). By understanding these modern parallels, readers discern that persecution is not confined to ancient arenas but is woven throughout contemporary contexts, challenging us to ask whether our faith is robust enough to weather these digital and physical storms.

5.3 Post-Resurrection Challenges to Belief

5.3.a Thomas: From Empirical Doubt to Embodied Worship (John 20:24–29) When Thomas heard the other disciples' report of

Jesus' resurrection, he insisted on empirical proof: "Unless I see in His hands the mark of the nails . . . and put my finger into the mark of the nails, and put my hand into His side, I will never believe" (John 20:25). His demand for physical evidence reflects a crisis many fans face when appealing to faith as merely a set of convictions rather than a relationship with a living Savior. The other disciples met behind locked doors in fear of Jewish authorities (John 20:19), but Thomas was absent for that initial appearance and thus missed hearing Jesus' reassuring words. A week later, Jesus deliberately invited Thomas into the same room, offering His hands and side as evidence. This private encounter addressed Thomas's specific doubts while also highlighting that Jesus honors honest questioning rather than punishing it. When Thomas exclaimed, "My Lord and my God!" (John 20:28), he showcased the transition from skeptic to worshiper—a journey that required direct confrontation with the risen Christ. His testimony, preserved in Scripture, invites readers to recognize that doubt, when brought to Jesus, can become a catalyst for deeper faith rather than a sign of weakness. Thomas's story also warns fans who rely exclusively on secondhand reports or sensational presentations: true belief may require personal encounter and vulnerability. By moving from skepticism to profound devotion, Thomas exemplifies that post-resurrection challenges refine faith by forcing a shift from reliance on signs alone to wholehearted surrender to the person of Christ.

Thomas's transformation underscores that the crucible of doubt can serve the Spirit's purpose of forging robust conviction. His subsequent witness likely emboldened early Christian communities, offering a powerful testament that encountering Jesus authentically overturns entrenched skepticism (John 20:30–31). For modern readers, Thomas's example confronts the temptation to dismiss faith as irrational; instead, it invites us to bring our questions honestly before Jesus, trusting that He will meet us at the point of uncertainty. As we transition to the Emmaus Road encounter, we will see how disappointment in unmet expectations can lead to renewed conviction as Scripture's power illuminates the heart.

5.3.b Emmaus Road: Reinterpreting Disappointment through Scripture (Luke 24:13–35) Two disciples walked from Jerusalem to Emmaus on the day of Jesus' resurrection, their hearts heavy with disappointment (Luke 24:17–18). They recounted to a stranger—the risen Jesus, concealed from their sight—how they had hoped He would redeem Israel, yet now His death seemed to have dashed their dreams (Luke 24:21). Their "Foolish and slow of heart to believe" response (Luke 24:25) reveals how shock and disillusionment can darken understanding, causing followers to miss the deeper narrative God was unfolding. As they walked, Jesus "opened to them the Scriptures," explaining how all Moses wrote, the prophets proclaimed, and psalmists anticipated the Messiah's sufferings and glory (Luke 24:27). This exposition reoriented their expectations: they realized that redemption did not exclude the cross but required it. When they invited Him to stay, breaking bread awakened them to His presence, and He vanished from their sight, leaving their hearts ablaze (Luke 24:30–31). This crisis of disappointment became a turning point: sorrow transformed into joy as the resurrected Lord redefined their understanding by the living Word. Their immediate response—gyrating back to Jerusalem to share the news—demonstrated that Scripture-guided interpretation of crises cultivates conviction rather than withdrawal. Unlike fans who walk away when hopes crumble, these disciples responded to disappointment by seeking illumination in God's narrative, emerging with renewed zeal. Their story invites modern believers to allow Scripture to reshape disillusionment into worship, trusting that God's purposes often operate beyond our initial expectations. As we move to Peter's restoration by the Sea of Galilee, we will see how post-failure encounters extend this theme of reorienting heart through Christ's mercy and word.

5.3.c Sea of Galilee: Peter's Restoration and Re-Commission (John 21:15–19) After Jesus' resurrection, Peter returned to the familiar rhythms of pre-Fishers-of-Men life, heading to the Sea of Galilee to fish all night, yet catching nothing (John 21:3). His return to old routines illustrates how fans often regress to former comforts when crises—like fear or guilt—undermine their initial zeal. At dawn, Jesus stood on the shore, instructing them to cast nets on the right side of the boat; when they obeyed, they caught so many fish their nets began to tear (John 21:6). This miraculous catch parallels their earlier first encounter with Jesus (John 1:39–51), highlighting that following crises often requires re-engaging foundational callings with divine guidance. After bringing the catch ashore and sharing a meal, Jesus asked Peter three times, "Do you love me?" (John 21:16–17). Each affirmation allowed Peter to atone for his threefold denial (John 18:15–27) and to hear the commission to "Feed my lambs" and "Tend my sheep." This restoration process demonstrates that failure in crisis—Peter's desertion—does not permanently derail those willing to return to Christ's presence. Instead, post-resurrection encounters rebuild confidence, reminding Peter his identity and mission remain secure despite past weakness. This re-commissioning underscores that followers, rather than fans, embrace God's grace, enabling them to move forward in mission rather than retreat into self-condemnation. In the same way, modern believers who experience ethical failures or moments of fear can return to Christ's loving restoration, reclaiming callings perhaps neglected during crises. As we transition to the Ascension period's waiting season, we observe that even after restoration, followers must learn patient obedience while awaiting further revelation from the risen Lord.

5.3.d Ascension and Waiting: Obedience in the Silence between Promises (Acts 1:4–14) Following His resurrection appearances, Jesus met with His disciples over forty days, teaching them about the kingdom of God and promising that before long they would be baptized with the Holy Spirit (Acts 1:3–5). Just as Mary's wait at the stable exemplified faithful anticipation of promised Messiah, the disciples' waiting period required trust that Jesus would fulfill His promise. Though fans often grow restless when answers do not come swiftly, followers learn to cultivate prayer and unity in the interim. Jesus' final words—"You will receive power when the Holy Spirit has come upon you, and you will be my witnesses" (Acts 1:8)— established a clear mission that hovered in tension until Pentecost. His ascension, marked by the cloud concealing Him from sight (Acts

1:9), created a crisis of absence: the risen Lord was no longer physically present, requiring the disciples to internalize His teachings and trust the promised Spirit. In the epochs of silence between His departure and the outpouring of Pentecost, the disciples devoted themselves to prayer with one accord, demonstrating that crisis waiting refines corporate faith and prepares them for empowerment (Acts 1:14). This period serves as a model for contemporary believers who face seasons of apparent divine quietude—embracing obedience, steadfast devotion, and communal prayer rather than capitulating to discouragement. Their eventual empowerment at Pentecost confirms that faithful waiting catalyzes greater boldness, creating followers who can withstand future persecutions. As we move from post-resurrection challenges to moral failures that force a fork in the road, we see that what unfolds in these waiting moments lays the foundation for enduring allegiance beyond crises.

5.4 Moral Failures that Force a Fork in the Road

5.4.a Judas vs. Peter—Despair or Repentance after Denial Both Judas Iscariot and Peter found themselves at a moral precipice following their betrayals of Jesus. Judas, having arranged the betrayal for thirty pieces of silver (Matthew 26:14–16), experienced profound remorse upon seeing Jesus condemned (Matthew 27:3). Yet instead of seeking forgiveness, he succumbed to despair, returning the silver to the chief priests and overdosing on guilt until his lifeless body lay in a field (Matthew 27:4–5). His actions reveal that even deep remorse, unaccompanied by seeking God's mercy, devolves into hopelessness and self-destruction. Peter, on the other hand, denied knowing Jesus three times (Luke 22:54–62), but when the rooster crowed and he remembered Jesus' prediction (Luke 22:61), he wept bitterly rather than despairing wholly. Following the resurrection, Peter's restoration by Jesus (John 21:15–19) reaffirmed that repentance leads to renewed purpose. The fork in the road emerges in these differing responses: Judas's failure to pursue forgiveness contrasts sharply with Peter's decision to repent and re-engage his calling. While both men faced acute crisis encounters, only Peter's acknowledgment of guilt and pursuit of grace led him to perseverance as a foundational apostle (Acts 2:14–41). Investigating these parallel failures highlights how fans of Jesus, unprepared for moral lapses, often collapse at the first hint of compromise, whereas followers who embrace repentance find restoration and recommissioning. The divergent trajectories of Judas and Peter caution readers to choose the path of confession over the path of despair, illuminating the transformative power of mercy that distinguishes fans from followers.

As we move from individual failures to corporate failures like Ananias and Sapphira's story, we see how ethical lapses not only force personal reckonings but also test communal integrity.

5.4.b Ananias & Sapphira: Spectator Generosity Exposed (Acts 5:1–11) In the early church's context of communal sharing, Ananias and Sapphira sold property with the intention of presenting a portion of the proceeds as if it represented the full amount (Acts 5:1–2). Their deception arose from a desire for public acclaim—fans crave recognition for their generosity—yet wanted to keep a secret portion for themselves. Peter confronted them individually, exposing their lie to the Spirit: "Why has Satan filled your heart to lie to the Holy Spirit?" (Acts 5:3). Their sudden deaths underscore that God's holiness does not tolerate hypocrisy masquerading as piety. This narrative painfully illustrates how a merely fan-like attachment to faith can motivate one to manipulate religious expression for personal gain. Their sin threatened the church's witness, prompting fear and reverence among observers (Acts 5:11). Ethical inconsistency at a corporate level jeopardizes communal trust, as both insiders and outsiders question the authenticity of shared devotion. While some brethren buried the couple, perhaps in an effort to restore dignity, the incident served as a sobering reminder that the unity and purity of the church must uphold transparency and truth. The church responded with boldness, continuing to testify to the resurrection even amid fear (Acts 5:41–42), demonstrating that the exposure of hypocrisy need not extinguish mission but can prompt deeper communal integrity. This episode moves us to consider how entire congregations face crises of moral failure—illustrated in Corinth.

5.4.c Corinthian Chaos: Church Discipline as a Line of Demarcation In Corinth, believers prematurely celebrated the resurrection by indulging in drunkenness during the Lord's Supper, neglecting the community's weaker members and mocking the poor (1 Corinthians 11:20–22). Paul rebuked them sharply: "When you come together, it is not the Lord's Supper that you eat" (1 Corinthians 11:20), indicating that their misguided exuberance desecrated sacred memorial. Furthermore, contentious divisions erupted over allegiances to different leaders, debasing the unity Christ intended (1 Corinthians 1:12). Moral scandals—such as a man living with his father's wife (1 Corinthians 5:1)—shocked even pagan observers, prompting Paul to demand church discipline: "Purge the evil person from among you" (1 Corinthians 5:13). These failures forced a fork in the road: either a community remains a loose collection of admirers, tolerating ethical lapses for the sake of harmony, or it becomes a disciplined body, willing to exclude unrepentant members to preserve testimony. Paul's insistence on holiness and unity underscored that genuine discipleship demands both loving correction and courageous separation from sin's contagion. The Corinthian church's journey from chaotic immorality to restored fellowship (2 Corinthians 2:5–11) demonstrates that crises of corporate sin, when addressed with a spirit of repentance, can lead to healing and deeper covenant commitment. As modern churches navigate scandals and division, they face similar choices: preserve reputation through tolerance or preserve mission through biblical discipline. This understanding transitions to exploring how intellectual crises and cultural pressures further test the resolve of fans and followers alike.

5.5 Intellectual Crises and Cultural Pressures

5.5.a Greek Philosophers on Mars Hill — Curiosity or Conversion? (Acts 17:18–34) When Paul arrived in Athens, he encountered Epicurean and Stoic philosophers who viewed his proclamation of Jesus and resurrection as either strange or sensational (Acts 17:18–20). They invited him to deliver the "babbler" message at the Areopagus, a crucible of intellectual scrutiny. Paul's sermon addressed the Greek quest for the unknown god by identifying the divine as Creator of all, "not served by human hands" (Acts 17:25), challenging Athens' pantheon and idolatry. This intellectual crisis forced the crowd to choose between familiar philosophies and a new revelation of a resurrected Savior. Some sneered, some deferred, but others believed, including Dionysius and a woman named Damaris (Acts 17:34). Their conviction emerged not from fan-like interest in philosophical novelty but from a willingness to reconsider deeply held assumptions in light of compelling truth. For fans who chase spiritual trends or "hot topics," this episode warns against applauding novelty without applying discernment. True followers, however, follow where truth leads, even if it dismantles previous worldviews and social standing. As our culture grapples with postmodern relativism, secular humanism, and scientism, contemporary believers face similar pressures: do we conform our faith to prevailing intellectual currents or allow the gospel to challenge and transform our thinking? The Areopagus sermon models a posture of winsome engagement—speaking truth with respect—demonstrating that intellectual crises can become entry points for gospel advance rather than triggers for retreat.

From the intellectual arena of Mars Hill, we move to the subtle allure of syncretism in Colossae, where cultural pressures threatened to dilute Christ's supremacy, showing that cultural compromise can be as deadly to faith as overt persecution.

5.5.b Colossian Syncretism — Choosing Christ over Trending Spiritualities (Colossians 2:6–10) In Colossae, a blend of Jewish legalism, Greek mysticism, and human philosophies threatened to supplant the Sufficiency of Christ. Ascetic regulations, angel worship, and dietary legalism enticed believers to pursue spiritual progress through extra-biblical practices (Colossians 2:18–23). Paul warned them not to be taken captive by empty philosophies grounded in human tradition rather than in Christ (Colossians 2:8).

He emphasized that believers are "complete in him" (Colossians 2:10), meaning Christ's work is sufficient for redemption and growth; no additional mystic mediators or legalistic rituals add value. This intellectual crisis forced the Colossians to evaluate whether their devotion lay with Christ's finished work or with religious and cultural fads that promised elevated status. Many fans of novelty gravitate toward practices that sound spiritual—yoga, meditation, crystals—without considering that Christ alone is the unique revelation of God. The Colossian model encourages followers to measure every spiritual trend against the person and work of Christ: is it rooted in Scripture or in syncretistic culture? By urging believers to focus on Christ-centered identity, Paul recalibrated their worldview from self-help spirituality to God-shaped trust. This crisis highlights that cultural pressures can seduce believers into believing spiritual authenticity comes through charismatic personalities or trendy rituals rather than through abiding in Christ. As we shift from ancient syncretism to modern digital doubt communities, we see that intellectual crises continue to test the resolve of fans and followers alike.

5.5.c Deconstructing Faith Online: Doubt Communities vs. Disciple Communities The Internet today hosts vast communities where individuals deconstruct their faith, often buoyed by anecdotal evidence, moral criticisms of the church, or intellectual objections. These "doubt" communities function much like 5.5.b's syncretistic pressures but amplified by algorithm-driven echo chambers. Participants may share stories of churches that failed them, controversies surrounding Scripture's reliability, or unresolved theological tensions, creating a crisis of belief. Fans, whose faith was built on cultural Christianity rather than personal conviction, often find these platforms validating their exit from the church. Conversely, disciple communities—small groups committed to Scripture study, mutual accountability, and honest dialogue—provide a counterbalance, offering space to process doubts under the guidance of seasoned believers. In these discipleship contexts, questions lead to deeper exploration of biblical truth rather than wholesale rejection of faith. Disciple communities resist the binary of "all or nothing" by modeling that struggles and questions can coexist with robust commitment to Christ. Participants learn to engage objections with humility and rigor, weighing historical evidence, textual criticism, and lived experience through a biblical lens. This holistic approach fosters resilience, transforming crises of deconstruction into opportunities for maturation rather than abandonment. The crisis of digital doubt thus serves as a clarifying moment: fans who seek easy answers exit the faith, while followers who courageously grapple under communal support emerge with clarified conviction. This modern parallel invites reflection on whether our digital engagements draw us closer to Christ or push us toward passive skepticism, guiding us to discern the locus of true community.

5.6 Suffering that Births Mission

5.6.a Prison Epistles: Chains as a Pulpit for Paul (Philippians 1:12–20) Paul's frequent imprisonments transformed adversity into fertile ground for gospel proclamation, illustrating how suffering can ignite rather than extinguish mission. While under house arrest in Rome, guarded by soldiers and confined within a rented home (Acts 28:16–20), Paul recognized that his chains had circulated Christ's message throughout the imperial guard and to all those visiting him (Philippians 1:12–13). Far from being a hindrance, his imprisonment provided a visible testimony: friends and foes alike observed his unwavering faith under duress. Paul rejoiced that Christ was preached whether from pure motives or from selfish ambition, acknowledging that God's purposes transcend human intent (Philippians 1:18). In this way, the apostle's circumstances exemplified Jesus' teaching that persecution could produce a harvest of faithful witness (John 4:35–38). Paul wrote to the Philippians not with lament but with gratitude, asserting that his imprisonment had emboldened others to speak the word of God more courageously and fearlessly (Philippians 1:14). His perspective challenges fans of comfort who imagine that mission requires peak conditions; instead, Paul's experiences reveal that adversity can function as a pulpit, carving out opportunities to preach Christ's sufficiency. The chains that bound his body became the very medium through which the gospel spread. Prisoners from Caesar's household—who had access to the Roman aristocracy—heard the gospel directly or secondhand, creating ripple effects the apostle could never have orchestrated from street corners. As a result, Paul's letters, composed under confinement, brim with theological insight tempered by humility and joy. In Philippians 1:21, he declares, "For to me to live is Christ, and to die is gain," showing that his identity was no longer anchored in circumstances but in union with Christ. This radical reorientation under duress invites modern readers to view personal crises not as terminators of mission but as pivot points for renewed purpose. Transitioning from Paul's example, we explore how John's exile on Patmos similarly transformed isolation into visionary commission.

5.6.b John on Patmos: Isolation Turned Revelation (Revelation 1:9–11) Exiled to the barren island of Patmos under Emperor Domitian's reign (Revelation 1:9), John endured harsh conditions that sought to silence his prophetic voice. Patmos, a penal colony for political prisoners, offered isolation, bleak terrain, and the constant threat of imprisonment for harboring Christian texts. Instead of succumbing to despair, John found himself in a crucible that primed his spirit to receive apocalyptic revelation. On the Lord's Day, as he worshiped, John was "in the Spirit," and he heard behind him a "loud voice like a trumpet" commanding him to "Write what you see in a book and send it to the seven churches" (Revelation 1:10–11). The solitude forced upon him by persecution became the backdrop against which he beheld visions of the risen Christ—described in majestic terms: eyes like blazing fire, feet like burnished bronze, and a voice as the sound of rushing waters (Revelation 1:12–16). This dramatic revelation reveals that God meets His people precisely in their suffering, providing both comfort and commissioning. John's subsequent struggle to write down what he saw demonstrates that the Holy Spirit transforms persecution into prophetic clarity. While Patmos was meant to silence him, it instead amplified his witness: Revelation would challenge and encourage churches facing severe trials—Pergamum's martyrdom, Smyrna's poverty, and Laodicea's complacency. The book's letters communicated timeless truths:

perseverance in the face of tribulation (Revelation 2:10), the call to holiness (Revelation 3:19), and the ultimate victory of Christ (Revelation 21:1–4). John's festering sores and isolation illustrate that trials need not isolate followers from God's presence; rather, they can intensify communion, sharpen spiritual vision, and embolden mission to a broader audience than originally intended. As modern believers grapple with social exile, censorship, or imprisonment, John's example assures them that crises can become conduits for divine revelation, prompting us to consider how contemporary testimonies echo this pattern of isolation birthing mission.

5.6.c Contemporary Witness: Testimonies from Persecuted Regions In our own era, believers in persecuted regions face daily reality of suffering akin to early church martyrs, yet their stories affirm that crisis continues to birth mission today. In parts of Central Asia, Christians meet secretly in homes, risking arrest if discovered by authorities that deem their gatherings illegal. These believers worship by candlelight, sometimes baptizing new converts in hidden streams at dawn. Their courage echoes Paul's chains motivating bold gospel witness; despite danger, they share faith with neighbors, including fellow Muslims, leading to surprising conversions amid oppression. In North Africa, house church networks thrive under close government scrutiny. Members memorize Scripture and share it orally in oral cultures wary of possessing banned texts. When arrests occur, letters written from prison articulate radical love and forgiveness—hastening gospel advance as authorities and prison guards alike marvel at their resilience. The testimonies from East Asia include students who, expelled from university for attending underground churches, establish new fellowships at other campuses, spreading the faith among classmates previously indifferent to Christianity. Each prison cell or forced labor camp becomes a makeshift seminary where believers deepen reliance on God's Word rather than on comfortable church buildings. In Latin America, where gang violence threatens Christian outreach, pastors lead congregations to pray for persecutors and negotiate cease-fires, demonstrating that love under fire stands as the strongest gospel witness. Across these diverse contexts, suffering births mission when persecuted believers choose to forgive captors, distribute food to neighbors, and share even on deathbeds, believing that their testimony will sow seeds for future harvest. International agencies record that while persecution intensifies in certain areas, local churches multiply rapidly, reflecting Christ's promise that "where the treasure is, there your heart will be also" (Matthew 6:21). These contemporary examples mirror John's Patmos experience: exile intended to silence becomes a platform for visionary mission. As we transition to Chapter 6, which examines practical steps for integrating crises into kingdom growth, these testimonies remind us that faith deepened through suffering equips us to bear fruit in every season, regardless of circumstance.

Conclusion

The crucible of crisis does more than sift out the fainthearted; it forges hearts into vessels fit for Christ's ongoing mission. When disciples face the agony of betrayal in Gethsemane, the stark reality of a resurrected Savior, or the heat of imprisonment, a threshold emerges—fans fall away, and followers press forward. Those who walked away at a hard saying discovered that mere approval of Jesus' benefits cannot sustain them when discomfort becomes inevitable. In contrast, believers who embraced their own brokenness found grace to proclaim the gospel from prison cells, on mountain peaks, and in hidden rooms. Post-resurrection doubts, moral failures, and intellectual challenges all converge to test whether faith is reducible to emotion or rooted in a covenantal relationship with the risen Lord. As the early church scattered under persecution, they carried the message into unreached corners, demonstrating that suffering births mission rather than silence. These testimonies remind us that the same Holy Spirit who kindles hearts in calm seasons empowers us in storms, equipping every follower to endure, to witness, and to testify. Ultimately, crises do not herald abandonment but invitation: an invitation to trade fan-level infatuation for a faith that stands firm amid trial, a faith that learns to say "My Lord and my God" after seeing stripped nails and an empty tomb.

Chapter 6 — Portraits of Authentic Followers in Scripture

Scripture offers rich, multidimensional portraits of those who moved beyond fleeting enthusiasm to build lives anchored in Christ's transformative power. Whether a fisherman who leapt from a boat to walk on stormy seas or a foreign widow who pledged allegiance to an unseen God, these figures exemplify what it means to follow when everything in them—panic, grief, social convention—urged them to retreat. Their stories unfold in moments of vulnerability, from private decisions to public proclamations, illustrating that authentic devotion is forged in the interplay of faith, failure, and redemption. As we trace lives marked by humility, steadfast prayer, and sacrificial love, we discover that genuine discipleship looks less like a polished résumé of accomplishments and more like a tapestry woven from ordinary choices made in extraordinary circumstances. These narratives remind us that following Jesus is not a one-time commitment but an ongoing journey that reshapes identity, priorities, and community.

6.0 Framing Authentic Discipleship

6.0.a Core Marks: Humility, Teachable Spirit, Missional Obedience Authentic discipleship begins with humility, the posture of heart that acknowledges one's need for God above all else. Humility resists the allure of self-exaltation and embraces a willingness to bow before divine wisdom. The prophet Micah captures this when he declares that the Lord requires "to do justice, and to love kindness, and to walk humbly with your God" (Micah 6:8), suggesting that true following is marked by a disposition that prioritizes God's will over personal ambition. In the New Testament, Jesus models humility by taking on the form of a servant, washing His disciples' feet (John 13:14–15) and teaching that "whoever wishes to be first among you must be your slave" (Matthew 20:27). A humble disciple does not insist on having all the answers but instead cultivates a teachable spirit—an openness to correction, instruction, and the unexpected ways God may speak through others. Proverbs exhorts, "The way of a fool is right in his own eyes, but a wise man listens to advice" (Proverbs 12:15), underscoring that wisdom in following Christ requires reliance on community and Scripture rather than personal intuition alone. Teachable spirits pay attention to the Spirit's nudges toward repentance and refinement, welcoming accountability from mentors and peers. This openness prepares the heart to embrace missional obedience, the practical outworking of faith in daily context. Jesus' commissioning of the Twelve (Matthew 10:5–8) and later all believers (Matthew 28:19–20) underscores that discipleship is never purely inward but always oriented toward God's redemptive purposes in the world. Missional obedience involves mundane acts of service—feeding the hungry, defending the orphans, caring for the stranger (Isaiah 1:17)—as well as bold proclamation of Christ's lordship when cultural conditions press in. Together, humility, teachability, and missional intent form the tripod on which authentic following stands, resisting superficial faith that coasts on enthusiasm without sustained transformation.

Transitioning from these foundational marks, we recognize that narrative portraits of disciples convey authenticity far more vividly than abstract definitions ever could. Stories of Peter's impulsiveness, Mary's devotion, and Paul's radical conversion enliven the virtues of humility and obedience in concrete contexts. By tracing these lives, we discover how discipleship unfolds in tension between failure and forgiveness, quiet worship and costly sacrifice. Narrative testimony clarifies doctrinal contours, showing readers not just what discipleship should look like but how it actually functions when lived out amid real-world trials and triumphs. As we turn to the first portrait—Peter's journey—we see how his impulsive heart, guided by humility and shaped by mission, evolves from fan-like admiration to commissioned shepherd, embodying the core marks we have described.

6.0.b Why Narrative Testimonies Trump Abstract Definitions

Abstract definitions of discipleship—lists of behaviors, creeds, or duties—can become disconnected from the messy realities of human experience. When pastors or authors outline bullet points for "what makes a disciple," the result can be a dry checklist that fails to resonate with individuals wrestling in their particular context. In contrast, narrative testimonies leverage the power of story to bridge cognitive understanding and emotional engagement, making the cost and joy of following Christ palpable. Consider the story of Peter's failure at Caesar's house (Matthew 26:69–75): his vehement denials of Jesus after professing loyalty expose the depth of his love and the weight of his weakness. As we watch Peter's emotional unravelling in real time—weeping bitterly when the rooster crows (Luke 22:61–62)—we recognize our own potential for compromise and the genuine anguish that ensues. This vivid portrayal invites empathy, prompting us to confess sincerely, "Lord, I am not more courageous than Peter." Similarly, Mary of Bethany's choice to sit at Jesus' feet (Luke 10:38–42) transcends a mere bullet point about "prioritizing worship over service" by showing us the relational stakes: Martha's frustration and Mary's single-minded devotion become tangible in a domestic setting, teaching that discipleship often entails difficult conversations about values and time allocation. Narrative keeps us anchored in lived reality: we see how disciples stumble, howl in grief, and emerge renewed—none of which is captured fully in doctrinal abstractions. Through stories, we internalize the rhythms of repentance, restoration, and mission, learning to navigate our own spiritual crises by observing how others did so. This approach not only informs our heads but also nurtures tender hearts, fostering a desire to risk obedience when circumstances mirror those ancient encounters. As we transition to exploring our first narrative portrait—Peter's transformation—we will witness how story demonstrates the synergy of humility, teachability, and missional obedience in a way that definitions alone cannot.

6.1 Peter: From Impulsive Admirer to Commissioned Shepherd

6.1.a Call by the Lake—Leaving Nets for Deeper Waters (Luke 5:1–11) Peter's initial encounter with Jesus unfolds beside the Sea of Galilee, where fishermen like Peter, Andrew, James, and John had spent countless dawns hauling nets for fish. On one such morning, the crowd press-jammed the shoreline to hear Jesus teach, prompting Him to borrow Simon's boat to gain leverage for His voice (Luke 5:3). After teaching, Jesus invited Simon to launch "into the deep and let down your nets for a catch" (Luke 5:4), instructions that perplexed Simon after an unproductive night of fishing (Luke 5:5). Nonetheless, Peter humbly acquiesced, recognizing Jesus' spiritual authority—an early sign of teachable obedience. When the nets bulged under an overwhelming catch (Luke 5:6), Peter's astonishment morphed into trembling as he knelt before Jesus, confessing his unworthiness: "Depart from me, for I am a sinful man, O Lord" (Luke 5:8). This moment of contrition contrasts sharply with worshipers who admire miracles but remain unmoved inwardly; Peter's response reveals that authentic following begins with acknowledging personal sin in light of divine holiness. Jesus then called him to "Behold, I will make you fishers of men" (Luke 5:10), reorienting Peter's vocation from earthly provision to spiritual harvest. This call demanded leaving both nets and fishermen behind—a rupture from comfort to mission. Peter and his partners left everything and followed Jesus (Luke 5:11), illustrating the cost of genuine discipleship: relinquishing familiar livelihoods for unpredictable itineration. The scene models how Christ's invitation often appears unreasonable in worldly terms yet suffices in heavenly logic. By casting his nets on Christ's word rather than his own experience, Peter displayed a kernel of faith that would grow through testing. Transitioning from this initial call, we see that the one who once doubted Jesus' instruction to fish at dawn would soon walk on stormy waters—a further stretch of faith and obedience.

6.1.b Walking on Water—Risk, Fear, and Rescue (Matthew 14:28–33) After withdrawing to pray alone on a mountain, Jesus saw the disciples struggling to row against a storm in the dark (Matthew 14:22–23). As they strained in fear, Jesus approached, walking on the turbulent sea (Matthew 14:25). Mistaking Him for a ghost, the disciples shrank back in terror, but Peter called out, "Lord, if it is you, command me to come to you on the water" (Matthew 14:28). Jesus beckoned, and Peter stepped from the boat, walking on water toward the Lord (Matthew 14:29). Yet when wind and waves assaulted his attentiveness, Peter's gaze shifted from Jesus to the howling tempest, and he began to sink (Matthew 14:30). His faltering faith, however, did not result in condemnation but in the immediate伸 reach of Jesus' hand: "O you of little faith, why did you doubt?" (Matthew 14:31). This dramatic rescue underscores that authentic discipleship confronts uncertainty not by retreating to safety but by trusting Christ's presence amid chaos. Peter's audacious step demonstrates the risk inherent in following Christ beyond comfort zones; his doubt reveals how easily fear can eclipse faith. The disciples in the boat witnessed this event and worshiped Jesus, confessing, "Truly you are the Son of God" (Matthew 14:33), evidencing that crisis-laden experiences of Christ's power precipitate deeper confession and devotion. Fans of Jesus might admire the miracle from afar, celebrating the spectacle without operating out of it; followers like Peter immerse themselves in risk, discovering that Jesus does not hesitate to meet amid their weakness. As Peter emerges from the sea, dripping and breathless, we see that the path of faith is not seamless but marked by intertwined moments of courage and fear, trust and doubt. This encounter sets the stage for a season of revelation on the mountain, where Peter learns to listen rather than perform.

6.1.c Mount of Transfiguration—Learning to Listen, Not Perform (Matthew 17:1–8) Following the ordeal on the sea, Jesus led Peter, James, and John up a high mountain (commonly identified as Mount Tabor or Hermon), where He was transfigured before them: "His face shone like the sun, and his clothes became white as light" (Matthew 17:2). Moses and Elijah appeared, conversing with Jesus about His approaching departure (Matthew 17:3), symbolizing the Law and the Prophets bearing witness to His messianic mission. Peter, overwhelmed by awe, proposed erecting three shelters for Jesus, Moses, and Elijah, revealing his impulse to cement mountaintop experiences rather than process their significance (Matthew 17:4). While well-intentioned, this urge to act—typical of fan-like reactions to transcendent moments—risked distracting from the substance of God's revelation. Suddenly, a bright cloud enveloped them, and a voice from the cloud declared, "This is my beloved Son, with whom I am well pleased; listen to him" (Matthew 17:5). This divine injunction highlights that authentic following prioritizes listening to Christ's voice over constructing physical monuments to spiritual highs. The disciples fell facedown, terrified, but Jesus gently touched them, bidding them not to fear and to rise (Matthew 17:7). When they lifted their eyes, only Jesus remained, reminding them that the essence of discipleship involves ongoing obedience to His words—rather than freezing in ecstatic worship on mountaintops. This moment catalyzed personal transformation, teaching Peter that spiritual experiences are not destinations but passages pointing toward Christ's redemptive pathway. As they descended, Jesus ordered them not to speak of the vision until after His resurrection (Matthew 17:9), indicating that revelation must be integrated through cross-centered context. From this transfiguration moment, Peter would learn that listening—attuned to Jesus' unfolding mission—far outweighs building visible shrines to spiritual sensations.

6.1.d Restoration after Denial—Love's Threefold Re-Affirmation (John 21:15–19) After Jesus' resurrection, Peter and several disciples returned to Galilee, resuming fishing on the Sea of Tiberias but catching nothing (John 21:3). At daybreak, Jesus appeared on the shore, instructing them to cast the net on the right side of the boat for a miraculous catch (John 21:6), reminiscent of their first call (Luke 5:4–6). Following this familiar encounter and shared meal, Jesus engaged Peter in a poignant dialogue that focused on genuine, sacrificial love (John 21:15–17). Three times Jesus asked, "Simon, son of John, do you love me?" (John 21:15, 16, 17), mirroring Peter's three denials (John 18:15–27) and granting him a path to restoration. Peter's repentant affirmation—"You know that I love you" (John 21:17)—reveals humility, honesty, and a desire for reconciliation rather than mere verbal loyalty. Each time Peter professed love, Jesus commissioned him to "Feed my lambs," "Tend my sheep," and "Feed my sheep," entrusting Peter with shepherding Christ's community (John 21:15–17). This sequence affirms that authentic discipleship is not a trophy lifted after failure but a restoration that equips for renewed mission. Peter's tears of repentance and his acceptance of pastoral responsibility illustrate that followers emerge from failure not with shame but with redirected purpose. The dialogue also underscores that following Jesus involves both devotion and duty: love for Christ translates into tangible care for others. As the conversation concluded, Jesus predicted Peter's martyrdom—"When you are old, you will stretch out your hands, and another will dress you and carry you where you do not want to go" (John 21:18)—reminding Peter that restoration does not guarantee a painless life but rather prepares him for a cross-shaped destiny. From denial to recommission, Peter's trajectory models how Christ's grace transforms brokenness into leadership, separating fans content with surface faith from followers whose lives bear the imprint of restorative obedience.

6.1.e Pentecost Courage—From Self-Preservation to Spirit-Empowered Preacher (Acts 2:14–41) Fifty days after the Passover, the disciples gathered in Jerusalem for the Feast of Weeks (Pentecost), and the promised Holy Spirit descended with a sound like a mighty rushing wind and tongues of fire resting upon them (Acts 2:1-4). Empowered by the Spirit, Peter stood in the midst of the assembled crowd—descended from various nations—and addressed them boldly (Acts 2:14). Where he had once fled at the moment of greatest danger (Matthew 26:56), Peter now spoke with clarity and conviction, declaring Jesus to be both Lord and Messiah, whose crucifixion had fulfilled God's determined plan but whose resurrection He raised to life (Acts 2:22-24). When the crowd recoiled, asking, "What shall we do?" (Acts 2:37), Peter offered a Spirit-birthed response: "Repent and be baptized every one of you in the name of Jesus Christ for the remission of sins" (Acts 2:38). Three thousand souls accepted the message that day (Acts 2:41), illustrating that Spirit-empowered testimony has catalytic potential. Peter's transformation—from impulsive admirer to authoritative preacher—demonstrates how Spirit filling aligns human frailty with divine purpose. Fans might admire his prior experiences but would balk at his newfound courage to confront religious leaders and challenge public groups. As he continued preaching, healings and signs accompanied his words (Acts 3:1-10), prompting more to believe. Yet Peter did not rest on popularity; he faced arrest (Acts 4:3) and rejection (Acts 4:18-21), yet rejoiced that God's name was glorified by the opposition (Acts 5:41). His trajectory epitomizes how authentic following, sustained by the Spirit, thrives not in self-preservation but in the willingness to be shaped, sent, and stretched, revealing that genuine discipleship hinges on empowering presence rather than mere attraction to spiritual highlights. As his leadership matured, Peter consistently pointed back to Christ—ever mindful that the gospel advances through Spirit-filled witness rather than personal prowess.

6.2 Mary of Bethany: Worship over Work

6.2.a Sitting at His Feet—Choosing Presence above Productivity (Luke 10:38-42)

When Jesus entered the village of Bethany, Mary welcomed Him into her home, and instead of joining her sister Martha in hospitality tasks, she chose to sit at Jesus' feet—listening to His teaching (Luke 10:39). In first-century Jewish culture, seating at a rabbi's feet signified disciple status, an honor typically reserved for male students. Mary's decision defied gender expectations and elevated her desire for Christ's presence above the cultural priority of domestic service. Martha, overwhelmed with the burden of preparing food and serving the guest, confronted Jesus, asking Him to make Mary help her (Luke 10:40). Jesus gently corrected her, saying, "Martha, Martha, you are anxious and troubled about many things, but one thing is necessary. Mary has chosen the good portion, which will not be taken away from her" (Luke 10:41–42). This "good portion" denotes relational intimacy with Christ that supersedes pragmatic concerns. For Martha, hospitality had become an idol, trapping her in a cycle of busyness that obscured the gift of presence. Mary's choice illustrates that authentic discipleship often looks countercultural: while fans prioritize productivity—doing more ministry tasks—true followers recognize that deep listening and worship serve as the wellspring for fruitful service. Mary's posture underscores that the foundation of obedience is being under the lordship of the Word—remaining rooted before venturing forth. When we build our lives around doing for Christ without first sitting at His feet, we risk substituting activity for spiritual formation. Mary's example models the way of contemplative devotion integrated with mission, showing that worship is not a luxury to be squeezed in but the anchor around which service coheres. As we transition to her next defining action—anointing Jesus with costly perfume—we see how devotion inevitably overflows into sacrificial worship.

6.2.b Grief and Faith at Lazarus' Tomb—Honest Lament That Invites Glory (John 11:32–44) Upon receiving news that her brother Lazarus was ill, Mary remained in Bethany while Lazarus died (John 11:5–6). When Jesus finally arrived four days later, Martha hurried to meet Him, but Mary remained in the house until summoned (John 11:20–21, 32). Arriving at the tomb, Mary saw Jesus, fell at His feet, and wept (John 11:32–33). Her tears and confession—"Lord, if you had been here, my brother would not have died" (John 11:32)—exposed her raw faith interlaced with grief. Jesus, moved deeply by her sorrow, wept Himself (John 11:35), demonstrating that authentic following embraces vulnerability rather than suppressing emotion. As onlookers questioned whether He could have prevented Lazarus' death (John 11:37), Jesus prayed and commanded Lazarus to come forth (John 11:41–43), illustrating that faith unafraid to express grief invites divine glory. Mary's lament did not undermine her trust in Jesus; instead, it underscored her conviction that even in death, Christ's word had power. This episode shows that authentic disciples do not feign stoicism but recognize that faith shows its strength precisely in Jesus' compassionate response to human pain. The tomb-cry "Lazarus, come out!" (John 11:43) echoes throughout history as a summons for believers to approach God with honest hearts, knowing He will respond with resurrection power. As Martha stepped forward, Jesus affirmed that He is "the resurrection and the life" (John 11:25), and Lazarus emerged bound in burial cloths (John 11:44), depicting how authentic faith emboldens both the mourner and the miracle. Mary's longing, expressed in tears, teaches that vulnerability before Christ does not reveal weakness but opens the door for divine intervention. Transitioning from grief to extravagant worship, we find Mary once again modeling that intimate devotion naturally translates into costly offerings of worship.

6.2.c Costly Perfume Offering—Extravagant Love Beyond Social Convention (John 12:1–8) Six days before the Passover, Mary anointed Jesus' feet with a pound of costly ointment made of pure nard and wiped His feet with her hair (John 12:3). The perfume's value equaled a year's wages, underscoring the extravagance of this act. The aroma filled the house (John 12:3), signifying that true worship emanates from every aspect of life—physical senses as well as spiritual sentiments. Judas Iscariot objected, calling it wasteful and suggesting the perfume should have been sold to aid the poor (John 12:4–5). Jesus corrected him, saying Mary had kept the perfume for the day of His burial, praising her foresight and devotion (John 12:6–8). Mary's willingness to break cultural norms—letting down her hair in public, an act of vulnerability for a Jewish woman—revealed a profound love that transcended convention. Her example underscores that authentic discipleship often appears foolish in the eyes of onlookers because it subordinates costly devotion to societal expectations. While fans seek recognition or affirmation, Mary's worship was directed solely at Jesus, with no desire for acclaim. The anointing prefigured Jesus' burial, linking extravagant love to redemptive sacrifice. Mary's gift reminds us that authentic following does not calculate cost in human currency but counts it all joy to lavish love on Christ (Philippians 2:17). Her act invites modern readers to consider what resources—time, money, reputation—they might pour out for Jesus as tangible expressions of worship. As we move from Mary's personal devotion to her influence on community faith, we see how one act of sacrificial worship fuels collective recognition of Christ's impending sacrifice.

6.2.d Quiet Influence—How Contemplative Devotion Shapes Communal Faith (Mark 14:9) In Mark's Gospel, Jesus declares that Mary's act of anointing will be remembered "wherever the gospel is preached in the whole world" (Mark 14:9). This pronouncement suggests that Mary's private devotion would have rippling effects far beyond the walls of Bethany. In the early church, this same perfume narrative inspired believers to cherish sacrificial worship as integral to gospel proclamation. Through her contemplative devotion—sitting at Jesus' feet (Luke 10:39), grieving honestly at Lazarus' death (John 11:32), anointing Him lavishly (John 12:3)—Mary shaped the way others perceived worship. Later traditions, such as the Eastern Orthodox Church's veneration of icons and the West's emphasis on eucharistic adoration, reflect this legacy of intimate contemplation. Mary's quiet example also provided a counterbalance to the world's fixation on frenetic activity; she demonstrated that genuine service flows from being rooted in Christ's presence. In communal settings, when stories of her devotion circulated, they stirred hearts to prioritize presence over performance. Mary's influence reminds us that authentic followers do not always lead from stages but often lead from footstools of humility, reshaping community practice through personal example. As modern faith communities seek to balance action and contemplation, Mary's portrait offers a template:

devotion that begins in hidden communion with Christ inevitably overflows into communal worship that testifies to His worth. This reflection on Mary's quiet influence provides a bridge to the next set of portraits—Saul's radical transformation, where solitary devotion collides with the mission of the church—illustrating how different temperaments contribute uniquely to the tapestry of authentic discipleship.

6.3 Saul to Paul: Radical Re-Orientation

6.3.a Damascus Encounter—Confronted by the Risen Lord (Acts 9:1–19) Saul of Tarsus, a zealous Pharisee educated under Gamaliel (Acts 22:3), had been notorious for persecuting the early church, approving Stephen's stoning (Acts 7:58) and hunting down believers in Jerusalem (Acts 8:3). Under letters from the high priest, Saul set out for Damascus with authority to arrest any followers of "the Way" (Acts 9:1–2). As he neared the city, a bright light from heaven flashed around him, and he fell to the ground, hearing a voice ask, "Saul, Saul, why are you persecuting me?" (Acts 9:4). Startled, Saul responded, "Who are you, Lord?" to which the voice replied, "I am Jesus, whom you are persecuting" (Acts 9:5). Struck blind, Saul was led by his companions into Damascus and remained without sight for three days, neither eating nor drinking (Acts 9:8–9). This physical blindness reflected his spiritual blindness to the truth of Jesus as Messiah. Meanwhile, the Lord spoke to a disciple named Ananias in a vision, instructing him to go to Straight Street to lay hands on Saul so that he might regain his sight (Acts 9:10–12). Ananias hesitated, knowing Saul's reputation, but the Lord assured him that Saul was a chosen instrument to bear His name before Gentiles, kings, and children of Israel (Acts 9:15). Obeying, Ananias found Saul praying; he laid hands on him, and something like scales fell from Saul's eyes, restoring his sight (Acts 9:17). Saul then rose, was baptized, and after taking nourishment, regained strength (Acts 9:18–19). Immediately he began proclaiming Jesus in the synagogues, declaring that He is the Son of God (Acts 9:20). The Damascus encounter thus marked a dramatic turning point: Saul transitioned from official persecutor to ardent proclaimer, demonstrating that authentic following sometimes begins with confronting our own malice and submitting to Christ's authority. This foundational crisis narrative sets the stage for understanding how periods of hidden formation in isolation further shape disciples for mission.

6.3.b Desert Formation—Years of Hidden Preparation in Arabia (Galatians 1:15–18) After his conversion, Saul did not immediately rejoin Jerusalem's fellowship; instead, he withdrew to Arabia, a period of solitude and reflection that lasted up to three years (Galatians 1:15–18). In this desert setting, removed from structured community and ritual observance, Saul immersed himself in prayer and contemplation, deepening his understanding of the gospel he had once violently opposed. His personal writing does not elaborate on the specific activities during this time, but it likely involved fasting, meditation on Scripture, and receiving revelatory insights into Christ's death, resurrection, and the implications for Jew and Gentile alike. The solitude of the Arabian desert stripped away distractions, much as a sculptor removes unnecessary material to reveal the figure within stone. Saul's transformation here underscores that authentic discipleship often requires seasons of hidden formation—times when outward ministry halts so inward transformation can germinate. When he emerged to visit Jerusalem, he stayed with Peter for fifteen days, meeting with other apostles but revealing little of the revelation he had received directly from Christ (Galatians 1:18–19). Only Barnabas took him under his wing, introducing him to the apostles throughout Judea (Galatians 1:19–24). This desert apprenticeship reveals that public ministry without prior internalization of Christ's call can lead to superficial service. Saul's example warns modern followers against skipping formative seasons, reminding us that God's call often precedes corporate endorsement. As we transition to exploring his cross-shaped ministry centered in "I have been crucified with Christ" (Galatians 2:20), we see how this period of solitude equipped Paul to embrace suffering as integral to his mission.

6.3.c Cross-Shaped Ministry—Living "Not I, but Christ" (Galatians 2:20) Upon his return to Antioch and eventual elevation as an apostle to the Gentiles, Paul's ministry embodied his declaration, "I have been crucified with Christ. It is no longer I who live, but Christ who lives in me" (Galatians 2:20). This verse captures the essence of cross-shaped ministry: the believer's identity dissolves into union with Christ, yielding a life that is both surrendered to and empowered by Him. Paul's missionary journeys, often initiated by visions and calls (Acts 16:9–10), led him through Asia Minor, Greece, and beyond, always inviting listeners to partake in the same cruciform life that he embraced. In Philippians 3:10, he wrote of his desire to "know Christ and the power of his resurrection, and may share his sufferings, becoming like him in his death." This longing reveals that authentic following involves a willing participation in Christ's sufferings, recognizing that the gospel is not merely good news for life here but also for death that leads to resurrection. Paul's numerous imprisonments—Philippi's inner prison, Roman house arrest—illustrate how he endured hardship while continuing to write epistles that guided churches he founded, exemplifying that cross-shaped ministry extends beyond physical ailments to spiritual encouragement. When arrested in Philippi, he and Silas prayed and sang hymns at midnight (Acts 16:25), causing an earthquake that opened the prison doors but also led to the jailer's conversion (Acts 16:26–34). Paul's commitment to living by faith—declaring "the life I now live in the flesh I live by faith in the Son of God" (Galatians 2:20)—transcended temporal circumstances. His letters reveal that he counted "everything as loss because of the surpassing worth of knowing Christ Jesus my Lord" (Philippians 3:8). This radical reorientation, from zealous persecutor to crucified co-worker with Christ, stands as a paradigm for followers who must choose daily surrender over fleeting comforts. As we transition to exploring Paul's partnerships, we see that cross-shaped ministry flourishes in community, when believers support one another rather than clinging to individualistic pursuits.

6.3.d Partnership over Platform—Barnabas, Timothy, and the Team Model (Acts 13:1–3; Philippians 2:19–22) From his earliest missionary ventures, Paul recognized that the gospel advanced most effectively through partnerships rather than solitary platforms. Barnabas, whose name means "son of encouragement" (Acts 4:36), partnered with Paul as they planted the church in Antioch (Acts 11:25–26), equipping new believers and providing crucial credibility for Saul before Jew and Gentile alike. Their commission by the Holy Spirit for the first European mission (Acts 13:1–3) exemplifies collaborative leadership: prophets and teachers in Antioch prayed, fasted, laid hands on Paul and Barnabas, and sent them out. This framework of mutual affirmation and shared responsibility contrasts sharply with modern celebrity Christianity, where platforms often overshadow partnerships. Barnabas's role extended beyond advocacy; he invested in Paul's mentorship, aiding reconciliation with the Jerusalem apostles (Acts 15:12–17). Later, Paul chose young Timothy, his "beloved and faithful child in the Lord" (Philippians 2:22), as a co-laborer. Paul's description of Timothy as someone who "shares in the gospel" and "genuinely cares for your welfare" (Philippians 2:20–21) underscores that true ministry partnerships require shared vision, equal sacrifice, and mutual affection. When Paul instructed Timothy to remain in Ephesus, charging him to preach, reprove, rebuke, and exhort with all patience (2 Timothy 4:2), he entrusted him with the continuation of community growth, illustrating how the baton of mission passes through relationships rather than isolated pulpit presence. This teamwork model fostered resilience during persecution: when Paul was imprisoned, Timothy's presence in Philippi provided comfort and support (Philippians 2:19–22). As we move to consider Paul's finishing well, we see how partnerships sustained him through decades of cross-bearing service, culminating in his confident anticipation of the crown of righteousness (2 Timothy 4:6–8).

6.3.e Finishing Well—Last Letters and the Hope of a Crown (2 Timothy 4:6–8) In Paul's final epistle, he likens his approaching death to a poured-out drink offering, indicating that his life was already being consumed for Christ (2 Timothy 4:6). Writing from a Roman prison, perhaps under Nero's tyranny, Paul exhibited a serene acceptance of martyrdom: "The time for my departure has come" (2 Timothy 4:6). He did not lament impending execution but looked forward to "the crown of righteousness" that the Lord will award to him and to all who have loved His appearing (2 Timothy 4:8). This perspective underscores that authentic discipleship concludes not with regret over missed opportunities but with confident hope resting on faithfulness to the end. Paul's departure stands in contrast to those who fade away from ministry when life becomes uncomfortable or dangerous. His last instructions to Timothy—encouraging him to bring Mark with him, to come before winter, and to bring his coat—reveal a tender affection that transcends the grave (2 Timothy 4:11–13). As he penned these words, his earthly platform might have been collapsing, but his heavenly hope shone brighter: he had fought the good fight, finished the race, and kept the faith (2 Timothy 4:7). His example invites modern followers to aspire beyond short-lived impact toward enduring legacies forged in suffering, grounded in divine promise, and sustained by partnerships. As we transition from Saul to Paul's narrative to the next portrait—Ruth's loyal love that steps beyond ethnic boundaries—we see that authentic following emerges not just in extraordinary calling but also in steadfast devotion across diverse contexts.

6.4 Ruth: Loyal Love That Transcends Ethnic Boundaries

6.4.a Brave Decision at Moab's Border—"Your God Will Be My God" (Ruth 1:16–18) In the midst of a famine in Bethlehem, Elimelech emigrated to Moab with his wife Naomi and their two sons, who took Moabite wives, Orpah and Ruth (Ruth 1:1–5). After ten years, Elimelech and his sons died, leaving Naomi alone with her daughters-in-law. Naomi, heartbroken, decided to return to her homeland upon hearing the Lord had visited His people by giving them food again (Ruth 1:6–7). She urged her daughters-in-law to remain in Moab with their families, but Orpah reluctantly kissed her mother-in-law goodbye and returned to her people (Ruth 1:14–15). Ruth, however, clung to Naomi, declaring, "Do not urge me to leave you or to return from following you. For where you go I will go, and where you lodge I will lodge. Your God will be my God" (Ruth 1:16). This counter-cultural pledge defied norms, as intermarriage between Israelites and Moabites was forbidden (Deuteronomy 23:3), and religious syncretism threatened Israel's purity. Ruth's commitment risked social ostracism, entailed severing family ties, and relocated her into hardship. Yet her loyalty to Naomi and faith in Yahweh transcended cultural and genealogical barriers. Naomi's initial resistance highlights the depth of Ruth's resolve: "Where you die, I will die, and there will I be buried" (Ruth 1:17), illustrating that genuine discipleship may require forsaking one's birthplace, traditions, and security. For fans of religious convenience, such total upheaval seems unwarranted; for followers of Christ's call, Ruth's example reveals that allegiance to God may demand crossing entrenched boundaries. Her journey back to Bethlehem is not merely geographical but theological: she steps from Moabite polytheism into covenant fidelity, planting the seed for her inclusion in David's lineage and ultimately Jesus' genealogy (Matthew 1:5). As we transition to exploring her gleaning in Boaz's fields, we see that Ruth's initial pledge—rooted in loyalty and faith—paves the way for a life that seamlessly integrates devotion with practical obedience.

6.4.b Gleaning in Hope—Faithfulness in Humble Labor (Ruth 2:2–12) Upon returning to Bethlehem with Naomi, Ruth sought permission to glean in the fields during barley harvest, a provision mandated by Mosaic law to care for the poor and sojourners (Leviticus 19:9–10; Deuteronomy 24:19–21). Ruth rose early and went out to glean behind the reapers, demonstrating industriousness and humility (Ruth 2:2). She happened to enter the field of Boaz, a prominent relative of Elimelech, who welcomed her warmly, instructing his workers to leave extra stalks for her to gather (Ruth 2:8–9). Boaz recognized Ruth's steadfast loyalty to Naomi and her commitment to the God of Israel, blessing her and praying that the Lord would recompense her for her deeds (Ruth 2:11–12). This divine interplay in the mundane task of gleaning illustrates how faithful obedience to God's social justice commands serves as a platform for extraordinary blessing. Ruth's work ethic and respect for local customs—humbling herself to glean under the threshers—signified that she was not merely seeking charity but was willing to labor under God's provision. Her respectful demeanor toward Boaz and his workers earned her protection and favor, reflecting the character of a true follower who honors both divine law and human relationships. Ruth's gleaning also underscores the theology of secondary blessing: by caring for Naomi through labor, she positioned herself to be cared for by God through Boaz. Her hope in action reveals that authentic following transforms daily tasks into expressions of trust and service. As the harvest season continued, Ruth gleaned from morning until evening, returning with a handful of barley sufficient to sustain herself and Naomi (Ruth 2:17). Through her obedience in the field, Ruth became the model for how marginalized individuals, bound only by their devotion to God and covenant loyalty to family, can inaugurate redemptive narratives. This gleaning scene transitions naturally into the midnight proposal, where her faithfulness positions her for invitation into Boaz's protective kinsman-redeemer role.

6.4.c Midnight Proposal—Risking Reputation for Redemptive Kinship (Ruth 3:7–11) Under Naomi's guidance, Ruth prepared herself to meet Boaz at the threshing floor, partaking in ancient customs of levirate redemption (Ruth 3:1–5). She bathed, anointed herself with perfume, and dressed modestly, demonstrating reverence and intentionality (Ruth 3:3–5). At twilight, Naomi instructed Ruth to wait until Boaz finished eating and drinking before he lay down, then to uncover his feet and lie down, allowing Boaz to discern her petition for protection and redemption (Ruth 3:6–8). While the threshing floor setting carried risk—an unmarried woman miring herself in vulnerability could incur scandal—Ruth trusted Naomi's counsel, acting in faith rather than fear. When Ruth lay at Boaz's feet, he awoke startled (Ruth 3:8), and she boldly requested that he spread his cloak over her, signaling his role as kinsman-redeemer (Ruth 3:9). Boaz praised her virtue, noting that she had not turned to young men but remained loyal to the poor and needy, conforming to the law of the Lord (Ruth 3:10–11). He acknowledged that a nearer kinsman-redeemer existed but pledged to fulfill his duty if the nearer relative declined (Ruth 3:12–13). Ruth's willingness to risk personal reputation, foreshadowing Hannah's silent prayer at the tabernacle (1 Samuel 1:9–11), illuminated her unparalleled devotion to familial loyalty and covenant faithfulness, portraying a model of godly courage. By embracing this risky proposal, Ruth further demonstrated that authentic discipleship sometimes requires stepping beyond social safety to enact love that looks forward to redemption. As she departed and returned to Naomi full of hope, the narrative conveyed that courageous faith often thrives in the nighttime of uncertainty. This midnight encounter lays the groundwork for the redemptive ceremony at the city gate, where legal and communal obligations converge to bring closure and legacy.

6.4.d Legacy of Messianic Lineage—From Field Worker to Foremother (Ruth 4:13–22; Matthew 1:5) After Boaz fulfilled his obligation as redeemer, he married Ruth, and she bore a son named Obed (Ruth 4:13). The women of the community praised the birth, proclaiming, "May he be to you a restorer of life and a nourisher of your old age" (Ruth 4:14). Obed became the father of Jesse, who fathered David, forging an unbroken lineage leading to the Messiah (Ruth 4:17; 1 Samuel 16:13). Naomi found her identity restored through Ruth's son, linking personal restoration with national destiny. The genealogy in Matthew 1:5 underscores Ruth's elevation from Moabite outsider to honored ancestor of King David and ultimately of Jesus Christ himself, demonstrating that authentic following transcends ethnic boundaries and reshapes redemptive history. Ruth's story foreshadows the inclusion of Gentiles into the new covenant community (Ephesians 2:11–22), highlighting that kingdom faithfulness expands beyond inherited privilege to embrace foreigners who cling to the living God. As Ruth's narrative preserves her loyalty, humility, and sacrificial risk, it also testifies that God exalts those who honor covenant fidelity, no matter how unlikely. Her presence in the Messiah's genealogy stands as a powerful affirmation that God's redemptive plan incorporates the devoted outsider into the heart of divine promise. As we transition to examine Daniel, we see another model of cross-cultural faithfulness—one where adherence to God's law, even in exile, yields lasting influence and prophetic insight.

6.5 Daniel: Integrating Conviction with Cultural Influence

6.5.a Resolute Diet—Small Choices That Guard Holiness (Daniel 1:8–17) In the first year of Nebuchadnezzar's reign, Judah's elite, including young Daniel, Hananiah, Mishael, and Azariah, were exiled to Babylon to be trained in the king's court (Daniel 1:1–3). Part of this training involved daily meals from the king's table, likely prepared according to Babylonian dietary practices and pagan rituals (Daniel 1:5). Daniel resolved not to defile himself with the king's food and wine, requesting permission from the chief official to eat only vegetables and drink water (Daniel 1:8). This request risked royal displeasure and possible death if perceived as rebellious. Nonetheless, Daniel's integrity stemmed from a deep conviction that honoring God's dietary laws, even in exile, preserved his covenant identity. God honored Daniel's resolve: after ten days, he and his friends appeared healthier and better nourished than those who ate the royal provisions (Daniel 1:15). Their wisdom and understanding surpassing all others (Daniel 1:17) demonstrated that faithfulness in small matters—including daily nutrition—paved the way for God to bestow extraordinary gifts. Daniel's choice reveals that amid cultural pressures, authentic discipleship begins with concrete decisions aligning life with God's commands. These decisions set a pattern for daily dependency on God rather than assimilation to prevailing norms. As Daniel's wisdom later flourished under Nebuchadnezzar and subsequent rulers, it became evident that small, consistent convictions can accumulate into profound cultural influence. Transitioning from this stage of personal integrity, we recognize how Daniel's dependence on prayer and Scripture equipped him for interpreting dreams, guiding us into the next episode of prayer-fueled insight.

6.5.b Night of Dreams—Prayer-Fueled Wisdom before Power (Daniel 2:17–23) When Nebuchadnezzar experienced a troubling dream he could not recall, he summoned magicians, enchanters, and astrologers to interpret it without revealing the content, threatening them with death if they failed (Daniel 2:1–5). Uncertain how to proceed, Daniel turned to prayer, beseeching God to reveal both the dream and its interpretation (Daniel 2:17–18). He enlisted his companions—Hananiah, Mishael, and Azariah—to join him in this petition, highlighting communal intercession as foundational for extraordinary revelation (Daniel 2:18). In a vision that night God disclosed the mystery to Daniel, prompting him to bless the name of God who reveals secrets (Daniel 2:19–23). Daniel then went to the king, recounted the dream, and interpreted it, delineating a sequence of world empires symbolized by a great statue with various metals (Daniel 2:31–45). Recognizing that political power alone is transient, Daniel declared that God's eternal kingdom would ultimately prevail, bringing hope to those oppressed under successive regimes. The contrast between Babylon's might and God's sovereign purpose underscores that authentic following seeks divine perspective, especially when worldly power appears overwhelming. Daniel's prayer-fueled wisdom proved superior to Babylon's soothsayers, earning him and his companions high positions in the kingdom (Daniel 2:46–49). This event demonstrates that when followers align their petitions with God's purposes, they can access revelation that informs and transforms cultures, whereas fans rely on earthly elites and transient human insights. As we move from Daniel's interpretive ministry to his stand in the lion's den, we see how his commitment to prayer undergirded resilience amid direct threats to his life.

6.5.c Lion's Den—Public Obedience under Legal Persecution (Daniel 6:6–23) During the reign of Darius the Mede, Daniel's exceptional qualities as an administrator prompted jealous rivals to conspire against him, persuading the king to issue a decree that anyone who prayed to any god or man other than Darius over the next thirty days would be cast into the lions' den (Daniel 6:6–9). Aware of the decree, Daniel continued his practice of praying three times a day, kneeling toward Jerusalem with windows open (Daniel 6:10), demonstrating that obedience to God superseded loyalty to human legislation. His rivals, catching him in the act, reported the violation to King Darius, who, despite his regard for Daniel, had to uphold the written law of the Medes and Persians (Daniel 6:14–15). Daniel was cast into the den, and the king spent a sleepless night fasting, hoping for Daniel's deliverance (Daniel 6:18–19). At dawn, Darius rushed to the den and, upon hearing Daniel's voice unharmed, rejoiced (Daniel 6:20–23). Daniel explained that God had sent His angel to shut the lions' mouths because he was found blameless before God and had done no wrong (Daniel 6:22). In response, Darius issued a decree that all must "tremble and fear before the God of Daniel," acknowledging His power to rescue (Daniel 6:26–27). Daniel's unwavering obedience in the face of death illustrates the essence of authentic following: refusing to compromise core convictions even when cultural pressures criminalize godly practices. Fans of faith might applaud from a distance but shrink when obedience entails public risk. Daniel's example encourages modern believers to assess whether our daily practices—prayer, witness, ethical stands—would withstand legal or social decree. As we transition to his intercessory prayer in Daniel 9, we recognize that Daniel's lifestyle of prayer, like his commitment to dietary purity, prepared him to stand firm amid the most severe trials.

6.5.d Apocalyptic Insight—Intercession for Future Generations (Daniel 9:1–19) In the first year of King Darius's reign, Daniel studied Jeremiah's prophecy concerning the seventy-year desolation of Jerusalem and realized that the time for Israel's exile was drawing to a close (Daniel 9:1–2). He turned to God in prayer and fasting, pulling "noodles" (likely sackcloth) upon his loins and placing dust upon his head—a posture of intense mourning and intercession (Daniel 9:3). From morning to evening, Daniel confessed the sins of Israel, pleading God's mercy for Jerusalem's sake (Daniel 9:4–19). His prayer reflects an acute awareness that communal restoration requires corporate repentance, underlining the principle that authentic discipleship attends not only to personal holiness but also to corporate intercession. As Daniel repented in the first person plural—"we" have sinned—he positioned himself within the covenant community, demonstrating solidarity with the exiled people. In response, the angel Gabriel arrived in the evening, providing Daniel with insight concerning "the vision" (Daniel 9:22)—a prophetic timetable outlining the coming of Messiah and the ultimate redemption of Jerusalem (Daniel 9:24–27). Daniel's apocalyptic revelation linked his intercessory prayer to God's redemptive timeline, illustrating that fervent petitioning aligns the heart with heaven's purposes. For modern readers, Daniel's model shows that amid uncertainty—whether political upheaval, moral decay, or persecution—prayerful engagement unlocks divine perspective that transcends temporal concerns. His example challenges fans who shy away from the esoteric or the communal weight of intercession, inviting followers to invest in seeking God's face for generational transformation. As we conclude Daniel's portrait, we see that his integrity, prayer rhythms, and prophetic vision combined to shape him into a powerful witness whose influence extended far beyond his immediate context, instructing us to ground authenticity in both personal devotion and corporate intercession.

Conclusion

The lives we have encountered—men and women who surrendered comfort, clung to hope in exile, and laid down personal agendas for God's purposes—illuminate a path that transcends mere admiration. Their faith was not an ideological posture but a living reality that bore fruit in perseverance, generosity, and cross-shaped service. By witnessing how each responded to doubt, loss, or cultural pressure, we glean that authentic following always involves vulnerability, teachable obedience, and a willingness to be shaped into agents of reconciliation and justice. As these portraits converge, they reveal a consistent thread: Christ's presence transforms ordinary individuals into vessels of grace, equipping them to navigate every season with courage. May their examples inspire us to embrace our own callings with humility, to risk obedience in small matters, and to trust that the same Spirit who empowered them remains our guide and source of endurance.

Chapter 7 — Marks of the Follower: Identity, Intimacy, Imitation

True discipleship unfolds not in fleeting bursts of enthusiasm but in the gradual reshaping of who we are, how we commune with God, and the ways we reflect Christ's character in daily life. The journey begins with discovering our new identity, a reality that liberates us from the shifting definitions imposed by culture and our own anxieties. When we see ourselves as beloved children of the Trinity—chosen, redeemed, and empowered—we no longer scramble for affirmation or chase hollow ambitions. From this secure foundation, our hearts learn to draw near through spiritual practices that nurture ongoing intimacy. Prayer, Scripture meditation, fasting, and rhythms of rest invite us into conversations and communion with the living God, transforming duty into delight. As our affections reorder, imitation of Jesus naturally flows—not as hollow mimicry but as a cross-shaped pattern of service, forgiveness, generosity, and sacrificial love. In a world that often values power, comfort, and performance, followers instead embody a kingdom logic that values descending leadership, radical compassion, and whole-life witness. Each of these dimensions—identity, intimacy, and imitation—interweaves, forming the tapestry of a life conformed to Christ. Rather than offering dry prescriptions, this chapter traces how the gospel's core truths become tangible in the everyday choices of those determined to walk in Christ's footsteps.

7.0 Laying the Groundwork for Christ-Shaped Growth

7.0.a The Trinitarian Basis: Loved by the Father, In Christ, Empowered by the Spirit Healthy discipleship begins inside the life of God Himself: the Father's electing love, the Son's redeeming grace, and the Spirit's indwelling power form the atmosphere in which followers breathe. Before any command is given or obeyed, Scripture announces that the Father "chose us in him before the foundation of the world" (Ephesians 1 :4), rooting identity in eternal affection rather than performance. Christ then gathers us into Himself—"in Christ" appears more than 150 times in Paul's letters—so believers share His righteousness, status, and inheritance (2 Corinthians 5 :21; Romans 8 :17). The Spirit completes this movement by pouring the Father's love into our hearts (Romans 5 :5) and sealing us for future glory (Ephesians 1 :13–14); thus the whole Trinity takes responsibility for birthing and nurturing authentic disciples. Because the gospel's starting point is divine initiative, every spiritual discipline becomes a response of gratitude rather than an attempt to earn favor. Trinity-shaped identity also dethrones self-sourced spirituality: the Father authors the story, the Son accomplishes the work, and the Spirit animates obedience, guarding disciples from pride when growth is evident or despair when weakness surfaces.

This Trinitarian framework means the Christian life is essentially participatory—sharing in the Son's communion with the Father through the Spirit (John 17 :23). Prayer is therefore conversation within a family, not negotiation with a distant deity; Scripture meditation becomes listening to a Father's voice carried by the Spirit rather than sifting data for religious trivia (1 Corinthians 2 :12). Even suffering is reinterpreted: the Father disciplines those He loves (Hebrews 12 :6), the Son walks with us in fiery trials (Daniel 3 :24–25 fulfilled in Matthew 28 :20), and the Spirit groans with us when words fail (Romans 8 :26). Because disciples are enfolded into divine relationship, obedience flows from belonging; we become reflectors of Trinitarian love in families, workplaces, and the public square (John 13 :34–35). Every subsequent mark of the follower—identity, intimacy, imitation—springs from this fountainhead, ensuring that growth is relationally fueled and theologically tethered to God's own life.

7.0.b Relationship before Rule-Keeping: Grace as the Engine of Transformation Grace is not a thin layer of forgiveness sprinkled over moral striving; it is the animating power that turns dead hearts into living temples (Ephesians 2 :4–6). Jesus established this order when He called fishermen to follow Him before they understood all He would require (Luke 5 :10–11), and when He forgave an adulterous woman prior to urging her to "go, and from now on sin no more" (John 8 :11). Paul follows the same pattern: the first eleven chapters of Romans proclaim mercy, and only then does chapter 12 exhort believers to present their bodies as living sacrifices. Grace, then, is both pardon and propulsion—freeing us from condemnation (Romans 8 :1) and empowering us to walk in newness of life (Romans 6 :4). Rule-keeping devoid of relationship breeds either pharisaic pride or perpetual shame; relationship saturated with grace produces fruit that law alone could never grow (Galatians 5 :22–23). Because disciples know they are already accepted, they can confess sin quickly, obey joyfully, and risk boldly without the dread of rejection.

Living from grace also reshapes how we engage spiritual disciplines. Prayer morphs from box-checking into shared life with a loving Father; fasting becomes desire-retraining rather than punitive self-denial; Scripture reading shifts from duty to delight (Psalm 1 :2). Grace undercuts comparison—nobody's résumé outranks another's at the foot of the cross—and fuels perseverance, for the same power that raised Jesus works in those who believe (Ephesians 1:19–20). It dismantles the lie that growth depends on sheer willpower and instills humble confidence that "He who began a good work... will bring it to completion" (Philippians 1:6). With the Trinity's embrace and grace's engine established, we can now explore the practical contours of identity, intimacy, and imitation that characterize authentic followers.

7.1 Identity in Christ over Social Labels

7.1.a Adoption Imagery — Heirs, Not Hirelings (Romans 8:15-17) The gospel replaces spiritual orphanhood with adoption, granting believers the astonishing right to call God "Abba, Father." Paul declares that we have not received "a spirit of slavery to fall back into fear," but the Spirit of adoption who testifies that we are God's children and co-heirs with Christ. Adoption reframes value systems fixed on résumé, ethnicity, or economic status, teaching that worth is received rather than achieved. Because heirs inherit by birthright, not merit, disciples can cease scrambling for validation through accolades or social media applause. This identity relieves anxiety—no promotion, demotion, or political shift can annul family ties sealed by the Spirit. It also injects holy courage: heirs steward the Father's estate, so risk-taking in mission reflects family business rather than reckless adventure. Suffering is reinterpreted as well, for heirs share both Christ's sufferings and His glory; hardship becomes proof of legitimate sonship, not divine displeasure.

Adoption fuels relational wholeness. Siblings in the family of God may differ racially, generationally, or ideologically, yet shared paternity dismantles superiority complexes and inferiority wounds. Knowing the Father's infinite resources frees believers to celebrate another's success without envy and serve unseen without resentment. Moreover, adopted identity resists the orphan spirit that hoards blessings for self-protection; instead it releases generosity, mirroring the Father who "did not spare His own Son" (Romans 8:32). Prayer shifts tone from transactional pleading to filial trust, as children confident of love ask boldly, "Give us this day our daily bread" (Matthew 6:11). Evangelism becomes an invitation into a family, not a sales pitch for a worldview. All other aspects of Christian identity grow out of this foundational reality: we are beloved heirs, not expendable hirelings.

7.1.b New-Creation Reality — "Behold, the Old Has Gone" (2 Corinthians 5:17) Paul's assertion that anyone in Christ "is a new creation" announces more than moral improvement—it describes ontological overhaul. The verb tense indicates a completed act with ongoing impact: the old has definitively passed, yet its implications unfold progressively. This new-creation status delivers freedom from shame attached to past sins or labels, because identity now flows from resurrection life, not previous failures or accolades. Baptism dramatizes this reality: immersion symbolizes burial of the old self; emergence pictures new life empowered by the Spirit (Romans 6:3–4). Disciples therefore confront temptation by remembering who they already are, not by mustering willpower to become what they are not. Crucially, new-creation identity carries corporate dimensions; Paul links it to a ministry of reconciliation, urging believers to regard no one "according to the flesh." Racial, gender, and socioeconomic divisions lose ultimacy because every believer bears resurrection DNA.

This identity also spurs ecological and societal renewal, for if God is making all things new, followers join His restorative agenda—advocating justice, stewarding creation, and healing broken systems. Fans who cling to status quo comforts may trivialize discipleship as inner serenity, but new-creation people expect concrete change in neighborhoods and nations. They view art, science, and civic engagement as arenas for manifesting resurrection creativity. Prayer becomes a laboratory for dreaming with God about what "on earth as it is in heaven" might look like on their street (Matthew 6:10). Thus, new-creation identity propels believers outward, integrating spiritual vitality with social imagination.

7.1.c Citizenship of Heaven amid Earthly Polarization (Philippians 3:20) Paul's claim that "our citizenship is in heaven" challenged Philippian believers proud of their Roman status; it likewise confronts modern Christians tempted to anchor hope in passports or political parties. Heavenly citizenship does not negate earthly responsibilities—Paul still appeals to Caesar (Acts 25 :11)—but it relativizes them. It calls disciples to embody kingdom ethics in public discourse: truth-telling over spin, dignity for opponents, and allegiance to Christ's justice agenda over partisan expedience. This orientation prevents despair when cultural tides turn hostile or triumphalism when they seem favorable, for the Savior we eagerly await will transform all bodies—societal and physical—by His resurrection power (Philippians 3 :21). Practically, heavenly citizens steward earthly influence for common good while resisting idolatry of nation, ethnicity, or ideology. They pray for leaders (1 Timothy 2 :2) yet remember that no human ruler is ultimate; Jesus alone wields the name above every name (Philippians 2 :9).

Citizenship of heaven nurtures cross-cultural solidarity. Believers in different nations recognize each other as compatriots even when geopolitical tensions arise. Shared liturgy and communion transcend linguistic and economic barriers, reminding worshipers that flags will fade while Christ's reign endures. This perspective equips disciples to engage civic debates with gentleness and respect (1 Peter 3 :15), confident that their primary polity is unshakeable. It also safeguards against culture-war fatigue: when ultimate victory is secured in Christ, believers can labor for justice without succumbing to apocalyptic angst.

7.1.d One Body, Many Members — Interdependence as Identity (1 Corinthians 12 :12-27) Paul likens the church to a human body where each member, though distinct, is indispensable. The eye cannot say to the hand, "I have no need of you," nor the head to the feet, "I have no need of you." This metaphor confronts consumer Christianity that treats church as a weekly product rather than an organism. Disciples discover identity not only vertically with God but horizontally with siblings; spiritual gifts are distributed "for the common good" (1 Corinthians 12 :7), making isolation antithetical to purpose. Interdependence cultivates humility—gifted teachers need mercy givers; prophetic voices need administrators; wealthy patrons need those with faith to challenge material security. Suffering is shared too: "If one member suffers, all suffer together" (1 Corinthians 12:26). In a culture praising self-sufficiency, the body image liberates believers to ask for help without shame and to offer help without condescension.

Corporate identity also provides a laboratory for practicing forgiveness, patience, and mutual submission—virtues impossible to develop in spiritual solitude. When quarrels arise, reconciliation becomes a gospel demonstration, proving that Christ's peace can dismantle hostility (Ephesians 2:14–16). In communal discernment, diverse gifts converge, preventing doctrinal drift and burnout. Fans may attend church yet abandon it when inconvenience surfaces; followers remain, trusting that sanctification often hides inside messy relationships. Ultimately, the body grows as "each part does its work" (Ephesians 4:16), revealing Christ's fullness to the world.

7.1.e Battling Identity Theft — Spiritual Warfare in the Mind (Ephesians 6:12-14) Even though identity is bestowed, it is contested by spiritual forces that whisper counterfeit narratives: God is distant, you are unworthy, sin defines you. Paul alerts believers that our struggle is not against flesh and blood but against rulers and powers in heavenly realms. The primary battleground is the mind, where fiery darts of accusation target assurance of adoption and new-creation reality. The belt of truth, breastplate of righteousness, and helmet of salvation stabilize identity by anchoring it in God's verdict, not emotional flux. Practically, disciples rehearse Scripture aloud, wielding the sword of the Spirit against lies—Jesus modeled this in the wilderness by countering each temptation with "It is written" (Matthew 4:4–10). Community plays a vital defensive role: when believers forget who they are, others remind them through prayer, prophetic encouragement, and sacramental confession.

Identity warfare often intensifies during transitions—career shifts, relational breakdowns, moral failures—when old labels resurface. Followers combat these assaults by lamenting honestly, then returning to gospel promises: "There is therefore now no condemnation" (Romans 8 :1). They also practice gratitude, which disarms envy, and Sabbath rest, which dismantles performance idolatry. Victory is less dramatic than Hollywood exorcisms; it is daily resilience in truth, gradually fortifying neural pathways around Christ's sufficiency. As identity settles, intimacy with God becomes the natural next pursuit.

7.2 Intimacy through Spirit-Formed Disciplines

7.2.a Prayer Patterns of Jesus — Solitude before Service (Mark 1 :35) Mark records that Jesus, after a full day of preaching, healing, and casting out demons, rose "very early in the morning, while it was still dark," and went to a desolate place to pray. This rhythm—withdrawal before engagement—reveals intimacy as the wellspring of effective ministry. Jesus did not treat prayer as a break from real work; communion with the Father was the work that governed every subsequent step. Disciples who mirror this pattern find their agendas sifted: some tasks remain urgent but unnecessary; others, previously ignored, rise to primary importance. Solitude exposes hidden motives—ambition, fear, comparison—and allows the Spirit to recalibrate desires toward kingdom priorities. It also fosters emotional honesty, enabling lament, gratitude, and intercession to mingle freely. Fans may admire prayer quotes but rarely schedule solitude; followers guard it, knowing public fruit depends on private roots.

Consistent early-morning or scheduled prayer creates a baseline of peace that outlasts daily turbulence. It trains ears to recognize the Shepherd's voice amid competing digital noise. Intercessory thrust broadens beyond personal needs to global concerns, aligning hearts with God's expansive mission (1 Timothy 2 :1–4). Over time, prayer becomes less wordy monologue and more attuned listening, echoing Samuel's "Speak, Lord, for your servant hears" (1 Samuel 3 :10). Spiritual lethargy often signals neglected prayer rhythms; rekindling them revives vitality. Thus Jesus' pattern invites disciples into dynamic friendship with the Father that fuels courageous obedience.

7.2.b Meditating on the Word — Roots Planted by Streams (Psalm 1:2-3) Psalm 1 portrays the blessed person as delighting in the law of the Lord, meditating day and night, like a tree whose roots draw constant nourishment from a river. Biblical meditation differs from emptying the mind; it fills imagination with Scripture's textures, allowing phrases to seep into memory and shape reflexive responses. Practically, disciples slow-read passages, emphasize verbs, paraphrase verses, or pray them back to God. Over time, the Spirit surfaces connections—linking a psalm to a gospel scene or an epistle command to a prophetic promise—forming a tapestry of revelation. Such rootedness yields fruit in season; when crises hit, stored truth surfaces to stabilize emotions and guide decisions (Matthew 4:4).

Meditation also dismantles false narratives planted by culture. If advertising insists "you are what you buy," slowly ingesting texts like Isaiah 55—"Come, buy without money"—re-narrates value around grace. Cognitive psychologists note that rehearsed thoughts carve neural pathways; Scripture meditation therefore rewires brains toward hope and holiness (Romans 12:2). Fans skim verses for motivational boosts; followers linger until the Word reads them, exposing hidden biases and birthing repentance (Hebrews 4:12–13). Meditation naturally feeds prayer, turning insights into adoration or petition, and prepares hearts for obedience: "I have stored up your word in my heart, that I might not sin against you" (Psalm 119:11). As roots deepen, fasting and other disciplines amplify thirst for God, creating integrated intimacy.

7.2.c Fasting and Holy Hunger — Re-calibrating Desire (Matthew 6:16-18) Jesus assumed His followers would fast—"When you fast," not "if you fast." Fasting trains desires by abstaining from legitimate pleasures—food, media, or entertainment—to feast on God's presence. It exposes how quickly comfort becomes necessity and reminds the body that "man shall not live by bread alone" (Matthew 4:4). During a fast, physical hunger signals deeper spiritual hunger, redirecting attention to prayer and Scripture. When practiced with humility—avoiding performative gloom—fasting aligns hearts with God's compassion; Isaiah 58 links true fasting to justice for the oppressed and food for the hungry. Physiologically, fasting quiets sensory overload, granting clarity for hearing the Spirit's whispers about hidden sin or fresh assignments. Fans may dismiss fasting as legalistic or inconvenient; followers view it as a formative grace that sharpens spiritual sensitivity.

Regular rhythms—one meal weekly, a media fast during Lent, quarterly extended retreats—build stamina for crisis moments when Spirit-led fasting becomes urgent. Corporate fasts unite communities in repentance or breakthrough petition, as with the church at Antioch before commissioning missionaries (Acts 13 :2–3). Re-calibrated desire also curbs materialism; contentment grows when bodies learn they can thrive without constant gratification. Fasting therefore complements prayer and meditation, forging holistic intimacy through disciplined appetite.

7.2.d Gathered Worship & Sacraments — Table, Font, and Fellowship (Acts 2 :42; 1 Corinthians 11 :26) The early church "devoted themselves to the apostles' teaching and the fellowship, to the breaking of bread and the prayers." Corporate worship is more than inspirational music; it is a formative liturgy rehearsing the gospel. Baptism (the font) publicly unites believers with Christ's death and resurrection, anchoring identity in communal memory. The Lord's Supper (the table) proclaims Jesus' death "until He comes," welding past sacrifice to future hope. Regular participation nourishes faith, confessing that salvation is received, not self-generated. Singing psalms and hymns embeds doctrine in melody, enabling hearts to remember truth in valleys of despair (Colossians 3 :16). Laying on of hands for prayer reinforces bodily solidarity; believers become tangible means of grace for one another.

Gathered worship also confronts individualism. In congregational confession, believers jointly acknowledge sin; in corporate intercession, they carry each other's burdens. Fans who attend sporadically treat worship as a consumer product; followers commit to rhythms even when preferences aren't met, trusting that the Spirit forms character through inconvenience. Sacraments act as "visible words," assuring wavering hearts that God's promises stand, especially during seasons when emotions feel numb. Thus corporate worship sustains intimacy both vertically with God and horizontally with His people.

7.2.e Sabbath Rest & Rhythms of Margin — Entering God's Ongoing "It Is Finished" (Hebrews 4 :9-11) Hebrews declares a Sabbath rest remains for the people of God, urging believers to "strive to enter" that rest. Sabbath is not merely a day off; it is an embodied declaration that God's work is sufficient and human worth is not measured by productivity. Practicing Sabbath confronts hurry sickness, screens' relentless demands, and the subconscious creed "I am what I accomplish." The pattern originates in creation—God rested, not from fatigue but to delight (Genesis 2 :2–3)—and is redeemed in Christ, who cried "It is finished" (John 19 :30). Ceasing from labor 24 hours each week mirrors the gospel every seven days, preaching to anxious hearts that salvation and provision are secure. Sabbath includes worship, feasting, nap-taking, nature walks—activities that foster delight, cultivate gratitude, and replenish imagination.

Margin extends Sabbath principles into daily life: pacing meetings, turning phones off at meals, embracing silence on commutes. These practices create space for spontaneous prayer and relational presence. Fans often equate busyness with importance, risking burnout; followers adopt Jesus' unhurried cadence, where He could nap amid storms because inner rest anchored His mission (Mark 4 :38). Sabbath also fuels justice: by resisting exploitative rhythms, the church models a counterculture that values people over profit, echoing Deuteronomy's command to let servants and even animals rest. Entering God's rest therefore completes the cycle of intimacy—identity leads to disciplines, disciplines protect delight, and delight sustains imitation. With roots deep in adoption and branches reaching toward cross-shaped action, the follower's life blossoms into holistic witness that fans rarely understand but the world sorely needs.

7.3 Imitation Shaped by the Cross

7.3.a Servant Leadership — Descending Greatness (Philippians 2:5–8) Jesus, though existing in the form of God, did not cling to His divine privileges but emptied Himself, taking the form of a servant by being born in human likeness (Philippians 2:6–7). This model of descending greatness overturns worldly notions that leadership is achieved by climbing a hierarchical ladder. Instead, genuine authority emerges through humility and sacrificial service. When Jesus washed His disciples' feet (John 13:1–17), He illustrated that those who wish to lead must stoop to serve, valuing others' needs above their own comfort. Fans of leadership often seek visibility, applause, and titles, whereas followers learn that true greatness is measured by one's willingness to take the lowest place at the table, caring for the overlooked and marginalized.

Servant leadership is not a low-key option reserved for a spiritual elite; it is the essence of Christ-like influence. Paul told Timothy to "consider those who are in prison as though in prison with him, and those who are being mistreated as though you yourselves were suffering" (Hebrews 13:3), calling leaders to empathize deeply rather than maintain distance. In practical terms, churches that adopt servant leadership allocate resources to ministries such as food distribution and counseling rather than merely funding flashy programs. Business leaders who serve their employees by providing equitable wages, safe conditions, and ongoing training reflect Christ's example, demonstrating that organizational success does not depend on exploiting workers but on nurturing them.

Emulating servant leadership also reshapes how conflicts are resolved. Instead of resorting to power plays or manipulation, followers guided by Philippians 2 embrace a spirit of reconciliation, seeking the good of others even at personal cost. In families, parents prioritize children's spiritual formation above control, disciplining them through gentle guidance rather than authoritarian decrees. As we transition to the counterintuitive command to love enemies, we see that servant leadership prepares hearts to forgive and serve those who wish us ill, embodying the ultimate expression of cross-shaped following.

7.3.b Enemy-Love as Kingdom Signature (Matthew 5:44–45)
When Jesus commanded His followers to love their enemies and pray for persecitors (Matthew 5:44), He revealed the distinctive mark of kingdom citizenship. Loving enemies frustrates human instincts and societal norms, for natural inclinations lean toward retribution and self-protection. The command to "pray for those who persecute you" expands love from emotional warmth to intercessory compassion, asking God to transform persecutors rather than allowing bitterness to take root. Loving enemies does not mean affirming their evil deeds but embodying the restorative posture of the cross, where Jesus prayed, "Father, forgive them, for they know not what they do" (Luke 23:34). This kind of love grants space for repentance and models the mercy that God shows to undeserving sinners.

Practically, loving enemies disrupts cycles of violence. In contexts of deep-seated conflict—ethnic, political, or personal—believers who bless adversaries rather than curse them introduce a new dynamic that can break mutual hostility. Pastors ministering to congregations divided by tribal affiliations foster reconciliation by organizing dialogues where each party articulates pain and receives prayers for healing. Loving enemies also extends to daily interactions: drivers who cut us off, coworkers who gossip, or individuals who slander us become subjects of our intercessions instead of targets of our anger. When congregations adopt enemy-love as a shared value, they witness together in public spaces by refusing retaliation, choosing instead to feed or shelter those who might compel harmful behavior against them.

The discipline of enemy-love matures over time through repeated acts of forgiveness and prayer. Even after extended seasons of persecution, followers who persist in blessing opponents demonstrate that Christ's love transcends natural limits. As we move from four marks of imitation to the integration of maturity—head, heart, and hands—we see how the practice of enemy-love integrates truth (knowing God's character), affection (cultivating compassion), and action (prayer and blessing), forging a holistic pattern of discipleship.

7.3.c Radical Generosity in Lean Times (2 Corinthians 8:1–5)

The Macedonian churches, despite extreme affliction and profound poverty, pleaded earnestly for the privilege of giving to the poor in Jerusalem (2 Corinthians 8:1–4). Their radical generosity amid need exemplifies cross-shaped imitation, for they gave beyond their means, voluntarily and joyfully, trusting that God, who supplies seed for sowing, would supply their needs (2 Corinthians 9:8). This generosity propels disciples beyond merely tithing from surplus; it invites them to consider sacrificial giving, even when resources are tight. Contemporary parallels abound: single parents who skip a recreational meal to provide for a struggling neighbor, young adults who forego an expensive vacation to support a refugee family, and retirees who downsize to allocate funds to local ministries. Radical generosity disrupts cultural assumptions that one must acquire wealth before giving generously, reaffirming that God often entrusts resources to demonstrate His provision and to build community.

The Macedonians' example also challenges Christian leaders to steward offerings transparently and equitably. When churches channel funds into systemic change—supporting transitional housing, microenterprise ventures, or healthcare clinics—giving transcends individual charity and pioneers shared prosperity. Moreover, radical generosity fosters interdependence: recipients become contributors when circumstances shift, breaking cycles of dependency and reinforcing the body's mutual care. Families who model sacrificial giving instill in children the values of trust and compassion, shaping future generations to prioritize others' welfare over material accumulation.

As this generosity flourishes, disciples learn to measure wealth by kingdom impact rather than bank statements. They celebrate God's provision for the needy as shared triumph. As we transition to forgiveness and reconciling posture, we observe that generosity and forgiveness operate in tandem—both require releasing claims on personal assets, whether material or relational, and both yield abundant harvests of grace.

7.3.d Forgiveness & Reconciling Posture (Colossians 3:12–13)

Colossians calls believers to clothe themselves with compassion, kindness, humility, gentleness, and patience, forgiving one another as the Lord forgave them (Colossians 3:12–13). Forgiveness stands at the center of cross-shaped imitation, for Christ's blood shed on the cross inaugurated forgiveness for sins, freeing us to release grievances rather than nursing grudges. Forgiveness does not mean minimizing hurt or granting carte blanche for abuse; rather, it means relinquishing the right to personal revenge, trusting God's justice and healing. In congregations, practicing forgiveness requires teaching about boundaries and accountability alongside grace. When church members confess sin, leaders facilitate genuine repentance and restoration rather than applying shaming tactics that perpetuate guilt.

Reconciliation extends forgiveness into relationship restoration. When siblings feud or business partners betray trust, disciples step into mediatory roles, reflecting God's reconciling work through Christ (2 Corinthians 5:18–19). They facilitate conversations where grievances are aired respectfully, apologies are offered sincerely, and restitution plans are established. This posture aligns with Jesus' teaching that if we hold anything against a brother, we must first reconcile before offering gifts at the altar (Matthew 5:23–24), indicating that unresolved conflict inhibits worship. In workplaces, reconciling posture means initiating conversations with offended colleagues, seeking to repair working relationships rather than nurturing silent resentment.

Forgiveness and reconciliation also cultivate emotional health. Those who forgive report lower stress, reduced anxiety, and greater sense of peace. Communities practicing these disciplines enjoy deeper unity, as members transcend gossip or scapegoating. As forgiveness teaches us to embrace others' imperfections, it primes us for the next kingdom mark—missional witness—equipping believers to display the gospel's reconciling power to a fractured world.

7.3.e Missional Witness in Word + Deed (1 Peter 2:12; Matthew 28:18–20) New Testament teaching never separates proclamation from demonstration. Peter instructs believers to maintain honorable conduct among pagans, so that even if they accuse us of wrongdoing, they see our good deeds and glorify God (1 Peter 2:12). Similarly, the Great Commission charges followers to make disciples by teaching them to obey all Christ's commands, a process that naturally integrates acts of compassion with verbal proclamation (Matthew 28:18–20). Missional witness therefore requires adequate theological training—knowing the gospel story—and simultaneous involvement in tangible kingdom work—caring for widows, advocating for justice, and feeding the hungry.

Churches that excel in missional witness structure ministries combining evangelism with social outreach. For instance, community health fairs offer basic medical services while volunteers share testimonies of personal transformation. In urban contexts, tutoring programs serve as relational bridges between congregants and neighborhood families, opening doors for meaningful spiritual conversations. Cross-cultural missions similarly resist parachute approaches; they prioritize long-term partnerships that equip local leaders rather than deploying short-term teams focused solely on visible celebration events.

At the individual level, missional witness means neighbors notice genuine care before they hear any sermons. A family inviting international students for meals embodies hospitality, setting the stage for faith discussions. Employees modeling ethical conduct and kindness in the workplace spark curiosity about underlying convictions. Such integrated witness avoids the hypocrisy of "walk out one door with a Bible and out the other with a cynical sneer." Emulation of Christ involves embodying the gospel's holistic truth, ensuring that words and deeds converge to create credible, attractive, and transformative testimony.

7.4 Integrated Maturity: Head, Heart, and Hands

7.4.a Renewed Thinking — Non-Conformity to the Age (Romans 12:2) Paul exhorts believers to not be conformed to the world's pattern but to be transformed by renewing the mind, enabling them to discern God's will—what is good, acceptable, and perfect (Romans 12:2). This transformation is cognitive: it intentionally replaces fallen thought patterns—self-centered ambition, fear-based insecurity, consumerist logic—with perspectives grounded in Scripture. For instance, where culture says "acquire more to feel secure," transformed minds ask "If God is my provider, why hoard beyond my family's legitimate needs?" Studying passages like Matthew 6:25–34 on God's provision trains the mind to release anxiety over tomorrow, shifting focus to seeking God's kingdom first.

Non-conformity also applies to resisting ideological polarization. When political discourse devolves into us-versus-them camps, followers practice critical discernment, evaluating ideologies through scriptural prisms rather than tribal loyalties. They avoid echo chambers by engaging diverse viewpoints prayerfully, testing them against biblical truth (Acts 17:11). This mental renewal frees believers from formulaic responses, equipping them to love enemies and seek the welfare of all, regardless of partisan affiliation (Jeremiah 29:7).

Renewed thinking extends to eschatology: instead of despairing over societal ills, matured minds view history as God's arena for redemptive progress, trusting that Christ's return will perfect what remains broken. Studying Revelation's vision of a new heaven and earth equips disciples to balance engagement with patience, working for justice today while longing for ultimate restoration. Ultimately, renewing the mind fosters both stability in a shifting world and creative participation in God's kingdom agenda, linking head-level clarity with heart-level trust and hand-level action.

7.4.b Ordered Affections — Loving God with All (Matthew 22:37–38) Jesus identified the greatest commandment as loving God with all one's heart, soul, and mind, followed by loving neighbor as oneself (Matthew 22:37–38). Loving God wholeheartedly means our affections are arranged to delight most in Him. Ordered affections prioritizes relationship over religion: Sunday attendance, prayer habits, or theological knowledge become expressions of love, not substitutes for love. When desired consistently more than pleasure, wealth, or acclaim, God occupies the supreme place in the heart, directing emotional energies toward what endures (Psalm 73:25–26).

This reordering counters spiritual neglect common among fans who attend church yet reserve deep affection for hobbies, finances, or reputations. The formative process of worship—singing, prayer, reading Scripture—targets the heart, shifting desires from finite to infinite objects. Reflecting on God's beauty in creation, grace in salvation, and hope in resurrection, disciples cultivate holy wonder that shapes everyday choices: spending time with God rather than scrolling feeds, giving funds to kingdom work rather than indulgent consumption, and valuing community over celebrity.

Love for neighbor emerges from this ordered affection, unfolding in acts of compassion that flow naturally when God's love saturates the heart. Disciples whose affections are rightly ordered tolerate slights, forgive quickly, and give lavishly because their love tank is filled by Christ, not by human approval. These affections prepare them to endure trials—when sickness or relational betrayal threatens, the love of Christ sustains them, preventing despair or bitterness. Nowhere is ordered affection put to test more vividly than in the rejection and suffering chapters ahead, where only a heart anchored in Christ remains steady.

7.4.c Kingdom Action — Religion That Visits the Vulnerable (James 1:27) James' concise definition of pure religion—visiting orphans and widows in their affliction and keeping oneself unstained from the world—underscores that authentic faith manifests in tangible care. Kingdom action elevates compassion to a sacrament:

feeding a single mother or befriending a refugee models Jesus' love more powerfully than remote prayers alone. Systemic injustice is addressed when disciples advocate for fair wages, work to abolish human trafficking, and partner with organizations offering healthcare in underserved regions. Local churches embody this by running after-school mentorship programs, providing transitional housing for the unhoused, and offering trauma-informed counseling for abuse survivors.

Visiting the vulnerable also includes emotional presence: sitting with someone in grief, offering consistent support for those in recovery, and celebrating milestones with those who often go unnoticed. These actions require humility, time, and sacrificial use of resources, reflecting Christ's own ministry to the broken. When Kingdom action informs budget allocations—prioritizing feeding programs over property upgrades—congregations demonstrate that Christ's priorities shape their financial stewardship.

Integrating kingdom action with head-level discernment and heart-level devotion yields balanced maturity: disciples act thoughtfully to avoid enabling dependency, while maintaining relational boundaries that protect both giver and recipient. They learn local needs through listening and prayer, then respond with culturally appropriate strategies. Kingdom action also influences vocational choices: teachers become advocates for equitable education, lawyers champion pro bono cases for the marginalized, and entrepreneurs create inclusive job training programs. This integration ensures that head, heart, and hands collaborate seamlessly, making faith unmistakable in a world worn by cynicism.

7.5 Obstacles and Aids on the Journey

7.5.a Cultural Lies & Identity Confusion Contemporary culture bombards individuals with lies that erode gospel truths: "You are what you own," "Sexual pleasure equals significance," "Power defines worth," and "Anxiety is normal." These false narratives entice the mind toward idolatry, eclipsing identity in Christ. Fans often absorb these messages uncritically, building identities around career success, social media personas, or romantic relationships. When these foundations crumble—job loss, public scandal, relationship breakdown—identity crises ensue, leaving lives adrift.

Countering these lies requires regular immersion in the gospel's corrective narratives. Preaching, teaching, and personal Bible study present alternative realities: "You are chosen (Ephesians 1:4), loved (1 John 4:10), and empowered to walk in newness of life (Romans 6:4)." Community also provides corrective mirrors: friends and mentors call out idols lovingly, reminding one another of who they are in Christ when they flounder. Spiritual formation groups that study identity passages like Ephesians 2 and Colossians 3 expose cultural lies and reinforce biblical self-understanding.

Discernment training sharpens the mind to identify the world's deceptions. It involves comparing prevailing messages—such as "Follow your heart; it knows the way"—with Scripture's caution that "The heart is deceitful above all things" (Jeremiah 17:9). By internalizing God's voice through repeated meditation, believers detect subtle deceptions before they become entrenched. This process combats identity theft: reclaiming the name "child of God" whenever the enemy whispers, "You are worthless," thus preserving spiritual integrity amid cultural disorientation.

7.5.b Discipline Fatigue & Dry Seasons Even well-intentioned followers experience seasons when spiritual disciplines feel fruitless or burdensome. Prayer sessions become mechanical monotony, Scripture reading yields no immediate insight, and corporate worship feels hollow, leading to discouragement. These "dry seasons" test the conviction that God's promises remain true even when sensory evidence seems lacking. Discipline fatigue arises when believers attempt to produce holiness through sheer willpower rather than by relying on the Spirit's grace.

Navigating these seasons involves remembering that spiritual growth often transpires beneath the surface, akin to a seed germinating unseen. Faithfulness to disciplines—setting aside time for prayer, joining a Bible study group, or fasting—sows seeds of grace that later bloom. Identifying checklists of disciplines rather than internal motivations can exacerbate fatigue; instead, disciples focus on worshiping in spirit and truth (John 4:23–24), trusting that the Spirit breathes where He wills. Encouragement from peers proves critical: sharing testimonies of perseverance during past dry spells restores hope and accountability. Pastors and spiritual directors who offer personalized guidance can help recalibrate expectations and prevent legalistic trapdoors—disciplines become less "must-dos" and more "waiting with God."

Recognizing patterns of spiritual ebb and flow prevents despair. Even Elijah's despair beneath the broom tree (1 Kings 19) did not nullify his prophetic calling—God met him in gentle whispers, recommissioning him. Similarly, disciples return to God's voice during dry seasons, allowing grace to sustain them until joy and spiritual vitality return. As heart disposition shifts from performance to dependence, disciplines become lifelines rather than burdens.

7.5.c Suffering as an Unwanted but Potent Tutor Jesus warned that "in this world you will have tribulation" (John 16:33), preparing followers for inevitable suffering. Whether from illness, relational rupture, or spiritual opposition, suffering exposes the fragility of human plans and cultivates deeper reliance on God's presence. While fans often abandon faith when trials strike, genuine followers discover in suffering a potent tutor who reveals God's sufficiency. Paul calls suffering "light momentary affliction" producing "an eternal weight of glory" (2 Corinthians 4:17), reframing pain as a refining process rather than meaningless cruelty.

In practice, disciples facing suffering resist isolation by seeking community, carrying one another's burdens (Galatians 6:2). They also resist trying to explain away suffering entirely; the Book of Job models lament as a valid response, expressing honest anguish while refusing to renounce God (Job 1:21; 2:10). Vulnerability in suffering opens doors for powerful empathy, enabling followers to comfort others with the comfort they themselves received from God (2 Corinthians 1:3–4). Rates of mental health crises prompt faith communities to integrate pastoral care, counseling, and support groups to accompany individuals through grief, depression, and trauma. By addressing the spiritual and emotional dimensions of suffering holistically, congregations become sanctuaries of healing rather than echo chambers of platitudes.

Over time, faithful endurance fosters maturity—James writes that "the testing of your faith produces steadfastness" (James 1:3). This steadfastness in turn becomes a beacon to a broken world. Whereas fans might retreat under suffering, followers become living epistles under the tutelage of trials, embodying a robust, hope-infused faith that invites others to experience God's grace amid their own struggles.

7.5.d Spirit-Empowered Community & Mentorship Practices

No disciple matures in isolation. From Paul and Barnabas (Acts 13:2–3) to Jesus' relationship with Peter, James, and John, the New Testament overflows with examples of relational discipleship. Spirit-empowered community provides accountability, diverse perspectives, and encouragement when personal resolve falters. Small groups that integrate prayer, Bible study, and mutual confession model the early church's devotion to "the apostles' teaching and the fellowship" (Acts 2:42). Mentorship pairs experienced believers with newer followers, replicating Paul's investment in Timothy (2 Timothy 2:2) and Aquila and Priscilla's training of Apollos (Acts 18:26).

These relationships resist fan-like entitlement and impulsive isolation by urging perseverance and celebrating incremental growth. Mentorship also helps identify and cultivate spiritual gifts, ensuring that no one remains unaware of how God may be equipping them for service. Debriefs of ministry experiences—both successes and failures—foster humility, wisdom, and refined practices for future engagement. In crises of doubt or moral failure, mentors guide mentees toward honest lament and effective repentance, offering insights from their own journeys.

Spirit-empowered community and mentorship practice highlight that discipleship is less an educational program and more an apprenticeship in Christlikeness. When believers lean into each other's strengths and weaknesses, they form a dynamic ecosystem that nurtures identity, intimacy, and imitation. As we move to the final epilogue, the combined power of Trinitarian grounding, disciplined formation, cross-shaped imitation, and communal support reveals how the follower's life becomes a continuous unfolding of Christ's image for the world.

Conclusion

The marks of true following are less visible at a glance than they are woven into the fabric of ordinary decisions—how we respond when provoked, where we place our hope, and whom we serve with our time, resources, and emotions. When we internalize our status as adopted heirs, reject the world's frantic enticements, and anchor ourselves in the Trinity's love, our inner compass points steadily toward devotion rather than distraction. Intimacy with God, cultivated through prayer, Scripture, and surrendered rhythms of rest, fuels the endurance needed to live out the difficult commands of enemy-love, forgiveness, and sacrificial generosity. In turn, imitation rooted in Christ's example transforms our public witness: servant-hearted leadership replaces ego-driven ambition, and reconciling outreach becomes the engine of our mission. Along the way, we face distractions, spiritual dryness, and cultural pressures that threaten to pull us off course. Yet the same gospel that calls us into this way equips us to persevere, for it promises ongoing transformation by the Spirit. As we step forward, may this integrated portrait of identity, intimacy, and imitation inspire us to press on, confident that each small act of faithfulness carries forward the work of the One who finished it all on the cross and invites us into a life that bears His image for a watching world.

Chapter 8 — Contemporary Obstacles to Wholehearted Discipleship

Every generation of believers has faced forces that can shrink vibrant faith into half-hearted habit, yet the shape of those forces continually evolves. In the twenty-first century they arrive less like overt persecution and more like invisible currents—shopping-mall spirituality, algorithm-driven distraction, ethical gray zones at work, identity confusion, chronic exhaustion, and an increasing drift toward screen-mediated relationships. Because these pressures often masquerade as normal life, they can infiltrate hearts and congregations before anyone notices the slow erosion of joy, courage, and attentiveness to God. This chapter peers beneath the surface of modern culture to name those subtle currents, trace how they sap affection for Christ, and explore practices that re-train desire, attention, and moral imagination toward wholehearted discipleship. By diagnosing the landscape honestly, we ready ourselves to turn obstacles into invitations for deeper dependence on the Spirit and more creative expressions of the kingdom in everyday spaces.

8.0 Mapping Today's Discipleship Landscape

8.0.a From First-Century Persecutions to Twenty-First-Century Pressures The opening decades of the church were shaped by overt hostility—stonings in Jerusalem (Acts 7:54-60), flogging in synagogues (2 Corinthians 11:24), and Roman executions in arenas—yet the gospel still flourished. Today, in many Western contexts, believers face a subtler environment: social scorn replaces Caesar's sword, and cultural conformity replaces physical chains. While martyrs like Polycarp died at the stake rather than deny Christ, modern disciples are more often tempted to dilute conviction in the boardroom or scroll past injustice on a phone. The setting has changed, but the challenge remains: will we love Christ more than reputation or comfort? Jesus warned the first disciples to expect hatred because they were "not of the world" (John 15:19); His words echo across centuries into office corridors, lecture halls, and online spaces. Early Christians wrestled with emperor worship; we confront the cult of self-worship, where personal branding competes with the call to bear a cross. The old arenas rang with cheers as lions mauled believers; today's arenas are digital, where mockery goes viral in seconds and reputations are shredded by strangers. Both ages reveal that following Jesus invites collision with prevailing values. Paul urged the Thessalonian church to "stand firm and hold to the traditions" (2 Thessalonians 2:15); in our era, that steadiness is tested not by legions but by relentless notifications that catechize the imagination toward hurry and self-absorption. Appreciating historical continuity helps us see that our circumstances are new in form but not in essence, and Scripture still equips for every cultural turn. This perspective cultivates humility—we are heirs of a long resistance movement—and courage, for the same Spirit who emboldened Stephen lives in us.

Crucially, recognizing this lineage prevents nostalgia for an imagined golden age. First-century congregations battled false teaching, class division, and racial suspicion even as they faced persecution (Acts 6; Galatians 2). Likewise, contemporary churches carry internal weaknesses that external pressure exposes. Remembering God's faithfulness across epochs recalibrates expectations; adversity is neither surprising nor fatal to mission. As disciples grasp this continuity, they grow wary of both alarmism and complacency. Instead of retreating, they discern how to translate timeless conviction into current idiom. This historical sweep prepares us to explore the "triple threat" shaping the modern landscape—forces less obvious than gladiators yet equally capable of muting wholehearted devotion.

8.0.b The "Triple Threat": Consumerism, Hyper-Connectivity, and Moral Pluralism Consumerism promises happiness through acquisition, reducing every experience—even church—to a commodity. Hyper-connectivity keeps minds buzzing with ceaseless stimuli, making sustained attention to God's voice feel tedious. Moral pluralism declares that conflicting truth-claims can all be valid, disorienting believers who confess that Jesus alone is "the way, the truth, and the life" (John 14:6). These three pressures often intertwine: digital platforms monetize attention, feed consumer appetites, and amplify relativistic narratives. In malls and feeds alike, identity is marketed as a purchasable aesthetic, subtly eroding the identity in Christ described in Ephesians 1:4-14. Smartphones glow late into the night, crowding out meditative prayer that once framed the day (Psalm 63:6). Algorithms curate content to confirm biases, making it harder to pursue the Berean habit of examining all ideas against Scripture (Acts 17:11).

Because each threat targets a distinct aspect of discipleship—desire, attention, and conviction—addressing them requires holistic formation. Fasting exposes consumerism's illusion, digital sabbaths retrain restless minds, and robust catechesis anchors truth amid relativism. Yet the threats also present opportunities: economic fatigue can awaken hunger for kingdom simplicity (Matthew 6:19-24); screen exhaustion can spark longing for embodied community (Hebrews 10:24-25); ideological confusion can drive seekers toward the coherence of the gospel story. The church's task is not merely defensive but creative—crafting counterliturgies that redirect imagination toward Christ. As we shift from mapping the landscape to examining consumer Christianity inside the sanctuary, we will see how marketplace logic infiltrates worship and how congregations can recover participatory life with God.

8.1 Consumer Christianity and Spectator Worship

8.1.a Worship as Entertainment Syndrome—Lights, Cameras, Shallow Engagement Stage lights swirling across fog machines can stir emotions, but when sensory spectacle eclipses spiritual substance, worship devolves into a concert where congregants watch rather than adore. This syndrome tempts leaders to measure success by crowd size and social-media impressions instead of repentance and transformed living. The psalmist calls us to "ascribe to the Lord the glory due his name" (Psalm 29:2), yet when applause for performers exceeds awe for the Savior, the sanctuary mirrors a theater. Attendees slip into passive observation, mouthing lyrics without yielding hearts, echoing Isaiah's lament—"This people draw near with their lips while their hearts are far" (Isaiah 29:13). Over time the soul becomes conditioned to seek adrenaline spikes, making the quiet humility of the Lord's Table feel anticlimactic. The entertainment impulse also shortens attention spans; sermons are trimmed to accommodate production cues, leaving little room for lament, silence, or lingering prayer. Meanwhile, vulnerable confession—so vital to authentic worship—feels risky under stage lights and live-stream cameras. When worship becomes a product, congregants evaluate songs by genre preference rather than theological depth, forgetting that hymns and modern choruses alike should root hearts in truth (Colossians 3:16).

Still, spectacle need not be enemy to substance. Artistic excellence can serve revelation when subordinated to Christ's glory. Congregations reclaim wonder by integrating historic practices—creeds, Scripture readings, and sung psalms—alongside creative visuals that point beyond themselves. Leaders can dim lights for communal prayer, shifting focus from stage to congregation. Testimonies interwoven with songs remind listeners that worship shapes lived obedience, not just Sunday emotion. As churches recalibrate toward participatory liturgy, they deny consumer instincts room to flourish. This corrective leads naturally to diagnosing the broader phenomenon of "church shopping," where preferences drive allegiance more than covenant commitment.

8.1.b "Church Shopping" and the Cult of Personal Preference In an age of infinite options, congregants often evaluate churches like streaming platforms: Which delivers the best experience for me? Drive-time convenience, children's amenities, preaching style, and coffee quality become decisive criteria. The apostle Paul envisioned the church as a family where members "have the same care for one another" (1 Corinthians 12:25), yet consumer logic conditions people to exit when preferences aren't met. Relationships stay shallow because deeper commitments would tether mobility, and discipleship programs struggle to gain traction when participants treat calendars as vending machines. Pastors, feeling pressure to retain attenders, may tailor sermons to felt needs rather than prophetic challenge, echoing the warning that itching ears will accumulate teachers to suit desires (2 Timothy 4:3).

Ironically, constant church shopping fosters spiritual malnutrition. Roots fail to sink into any soil, leaving believers vulnerable when trials strike and no community knows them well enough to shoulder burdens. Children raised in "rotating churches" rarely witness the messy work of reconciliation that a stable community requires. Remedy begins when congregations teach covenant membership— the biblical vision of belonging that transcends convenience. Practically, this involves public vows to submit to mutual accountability, contribute gifts, and persevere together through conflict. Designing pathways for service—welcoming newcomers, mentoring youth—helps move people from spectators to stakeholders. By prioritizing fidelity over variety, believers learn that love matures best in specificity. Addressing church shopping sets the stage to confront the celebrity pastor culture that often fuels consumer expectations.

8.1.c Celebrity Pastor Culture—Platform over Pasture Social media and podcast proliferation have elevated certain leaders into quasi-influencers whose charisma draws global audiences. While Paul urged believers to imitate him insofar as he imitated Christ (1 Corinthians 11:1), celebrity dynamics risk shifting focus from Christ to personality. Followers may quote pastors more than Scripture, and scandals among high-profile leaders can devastate faith for those who equate the messenger with the message. Celebrity culture also burdens pastors themselves; pressure to produce viral content leaves little margin for soul care or personal holiness. The shepherd image of John 10:11—laying down one's life for the sheep—mutates into brand management, conference circuits, and ghost-written bestsellers.

Counteracting this trend requires structural and spiritual shifts. Plurality of elders distributes authority, reminding congregations that no single voice embodies the whole counsel of God. Limiting platform time for any one leader and amplifying diverse voices—women, ethnic minorities, lay testimonies—breaks the monopoly of celebrity attention. Pastors cultivate anonymity disciplines: visiting hospitals without posting selfies, serving nursery rotation, or taking sabbaticals from social media. Congregants, for their part, examine heart motives: do we crave polished performance or humble shepherds who smell like sheep? Resisting celebrity allure clears space to reconsider transactional faith, where people view tithes and programs as quid pro quo deals with God.

8.1.d Transactional Faith: Tithes for Blessings, Programs for Loyalty When giving becomes a bargaining chip—seed money for guaranteed harvest—disciples slip into a contractual relationship with God. Prosperity teachers cite Malachi 3:10 out of context, promising financial windfalls for donors, ignoring Jesus' call to deny self and embrace suffering (Luke 9:23). Similarly, churches may entice members with robust programming, implying that involvement guarantees personal breakthroughs. Transactional paradigms distort grace, reducing the Father to a vending machine. In Acts 8:18-20, Peter rebuked Simon Magus for seeking to purchase spiritual power, exposing the mercantile impulse at odds with gospel economy.

Reorienting hearts starts with preaching God's generosity in Christ—He gave while we were still sinners (Romans 5:8)—therefore giving is gratitude, not leverage. Financial testimonies should celebrate generosity's impact on mission rather than trophies of material upgrade. Small-group curricula can trace themes of costly obedience, highlighting missionaries who sacrificed comfort to serve unreached peoples. On the program side, leaders ask whether ministries equip saints for works of service or entertain spectators. Simplicity often strengthens discipleship: fewer, deeper pathways foster maturity better than a buffet of options that fragment energy. As transactional assumptions lose grip, congregations can rediscover the Reformation doctrine of the priesthood of all believers, reclaiming active participation over passive consumption.

8.1.e Reclaiming Participatory Liturgy and Vocational Priesthood of All Believers First-Peter 2:9 names the church "a royal priesthood," implying every believer mediates God's presence through word and deed. Participatory liturgy embodies this by inviting congregants to read Scripture aloud, lead intercessions, and share testimonies. Communion servers drawn from diverse ages and backgrounds visualize that grace flows through ordinary saints. Worship planners can incorporate call-and-response prayers, symmetrical with the heavenly liturgy where multitudes cry, "Worthy is the Lamb" (Revelation 5:12). Children's voices reading psalms remind adults that the kingdom belongs to such as these (Matthew 19:14). Music teams teach congregations harmonies rather than overpowering them, reinforcing corporate song over stage performance.

Outside Sunday gatherings, vocational priesthood frames daily labor as sacred calling. Teachers impart wisdom as acts of worship; mechanics repair engines with integrity as service unto Christ (Colossians 3:23-24). Small groups commission members for

Monday worship—praying over lawyers before court or nurses before night shift—so discipleship inhabits cubicles and classrooms. As participatory practice expands, consumer Christianity loses its foothold, and believers hunger for deeper attentiveness to God. This shift dovetails into the next obstacle: digital distraction, where technology fragments attention and undermines the very participation we seek to recover.

8.2 Digital Distraction and Fragmented Attention

8.2.a Competing Narratives on Social Media—Scroll, Swipe, Forget Platforms curate endless content streams, each vying for emotional investment with sensational headlines and stylized images. Within minutes, users encounter stories of injustice, celebrity gossip, theological hot-takes, and product ads, producing cognitive whiplash. The parable of the sower describes seed choked by thorns—"the cares of the world" (Mark 4:19)—and social feeds function like a living briar patch, tangling attention in trivialities. Algorithms reward outrage because it spikes engagement, so believers risk being discipled into cynicism before breakfast. Scripture's grand narrative—from creation to new creation—demands sustained reflection, yet swipe culture trains us to process meaning in bite-sized meme theology. Consequently, doctrinal depth erodes, and convictions morph into reaction gifs.

The gospel offers an alternative story—one in which every click, like, or share is measured against the "whatsoever is true, noble, lovely" filter (Philippians 4:8). Practically, disciples audit feeds, unfollowing sources that incite envy or fear, curating spaces that foster edification. They practice slow scrolling, pausing to pray for individuals behind posts, transforming passive consumption into intercession. Sharing testimonies of digital fasting normalizes the choice to decelerate, resisting FOMO (fear of missing out) with JOMO (joy of missing out on noise). As believers gain narrative discernment, they become less reactive, able to engage cultural conversations with gentleness and informed conviction, setting the stage to explore how dopamine loops rewire the brain and spiritual life.

8.2.b Dopamine Loops and the Erosion of Contemplation
Neuroscientists explain that notifications trigger dopamine releases, reinforcing checking behavior much like gambling rewards slot players. This feedback loop cultivates compulsive scrolling, shortening attention spans and making lectio divina or prolonged silent prayer seem intolerable. Jesus often withdrew to lonely places (Mark 1:35) for extended communion with the Father; disciples steeped in dopamine cycles struggle to sit still long enough to hear even a whisper. Constant stimulation also hinders empathy: rapid image consumption leaves little emotional bandwidth to feel deeply for any story. Over time, brain circuits prioritize novelty over significance, so Scripture passages feel dull compared to viral videos.

Restoring contemplation involves deliberate friction—turning phone screens grayscale, disabling non-essential alerts, and charging devices outside bedrooms to permit tech-free mornings with God. Retreat settings where participants surrender devices for 24-48 hours reveal how silence revives imagination and prayer. Even micro-practices help: setting a timer for three minutes of breathing Scripture phrases ("The Lord is my shepherd," Psalm 23:1) can retrain attention muscles. Parents teach children analog delights—gardening, journaling—to counter digital captivity. As believers reclaim mental margin, they can confront algorithmic echo chambers with renewed discernment, resisting the lazy comfort of curated agreement.

8.2.c Algorithmic Echo Chambers vs. Scriptural Discernment
Recommendation engines feed content aligned with previous clicks, reinforcing ideological bubbles. Proverbs 18:17 warns that one side seems right until another comes and cross-examines, yet echo chambers silence that second voice, fortifying confirmation bias. The result is tribal rhetoric, where opposing viewpoints are caricatured, fueling division within the body of Christ. Acts 17:11 commends Bereans who examined Scriptures daily to verify Paul's

teaching, modeling critical engagement over blind acceptance. Today, Berean posture means cross-checking news with reputable sources, reading diverse theological voices, and anchoring all claims to biblical truth.

Churches host forums where members discuss culturally contentious topics—immigration, racial justice, technology ethics—through a biblical lens, practicing listening skills before rebuttal. Small groups can assign articles from differing perspectives, followed by prayerful dialogue. This intellectual hospitality counters algorithmic narrowing, creating space for Spirit-shaped conviction rather than feed-shaped reaction. Pastors also equip congregations with hermeneutical tools—genre awareness, historical context—to discern misused verses shared in viral memes. By cultivating scriptural discernment, believers break free from digital echo chambers, fostering unity amid diversity. Virtual friendships meanwhile promise connection but often intensify loneliness—a paradox addressed in the next subsection.

8.2.d Virtual Friendships, Real Loneliness—The Community Paradox Millions of followers may heart a post, yet genuine connection requires embodied presence—shared meals, eye contact, and physical touch. Sociologists note rising loneliness despite hyper-connectivity; God observed it was not good for Adam to be alone (Genesis 2:18), a truth screens cannot erase. Online interactions can supplement relationships but rarely replace covenant community where burdens are visibly borne (Galatians 6:2). Adolescents immersed in social media report heightened anxiety when digital affirmation fluctuates, revealing the fragile foundation of pixel-based identity. Couples seated together at dinner scroll separate feeds, missing opportunities for empathy. Even church engagement can become voyeuristic—watching livestreams while folding laundry may foster information transfer but not mutual edification.

Practices that restore embodiment include digital sabbaths during family time, phone-free zones at church gatherings, and intentional hospitality—inviting neighbors for backyard fires or potluck dinners. Congregations develop "tech tutoring" teams pairing digital natives with older saints, turning screens into intergenerational bridges rather than barriers. When believers prioritize embodied rituals—communion, laying on of hands, corporate singing—they taste relational fullness screens cannot supply. This embodied emphasis naturally leads into crafting tech-wise rhythms, the practical strategies we explore next.

8.2.e Crafting Tech-Wise Rhythms: Digital Sabbaths and Embodied Presence

Borrowing Sabbath's biblical rhythm of work and rest, digital sabbaths set predictable intervals—an evening, day, or weekend—when devices lie dormant, freeing attention for God, creation, and neighbor. Families light candles Friday night, signaling screens down and conversation up. Friends hike without phones, delighting in creation's unfiltered grandeur, echoing Psalm 19:1 that "the heavens declare the glory of God." Churches schedule post-service "linger hours," encouraging members to stay for shared meals instead of racing home to binge shows. Tech-wise rhythms also include rule-of-life practices: start days in prayer and Scripture before checking news, cap screen time an hour before bed to recite the Shema or examen.

Employers can champion focus by designating email-free blocks, mirroring Jesus' invitation to "come away and rest a while" (Mark 6:31). App-tracking tools reveal usage patterns, prompting repentance where digital indulgence steals affection from Christ. Conversely, technology becomes servant when harnessed for kingdom good—video calls uniting distant missionaries with home churches, translation apps enabling cross-cultural evangelism, and Bible apps facilitating daily reading plans. The goal is not digital asceticism but wise stewardship that keeps devices in their place under Christ's lordship. With attention reclaimed, believers are better prepared to resist the external ethical pressures explored in the next section, where marketplace conformity and cultural compromise challenge the integrity such tech-wise rhythms are meant to preserve.

8.3 Cultural Pressures and Ethical Compromise

8.3.a Marketplace Conformity vs. Kingdom Values — The Cost of Vocational Integrity In many workplaces the metrics that govern advancement—profit margins, consumer satisfaction, and rapid scalability—seem neutral until they clash with the ethics of the kingdom. A salesperson may be pressured to over-promise deliverables or quietly bury hidden fees, discovering that honesty can jeopardize quarterly bonuses. Scripture affirms diligent labor (Proverbs 22:29), yet it also warns that dishonest scales are an abomination to the Lord (Proverbs 11:1). When followers refuse to fiddle expense reports or pad billable hours, colleagues may label them naïve, but such resolve embodies Jesus' call to let "Yes" be yes and "No" be no (Matthew 5:37). Managers who resist discriminatory hiring practices might lose lucrative contracts, echoing Daniel who risked the lion's den rather than compromise prayer rhythms (Daniel 6:10–13). Faithfulness also involves advocating for equitable wages and humane schedules, reflecting the prophetic insistence that employers not withhold pay from workers (James 5:4). Kingdom integrity may cost promotions, yet it secures a clear conscience and a testimony that "those who honor me I will honor" (1 Samuel 2:30). Small acts—returning excess change, refusing to gossip in staff chat, insisting on truthful marketing—become countercultural witness in cubicles and boardrooms. Because economic systems often reward expedience, disciples must cultivate habits of daily examen, asking where profit endangers love of neighbor. As believers practice vocational integrity, they prepare themselves to withstand even sharper pressures in areas such as sexual ethics, where personal convictions collide with prevailing norms.

8.3.b Sexual Ethics in the Age of Expressive Individualism Contemporary culture catechizes citizens to view desire as destiny; fulfillment is framed as self-defined, immediate, and non-negotiable. Into that milieu the biblical vision speaks of covenant commitment, mutual self-gift, and bodily holiness, declaring that we are not our own but bought with a price (1 Corinthians 6:19-20). Followers who affirm marriage as a lifelong union between a man and a woman risk accusations of intolerance, yet they do so not to restrict joy but to safeguard it within God's design (Genesis 2:24; Hebrews 13:4). Singles who pursue chastity model hope-filled trust that their deepest identity is child of God, not object of conquest or consumption. Couples resisting cohabitation before vows bear witness that love is more than chemistry—it is promise. Pornography's easy access blurs consent and erodes intimacy; disciples counter by confessing struggles, installing filters, and seeking accountability, convinced that purity of heart enables sight of God (Matthew 5:8). Teaching teens bodily theology—God breathed life into dust, called it very good, and will one day raise it immortal (Romans 8:11)—arms them against reductionist messages that bodies are mere playgrounds. Churches that offer pastoral care for those experiencing same-sex attraction or gender dysphoria embody truth and tenderness, holding conviction while washing feet. When believers honor celibate saints and married couples equally, they shatter the myth that romance completes a person. Such counter-formation equips disciples to navigate cancel culture, where dissenting moral visions can trigger social ostracism, a challenge explored next.

8.3.c Cancel Culture, Fear of Dissent, and Courageous Witness
Digital platforms have amplified public shaming to the point where a single misstep—or even principled disagreement—can provoke calls for job loss and social exile. Early believers faced synagogue expulsion and imperial decrees; modern disciples face de-platforming, doxxing, or professional blacklists. Jesus foresaw such hostility, urging followers not to fear those who kill the body—or reputation—but to revere God (Matthew 10:28). Courageous witness today means speaking with grace and truth (Colossians 4:6), refusing both belligerent trolling and silent retreat. Practically, believers prepare by mastering issues thoughtfully, listening to critics, and framing convictions in narrative rather than slogans. House-church style gatherings where members rehearse tough questions foster rhetorical resilience. When backlash comes, believers bless persecutors (Romans 12:14) and examine feedback for any righteous rebuke worth heeding. Organizations can share the

burden—providing legal aid, mental-health support, and communal prayer for those under fire—mirroring the early church's care for jailed apostles (Acts 12:5). Over time, a track record of humility and service disarms caricatures, making it harder for mobs to reduce Christians to villains. Standing firm amid cancel culture exposes deeper idols of success that lure even ministries, segueing to prosperity metrics that threaten to distort gospel goals.

8.3.d Prosperity Metrics: Success Idolatry in Corporate and Ministry Spaces Whether on Wall Street or in megachurch hallways, numbers mesmerize—market share, streaming views, baptism counts. Metrics are useful servants but cruel masters, tempting leaders to inflate statistics or pursue flash over faithfulness. Jesus measured greatness by hidden obedience—mustard-seed influence, a widow's two coins, a cup of cold water given in secret (Mark 12:41-44). When ministries equate God's favor with growth charts, they risk commodifying souls and sidelining lament, discipline, and prophetic critique. Pastors may overwork, staff burn out, and volunteers become cogs in a production cycle, contradicting Jesus' rhythm of retreat (Mark 6:31). Businesses driven solely by quarterly profit may neglect environmental stewardship or employee flourishing, violating the dominion mandate to cultivate the earth (Genesis 2:15). Practicing sabbath economics—setting ceilings on campus expansion, celebrating faithfulness in small congregations, honoring bivocational pastors—defuses success idolatry. Companies that adopt triple-bottom-line accounting (people, planet, profit) embody kingdom values within competitive markets. Personal discipleship likewise rejects FOMO investing and status purchases, embracing simplicity that frees resources for mission. Cultivated this way, convictions can endure intense cultural winds without collapsing into sectarian withdrawal, the final task of this section.

8.3.e Developing Thick Christian Convictions without Sectarian Withdrawal Some believers respond to cultural heat by retreating into echo-chamber enclaves, shielding children from every dissenting idea. Yet Jesus prayed not for removal from the world but protection within it (John 17:15). Thick conviction combines doctrinal depth with cultural literacy, enabling engagement without assimilation. Households read Scripture alongside news articles, discussing where narratives diverge from kingdom ethics, teaching discernment rather than fear. Christian schools invite guest speakers with differing views, modeling intellectual hospitality anchored in truth. Local churches partner with city councils for neighborhood renewal, proving that convictional Christians can be civic blessing. Monastic-inspired practices—fixed-hour prayer, shared meals, hospitality to strangers—create counterculture without hostility. Study of church history reminds believers that vibrant faith has always negotiated minority status creatively. Mentors train emerging leaders to articulate beliefs publicly with charity, preparing them for boards, faculties, or laboratories. Thick conviction resists the allure to dilute doctrine or isolate; it remains porous enough for mission, resilient enough for ridicule. Such balanced posture provides an on-ramp to the identity crises explored next, where cultural flux intensifies personal confusion.

8.4 Identity Fluidity and the Quest for Self-Definition

8.4.a From Stable Roles to "Choose-Your-Own-Adventure" Selves Previous generations inherited relatively stable scripts—farmer's son, merchant's daughter—where identity cohered around family trade, faith, and locale. Today, digital mobility and expressive individualism invite constant reinvention: profile pictures shift, career pivots multiply, and geographical roots loosen. While freedom can foster creativity, it can also generate anxiety as people curate highlight reels to feel validated. Ecclesiastes laments the chasing of winds (Ecclesiastes 1:14), echoing modern dilemmas of endless self-optimization. Scripture counters by naming believers "chosen race… God's own people" (1 Peter 2:9), offering covenantal identity no algorithm can update. Apprenticeship to Jesus reorients self-expression toward self-surrender—who we are becomes gift received, not project engineered. Church communities help anchor wandering souls by celebrating vocation as service rather than status, hosting discernment retreats where members explore calling through prayer, feedback, and Scripture. Liturgical calendars tether identity to Christ's story—Advent hope, Lenten repentance—relieving pressure to invent significance. Mentors model faithfulness in ordinary roles, teaching that long obedience often outshines dramatic reinventions. As stable identity forms, disciples can tackle embodied questions of body image and gender beneath the surface of fluid self-construction.

8.4.b Body Image, Gender Dysphoria, and Theological Anthropology Social feeds bombard viewers with idealized physiques, fostering comparison and disordered eating, while contemporary discourse debates whether gender is fixed or self-assigned. Genesis presents humanity as male and female, image-bearers together (Genesis 1:27), and Psalm 139 extols God's intricate knitting of bodies in the womb. Yet fallen creation groans, and some experience distress over incongruence between gender identity and biological sex. Compassion compels the church to listen without caricature, while conviction affirms the goodness of embodied design. Pastoral teams establish support groups for those battling body shame or dysphoria, integrating counseling with robust theology of resurrection bodies (1 Corinthians 15:42-44). Teaching on fasting emphasizes gratitude for physical life rather than punitive self-hatred. Congregations celebrate diverse body types and abilities on stage, challenging narrow beauty standards. Parents coach children to critique media images through biblical lenses, reinforcing that worth rests in divine adoption, not digital likes. Engaging medical and psychological research with discernment enables holistic care rather than knee-jerk rejection or uncritical affirmation. This embodied discipleship paves the way for examining culture's exaltation of "authentic self," where performative identity competes with covenantal belonging.

8.4.c Performative Authenticity vs. Covenantal Belonging Popular mantras urge, "Be true to yourself" and "Live your truth," implying authenticity equals unfiltered self-expression. Yet Jeremiah warns that the heart is deceitful (Jeremiah 17:9), and Jesus insists that self-denial, not self-broadcast, is the path to life (Luke 9:23-24). Performative authenticity thrives on applause; covenantal belonging thrives on steadfast love. In church membership vows, individuals submit preferences to a broader body, promising to give and receive correction. Small groups that practice confession disrupt curated personas, replacing image management with shared weakness. Communion enacts belonging—believers approach the same table, regardless of résumé. Weddings and baptisms embody covenantal identity, anchoring life-stories in God's promises rather than shifting emotions. Mentors teach that feelings are real data, not ultimate dictators; Scripture adjudicates which impulses lead to flourishing. Artistic liturgy invites honest lament and exuberant praise, channeling authenticity toward worship instead of self-promotion. As disciples root identity in covenant, they can resist branding pressures that commodify the soul and discover baptismal story as the defining narrative explored next.

8.4.d Re-Rooting Identity in Baptismal Story rather than Personal Branding Baptism plunges believers into Christ's death and raises them into His life (Romans 6:4), marking identity with water, word, and communal witness. This sacrament tells a story older and more stable than any Instagram bio: sins washed, Spirit sealed, mission commissioned. Remembering baptism—touching fonts, tracing crosses on foreheads—anchors imagination during identity storms. Churches encourage yearly baptism anniversaries, inviting testimonies of God's faithfulness. Catechism classes unpack baptismal vows, linking them to daily ethics: renouncing devilish lies, embracing kingdom practices. When résumés falter or followers drop, baptism proclaims unshakeable belonging to Christ. Vocational discernment flows from baptismal identity; whether coding software or cleaning streets, disciples act as ambassadors of reconciliation (2 Corinthians 5:18). The marketplace values personal brand; the gospel brands with a cross, freeing believers from endless self-marketing. This liberation primes hearts to engage intellectual doubt honestly, an exploration taken up in the next section on skepticism and deconstruction.

8.5 Skepticism, Deconstruction, and Post-Truth Realities

8.5.a "Exvangelical" Movements and the Podcast Pulpit Disillusioned by scandal, political entanglement, or intellectual frustration, many join online communities that narrate exit stories from evangelicalism. Podcasts dissect deconversion tales, offering belonging to those nursing wounds. While some critiques uncover genuine abuses, others collapse orthodox belief with harmful subcultures, throwing out baby with bathwater. Jude urges believers to "have mercy on those who doubt" (Jude 22), inviting patient engagement rather than defensive dismissal. Local churches host listening circles where doubters voice concerns without fear of censure, mirroring Jesus' openness to Thomas' skepticism (John 20:27). Leaders repent publicly for past failures—cover-ups, power plays—demonstrating that reformation, not flight, is viable. Apologetics training addresses intellectual objections—science, violence in Scripture, sexual ethics—showing faith's coherence. Mentors accompany doubters through Bible reading plans that highlight lament and mystery, proving Scripture's capacity to wrestle honestly. Communities that welcome questions often see doubters reconstruct faith stronger than before. Recognizing this, we must also address conspiracy theories and misinformation that exploit distrust, threatening epistemic humility.

8.5.b Conspiracy Theories, Misinformation, and Epistemic Humility The digital age overflows with unverified claims—from medical hoaxes to political plots—spreading faster than fact-checked reports. Proverbs warns that the first story seems right until another perspective appears (Proverbs 18:17), urging cautious evaluation. When Christians propagate unfounded rumors, witness suffers, and neighbors doubt gospel credibility. Epistemic humility acknowledges human finitude: "We know in part" (1 Corinthians 13:9). Practically this means checking sources, reading across ideological lines, and consulting subject-matter experts before sharing. Bible study on truth-telling (Ephesians 4:25) complements media literacy workshops hosted by churches. Leaders model humility by correcting misstatements publicly, reinforcing integrity. Prayerful lament over society's fractured trust fuels peacemaking rather than polemics. As communities practice humility, they transform deconstruction from destructive skepticism to constructive refinement—an opportunity explored next.

8.5.c Deconstruction as Opportunity for Deep Reconstruction
Deconstruction originally described dismantling faulty frameworks to expose hidden assumptions. In spiritual journeys, it can reveal syncretism—nationalism, legalism, prosperity theology—cloaked as biblical faith. Jesus deconstructed Pharisaic traditions ("You have heard it said... but I say," Matthew 5), only to reconstruct fuller righteousness. Healthy deconstruction proceeds with Scripture, community, and Spirit, not in isolation. Retreats that pair silence with guided reading of the Sermon on the Mount allow participants to examine inherited beliefs under Jesus' lens. Spiritual directors ask clarifying questions: What is being deconstructed? What remains? What gospel truth might replace this rubble? Testimonies of saints who navigated crisis—Augustine, Teresa of Ávila—provide historical companions. Reconstruction emphasizes core creeds—Apostles', Nicene—as scaffolding. As disciples rebuild, they cultivate charity for those still tearing down. This journey calls for intellectual hospitality and orthodoxy, the final subsection.

8.5.d Cultivating Intellectual Hospitality and Historic Orthodoxy Paul implores Timothy to "guard the good deposit" (2 Timothy 1:14) while also urging servants of the Lord to be "kind to everyone... able to teach, patiently enduring evil" (2 Timothy 2:24). Intellectual hospitality embodies that balance: holding truth firmly yet welcoming conversation. Churches establish forums where scientists explain evolution alongside pastors who teach creation care, modeling gracious dialogue. Reading groups explore early church fathers, anchoring orthodoxy beyond contemporary fads. Seminaries integrate philosophy and cultural studies so pastors engage skeptics with rigor. Hospitality also entails acknowledging mystery—Trinity, incarnation—without resorting to simplistic analogies that breed heresy. When believers display confident humility, skeptics feel safe exploring faith claims. Over decades, such posture forms a resilient community able to face exhaustion, burnout, and hurry sickness addressed in the next part of the chapter, demonstrating that wholehearted discipleship depends on head and heart working in concert toward love of God and neighbor.

8.6 Exhaustion, Burnout, and Hurry Sickness

8.6.a Always-On Work Culture and the Myth of Limitless Productivity (Ecclesiastes 4:6) Smartphones have erased the boundary between office and bedroom, making the glow of late-night e-mail feel as compulsory as breathing. Employers praise hustle as virtue and craft mission statements that extol "round-the-clock responsiveness," but Scripture reminds us that "better is a handful of quietness than two hands full of toil and a striving after wind." The myth insists every hour can be optimized, so lunch breaks shrink into desk-side snacking while digital calendars fragment days into back-to-back blocks. Physiologically, chronic cortisol elevates blood pressure and weakens immunity, yet society calls it dedication. Disciples caught in the vortex often baptize overwork with spiritual language—calling endless tasks "servant leadership" rather than acknowledging addiction to affirmation. The early church countered empire time by gathering at dawn for prayer, declaring that Caesar's agenda would not dictate their pace. Re-reading Genesis 1 shows that God built pauses into creation itself; evening comes first, signaling that rest precedes labor. When believers ignore this rhythm, fatigue dulls discernment, temptation gains leverage, and relationships starve. Couples text from opposite ends of the couch instead of conversing, children grow accustomed to absent parents, and ministries equate full calendars with fruitful discipleship. The myth also fuels envy: scrolling LinkedIn, disciples compare output metrics, forgetting that John the Baptist rejoiced when his influence waned in favor of Christ's rise (John 3:30). Real freedom begins when people name the idol, admit limits, and recover the theology of finite creaturehood. Corporate teams can pilot e-mail curfews, tagging messages "delay send" until morning; such small acts confess that sleep is a gift, not a barrier to success. As communities practice limit-embracing rhythms, they expose the lie that worth equals productivity and open the door to examine how even ministry can mutate into another form of hurry.

8.6.b Ministry Fatigue: When Serving Replaces Abiding (Luke 10:38-42) Martha's frantic hospitality reflects millions of volunteers who sprint from planning meetings to livestream setup, whispering silent prayers that collapse under logistical weight. She welcomed Jesus, yet her anxieties swirled until resentment bubbled up toward Mary, who simply sat at the Rabbi's feet. Modern Marthas design sermon slides, manage children's check-in, and leave worship services dehydrated because they never paused to drink living water. Pastors preach self-denial but resist sabbaticals for fear attendance will dip, proving functionally they trust strategy over Spirit. Missionaries on the field report depression when support letters demand constant victory stories, reinforcing performance pressure. Jesus' gentle rebuke—"you are worried and upset about many things, but only one thing is necessary"—invites leaders to let ministry flow from union rather than hustle. Abiding vines bear fruit naturally; severed branches strain in vain (John 15:4-5). Practical safeguards include shared preaching rotations, mandatory retreat days, and peer supervision circles where burnout warning signs are addressed early. When teams replace lone-hero models with interdependent leadership, sabbath ceases to feel like abandonment and becomes worship. Naming ministry fatigue also dignifies ordinary vocations: nursery workers who change diapers for years mirror Christ's humility as profoundly as overseas evangelists. Recognizing that serving is gift, not badge, transitions us to consider restorative practices that mend weary souls and recalibrate speed.

8.6.c Restorative Practices: Sabbath, Silence, and Sustainable Pace (Mark 6:31) Jesus called His disciples to "come away… and rest a while" immediately after a mission trip, embedding recovery into the rhythm of outreach. Sabbath declares weekly that God runs the universe without our frantic assistance; lighting candles, blessing bread, and setting phones aside incarnate trust in divine provision. Silence deepens sabbath—five unhurried minutes each morning teaches the nervous system that value is bestowed before tasks begin. Communities adopt "quiet communion" segments in services, letting stillness preach louder than guitars. Rule-of-life templates help families plan margin: limiting extracurriculars, protecting one free evening, and scheduling nature walks that restore imagination. Pastors model sustainable pace by taking true days off—resisting sermon tweaks—and sending autoreplies that quote Psalm 127:2: "He grants sleep to those He loves." Workplaces experiment with "Focus Friday," cancelling meetings to privilege deep work, then release employees early. These practices do not romanticize laziness; they create capacity for resilient engagement during crisis. As rhythms settle, hearts become more attuned to unseen wounds—trauma and compassion fatigue that can linger even after schedules slow. Addressing those deeper fractures becomes the next imperative.

8.6.d Trauma, Compassion Fatigue, and the Need for Soul Care (Psalm 34:18) Frontline caregivers—counselors, teachers, medical staff, and pastors—absorb stories of abuse, illness, and war, often internalizing secondary trauma. Compassion fatigue surfaces as numbness, irritability, or cynicism, tempting servants to withdraw emotionally. David's assurance that "the Lord is near to the brokenhearted" includes healers themselves, inviting them to receive comfort before distributing it. Professional debrief groups, spiritual direction, and therapy normalize processing pain rather than spiritualizing it away. Prayer practices such as breath prayers—inhale "Come, Lord Jesus," exhale "Have mercy"—help release accumulated sorrow. Congregations budget for counseling stipends, signaling that mental-health investment is mission, not luxury. Rituals of lament offer corporate catharsis: lighting candles for victims of violence, reading imprecatory psalms, and shouting collective "how long" to God. These acts legitimize grief and remind caregivers they are conduits, not messiahs. When soul-care culture takes root, teams notice burnout earlier, intervening with respite or re-assignment. Renewed servants return to ministry grounded, compassionate, and less likely to replicate trauma through hurried leadership. This holistic healing prepares communities to confront another subtle threat: the disembodiment of faith that accelerated during pandemic lockdowns and continues to reshape church life.

8.7 Disembodied Faith in a Post-Pandemic World

8.7.a Livestream Liturgy and the Loss of Incarnational Fellowship (Hebrews 10:24-25) Stay-at-home orders moved sanctuaries into living rooms overnight, proving technology's capacity to extend reach while simultaneously exposing its limitations. Livestream sermons fed minds, yet tactile elements—handshakes of peace, collective singing, baptismal waters—vanished, and isolation gnawed at souls. Hebrews urges believers not to neglect meeting together because mutual encouragement depends on presence. Video delays mute spontaneous "Amen," children wander mid-sermon, and side-chat replaces hallway hugs. Some immunocompromised saints still rely on streams, reminding us inclusion matters; yet if convenience alone keeps healthy believers on couches, embodiment suffers. Church leaders redesign spaces to foster safe regathering—open-air services, micro-congregations in backyards—reclaiming eye contact as liturgical act. Testimony videos now include invitations to in-person prayer corners. Digital hospitality teams segue viewers toward local small groups, bridging pixels to pews. Acknowledging livestream's gift while grieving what it cannot supply readies us to consider the sacramental absence many endured: months without Eucharist, a gap that pressed theological questions into pastoral frontline.

8.7.b Eucharistic Absence: Sacramentality in Virtual Spaces (1 Corinthians 11:26) Paul ties the Lord's Supper to embodied proclamation—"whenever you eat this bread and drink this cup, you proclaim the Lord's death." During lockdowns, believers debated drive-thru communion, Zoom consecrations, and individually packaged elements. Some traditions discouraged remote sacrament, fearing disunity; others embraced provisional measures, trusting Christ to meet scattered flocks. This season surfaced hunger for tangible grace—crumb of bread on tongue, sip of wine warming throat—gestures that embed gospel deeper than words. Post-pandemic, congregations re-emphasize catechesis around the table: examining hearts (1 Corinthians 11:28), confessing sins corporately, and restoring extended moments of silence. Home-group Eucharists flourish with clergy oversight, reminding that location is flexible so long as community gathers around real presence. The experience also provokes creative liturgy: blessing of sourdough starters, garden-grown wheat for communion bread, linking daily labor to sacred meal. As Eucharistic practice regrounds bodies in grace, churches evaluate hybrid discipleship models, weighing digital gains against relational gaps.

8.7.c Hybrid Models: Opportunities and Limitations for Disciple-Making (Acts 2:46-47) Early believers met in temple courts and homes, a dual pattern suggesting flexibility in venue so long as fellowship, teaching, and breaking bread persisted. Modern hybrids mirror this rhythm: mid-week Zoom Bible studies allow commuters to attend; Sunday hubs gather locally for communal worship. Online Alpha courses draw seekers reluctant to step into sanctuaries, and recorded sermons bless night-shift workers. Yet screens cannot baptize, lay hands, or hear faint whispers of confession masked by mute buttons. Mentoring requires noticing body language, and prophetic ministry often emerges from lingering hallway conversation. Churches therefore define clear discipleship pathways: digital entry, embodied commitment. Membership classes blend e-modules with retreat weekends culminating in covenant vows. Small groups alternate online discussion with quarterly service projects, tethering theology to neighborhood need. Metrics shift from click-rates to participation in Eucharist, service, and giving. By integrating technology as supplement, not substitute, congregations safeguard incarnation while leveraging reach. Such intentional design points to the final movement: re-embedding worship in neighborhoods and households where digital habits find liturgical grounding.

8.7.d Re-embedding Worship in Neighborhoods and Households (Deuteronomy 6:6-9) Moses instructed Israel to recite God's words at home, on the road, and at the table, embedding worship into daily geography. Post-pandemic disciples recover this vision by turning living rooms into micro-sanctuaries: lighting advent wreaths, singing doxology at dinner, reading psalms during evening walks. Neighborhood prayer walks claim ground for peace, fostering relationships with baristas, teachers, and postal carriers. House-church networks complement larger gatherings, ensuring every believer is known by name. Families craft "screens-down" Sabbath dinners where Scripture is read and stories shared, reinforcing identity apart from devices. Local parishes adopt parish maps, assigning members to pray for specific streets, embodying Jeremiah's call to seek city welfare. Garden liturgies celebrate harvest with thanksgiving prayers, teaching children sacramental lens for creation. When worship springs from home soil, Sunday assembly becomes culmination rather than sole spiritual feeding. This reintegration steeps disciples in everyday sacraments—Christ recognized in the breaking of toast and embrace of neighbor—preparing believers to transform obstacles into formation pathways described in the chapter's closing epilogue.

Conclusion

The obstacles mapped here are formidable precisely because they entangle what we buy, how we work, when we rest, and even the stories we tell ourselves about who we are. Yet none of them is stronger than the grace that first called us or the Spirit who now empowers us. When consumer buzz yields to sacrificial worship, when fractured attention is reclaimed through sabbath rhythms, when ethical pressure meets the steel of kingdom convictions, and when lonely scrolling is exchanged for embodied community, the very challenges of our moment become chisels shaping mature followers of Jesus. The path forward is not withdrawal into fear or frantic activism but a patient, deliberate recalibration of loves and habits around the crucified and risen Lord. As we embrace that recalibration together—confessing where we have conformed, encouraging one another in counter-formation, and leaning into the Spirit's renewing work—we discover that today's pressures can forge tomorrow's resilient disciples, ready to bear faithful witness whatever the cultural weather.

Chapter 9 — Spiritual Practices for Crossing the Line

Stepping across the dividing line from nominal faith to wholehearted discipleship requires more than good intentions—it takes practical commitment to habits that reshape our very orientation toward God and neighbor. In the early church, believing without acting left congregations vulnerable to hypocrisy; James warned that faith without works is dead (James 2:17). Likewise today, it is not enough to recognize Jesus as Lord in theory; genuine transformation takes root when our routines—morning reflections, choices at work, hospitality around the table—align with the Spirit's leading. These practices cultivate a lived faith: repentance uncovers hidden loyalties, surrender rewires our affections for God's kingdom, obedient action bridges belief and behavior, perseverance sustains us through dry seasons, discernment helps us hear God's voice over cultural noise, and missional overflow turns inward devotion outward into tangible love. As disciples integrate head, heart, and hands in daily rhythms, they discover that ordinary rhythms—meal-sharing, workplace integrity, and storytelling—become conduits of grace. This chapter explores how simple, Spirit-empowered practices foster the kind of faith that doesn't just admire Jesus at a distance but follows Him through every moment, transforming both individual lives and communities.

9.0 Moving From Intention to Transformation

9.0.a Practice as Participation in Grace, Not Performance for Approval Spiritual practices are often misunderstood as checklists of sacred tasks that earn favor with God, yet the New Testament portrays them as means of participating in the grace already extended through Christ. Paul urges believers to present their bodies as living sacrifices, "holy and acceptable" to God (Romans 12:1), not so that God will start loving them, but to respond to the love He has already shown in sending His Son. This reorientation reshapes every practice—from prayer to fasting—into an act of communion rather than a legalistic ritual. When Jesus taught the Lord's Prayer, He modeled that prayer is a conversation between Father and children, not a scoreboard to tally petitions granted. This "grace-first" posture guards against the spiritual exhaustion that arises when disciplines become performance metrics. Instead of practicing humility to be recognized as humble, disciples practice it to dwell in the humility of Christ. When fasting arises from a desire to feel closer to God instead of to earn spiritual credentials, it restores reliance on God's sustaining presence rather than self-discipline alone. Similarly, scripture meditation ceases to be memory work and becomes listening work—letting the Spirit interpret the Word for the heart. This participation in grace also transforms confession. Instead of reciting sins to check a box, believers name shortcomings within a framework of assurance: "If we confess our sins, he is faithful and just to forgive us" (1 John 1:9). Recognizing the Spirit as the enabler of every good intention prevents self-condemnation when practices falter. Communities that foster this paradigm encourage one another in soft, grace-saturated language rather than scoring each other's devotion. Worship gatherings that begin with reminders of Christ's once-for-all atonement set a tone of gratitude, anchoring every subsequent petition in thanksgiving rather than desperation. This grace-driven approach to practice lays the groundwork for integration of head, heart, and hands, which sustains transformation beyond individual acts.

9.0.b Head–Heart–Hand Integration: How Habits Re-Script Desire, Imagination, and Behavior True transformation reshapes what we think, what we feel, and how we act—head, heart, and hands align around the gospel story that replaced shame with identity, fear with confidence, and selfishness with sacrificial love. In Romans 12:2, Paul calls for believers to be "transformed by the renewal of your mind," signaling that cognitive realignment precedes behavioral change. Yet renewed thinking works best when desires—our inmost affections—are also reoriented toward what God values, as captured in Psalm 37:4: "Delight yourself in the Lord, and he will give you the desires of your heart." When love for God becomes primary, imagination follows, picturing life in terms of faithfulness rather than fear. This inward shift then flows outward, prompting hands to serve neighbors because serving no longer feels like sacrifice but like overflow. Spiritual habits—such as reading the Gospels each morning—expose the mind to narrative truths that replace cultural self-concepts with Kingdom identity. Simultaneously, memorizing a Psalm occasions the heart to rehearse trust in God when distress arises, retraining emotional reactions away from anxiety. Putting hands to work—volunteering in shelters or caring for elderly neighbors—forms behavior that visually testifies to Gospel values. Pope John Paul II taught that truth leads to beauty and goodness; as disciples increasingly perceive the beauty of Christ in Scripture and community, their imaginations crave goodness in daily life. Conversely, practicing kindness in the workplace plants neural pathways that make compassion a reflex rather than an exception. In worship, singing creedal songs recalibrates beliefs; communal prayer lifts affections focused on gratitude and humility; breaking bread invites hands to enact fellowship. Over weeks and months, these integrated habits lend momentum to transformation that no single sermon could achieve. As head, heart, and hands collaborate, disciples become living testimonies of God's reconciling work, not merely hearers of instruction. With this framework in place, we pivot to the first essential practice—repentance—to see how reexamining daily life requires both reflection and concrete turning away from hidden drift.

9.1 Repentance: Re-Aligning the Heart's Affections

9.1.a Daily Examination — Naming Drift before it Becomes Defection (Psalm 139:23-24) David's prayer, "Search me, O God, and know my heart; test me and know my anxious thoughts" (Psalm 139:23), models the daily practice of self-examination. When the shepherd king invited inspection of his innermost life, he acknowledged that without God's scrutiny, hidden drift can lead to entrenched sin. In contemporary terms, drift may look like subtle envy toward others' success, a creeping reliance on technology for comfort, or the gradual silencing of prayer in favor of productivity. Daily examination flips on spiritual lights before shadows take root. Practically, believers carve out a few minutes each morning to review the previous day—asking where they felt disposable, loved, anxious, or resentful. Journaling these reflections provides tangible patterns: maybe they snapped at a spouse due to unaddressed fear, or neglected neighborly kindness in pursuit of personal goals. By naming these shifts quickly, disciples avoid the slow slide into rationalizing compromise. As realignment occurs, petitions follow: "Reveal where I trusted others instead of You," "Show me where I prioritized achievement over abiding." This humble posture sets the tone for confession, anticipates the need for grace, and fuels gratitude that God remains willing to correct. Through daily pruning, irreconcilable allegiances—status, security, or acclaim—are exposed while dependence on Christ deepens. Over time, what began as artificial discipline becomes longing for God's searching. When hearts submit regularly to the lamp of Scripture (Psalm 119:105), defiance loses momentum, replaced by joy in clarity. This morning practice naturally transitions to communal confession, where hidden sin becomes shared burden and assurance of forgiveness.

9.1.b Corporate Confession and Assurance — Community as a Mirror (James 5:16) James instructs believers to "confess your sins to one another and pray for one another, that you may be healed" (James 5:16). Unlike private maintenance, corporate confession harnesses community bandwidth to expose individual blind spots. When one person admits jealousy, another may realize they too have envied a coworker's promotion. Bystanders offering prayer create a context of intercession that resists isolation. Confession groups often meet weekly, opening with Scripture that highlights God's forgiveness—such as 1 John 1:9—thereby confirming that honesty precedes healing. As members share, the group practices active listening without immediate advice, modeling Christ's compassion. When confession leads to public accountability—naming a struggle with anger or dishonesty—other believers intervene with prayer, resource referrals to counselors, or mentoring for practical change. The assurance that "the blood of Jesus cleanses from all sin" (1 John 1:7) turns confession from slapping a spiritual Band-Aid to true reorientation of affections, for everyone witnesses grace meeting failure. When forgiveness is visible, trust grows, and the language of shame gives way to language of hope. Instead of burying transgressions that later erupt as bitterness, communities learn to uncover sin swiftly, preventing defection. Corporate confession also dovetails with liturgical elements: the congregational reading of a penitential psalm (Psalm 51) during worship sets a norm of transparency. Because human nature hides sin, the honesty of one member often grants courage to others to confess long-buried sins, sparking collective transformation. As wounds surface and heal, generosity increases, ministries flourish, and the light of Christ becomes more visible. From communal confession, attention shifts naturally to lamenting broken realities, where sorrow ushers in deeper repentance.

9.1.c Lament as Deep Repentance — Turning Grief into Godward Hope (Joel 2:12-13) Joel's call to "return to the Lord your God, for He is gracious and merciful, slow to anger, and abounding in steadfast love" (Joel 2:13) arises in the context of national catastrophe—locusts, drought, and invasion. Ancient Israel's lament paired grief with confession, acknowledging collective sin as root cause of judgment. In contemporary practice, lament provides a structured space to bring sorrow—over personal failure, social injustices, or ecological crises—to God's presence. Unlike superficial optimism, lament faces the pain directly, shaping cries like "My God, my God, why have you forsaken me?" (Psalm 22:1) as genuine hem of prayer. When individuals or congregations lament, they articulate truths often unspoken—racial injustice, economic exploitation, or betrayal by leaders. This honesty aligns with Revelation's image of the martyrs under the altar, crying out for justice (Revelation 6:9). As tears flow, participants claim hope in restoration, remembering that God turns mourning into dancing (Psalm 30:11). Liturgies of lament might include walking a labyrinth as a physical enactment of sorrow and repentance or writing prayers on paper and placing them in a "lament box" before the congregation, signifying trust that God hears. Music selections draw from the sons of Korah psalms, blending minor keys and plaintive melodies, guiding hearts toward trust in God's faithfulness. Corporate lament also breaks the idol of constant positivity that stifles confession; when churches publicly mourn community losses—gun violence, overdoses, or economic downturn—they embody solidarity with hurting neighbors. As lament gives voice to grief, it dissolves hardened hearts and opens them to renewed devotion. Emerging from lament, communities transition into acts of restitution—repairing relationships, advocating for policy change, or funding relief—making their repentance tangible.

9.1.d Embodied Acts of Turning — Fasting, Restitution, and Symbolic Gestures (Acts 19:18-19) The book of Acts recounts how many who practiced magic arts burned their scrolls publicly, amounting to fifty thousand pieces of silver worth of spells (Acts 19:18-19). This embodied act of turning—costly and visible—signified genuine repentance among Ephesians. Similarly, fasting serves as corporeal counterpart to lament, signaling that souls hunger for God more than bodily sustenance (Matthew 4:4). When believers fast, they break familiar routines, making space to refocus mortal appetites toward divine communion. Modern fasting might include giving up social media or coffee for a week, pairing the physical deprivation with extended prayer focused on areas previously ignored. At the same time, restitution addresses specific wrongs: someone who embezzled volunteer funds returns gifts or donates equivalent value to the church; a leader who spread false rumors publicly apologizes and meets personally with those harmed. Symbolic gestures deepen these acts of turning—shoes removed in reverence, public foot-washing ceremonies signifying humility, or placing coins in a "tithe for healing" box to support victims of betrayal. When a congregation stands in solidarity—laying hands on one who seeks reconciliation—it becomes a powerful visual of God's reconciling work. These embodied disciplines concretize the inner shift and broadcast to the world a faith that does not merely speak but also moves. As genuine turning culminates in tangible action, hearts are prepared to offer everything—time, energy, resources—in a full surrender that leads us into the next vertical step: surrendering the whole self to God's transformative purposes.

9.2 Surrender: Offering the Whole Self

9.2.a Living Sacrifice Imagery — Worship that Walks on Monday (Romans 12:1-2) Paul's urging to present our bodies as a living sacrifice suggests worship is not confined to moments of singing or prayer but extends into weekday activities—work, family life, civic engagement. In the Old Covenant, sacrifices were dead animals offered on altars; in Christ's once-for-all sacrifice (Hebrews 10:10), believers themselves become living altars. Surrendering the whole self begins with acknowledging that impulse, habit, and comfort zones often compete with allegiance to Christ's lordship. Instead of compartmentalizing spiritual devotion to weekends, disciples consecrate each meal, conversation, and decision as worship. This means negotiating office politics with integrity, viewing parenting discipline not as drudgery but as shaping image-bearers of God, and handling finances with generosity rather than greed. When individuals internalize scriptural rhythms—remembrance of the cross at midnight work shifts, prayer in traffic jams—they cultivate a posture where every fiber of being is oriented toward God's glory. This concept also tackles the knee-jerk tendency to serve God in spiritual tasks while neglecting everyday contexts. When a believer treats grocery-store checkout as mission, offering encouragement to cashiers or silently praying for customers, the worship transforms mundane moments into sacred ones. Over time, this lifestyle fosters alignment of values; decision-making filters through the lens of "What would Jesus do here?" rather than "What would my peers expect?" As hearts recognize Christ occupying every sphere of life, they find true freedom from performance-based religion; sacrifice becomes delight as breathing becomes natural. This holistic surrender then opens space to ponder God's will—an invitation to holy indifference essential for full surrender.

9.2.b Holy Indifference — Releasing Outcomes to God (Luke 22:42) In Gethsemane, Jesus demonstrates holy indifference: "Not my will, but yours, be done." This principle acknowledges that while humans must decide and act, ultimate control rests with the Father. Holy indifference does not mean apathy; it means holding plans, dreams, and desires with open hands, willing to embrace God's alternate path. When disciples launch new initiatives—church plants, social enterprises—they pray specific prayers but also whisper "Your kingdom come" over expected results. If outcomes diverge, holy indifference releases disappointment and reaffirms trust. This posture cures micro-managing tendencies that stem from fear of failure. In families, parents who practice holy indifference parent free from anxious agendas; they nurture children while letting God's Spirit shape character. In careers, believers offer job applications or pitches but rest in the knowledge that God ordains next steps, whether doors open or close. In missions, volunteers invest years in community development but accept if cross-cultural fruit emerges slowly. This balance of active responsibility and restful trust bridges the gap between hyperactivity and passivity, aligning hearts with Jesus' example of "working while trusting." When disciples cultivate holy indifference through prayer retreats, journaling surrender prayers, and practicing saying "Not my will" in daily devotions, they build resilience for unexpected twists. Holy indifference does not eradicate grief but transforms it into expectancy that God works all things for good (Romans 8:28). As surrender deepens into trust, disciples naturally arrange their lives around God's priorities, leading to intentional rhythms—a rule of life—that shape time, money, and energy.

9.2.c Rule of Life Crafting — Ordering Time, Money, and Energy around Kingdom Priorities A rule of life is a framework that deliberately allocates life's resources—time, finances, and physical vigor—so they align with gospel values rather than default cultural norms. Historically monastics patterned prayer, work, and rest according to rhythms that prioritized Christlikeness. Today, laypeople can adapt these principles: setting non-negotiable times for prayer and Scripture before career tasks, committing a percentage of income to tithing and compassion ministries, and ensuring weekly Sabbath practice despite hectic schedules. Household rosters might designate one "device-free evening" where family members gather to serve a meal or discuss Scripture passages, cultivating relational closeness. Financial rule of life elements could include budgeting for regular giving, emergency savings, and modest living to buffer against consumerist pressures. Energy management might involve establishing work boundaries—no emails after 7 p.m.—and scheduling physical exercise as stewardship of God's gift of health. A written rule of life serves as a covenant with oneself and community, providing clarity during hectic seasons: when back-to-back meetings threaten to crowd out prayer, another glance at the rule reminds the heart to uphold the established order. Crafting such a rule often begins with savior-defined priorities: abiding in Christ (John 15), nurturing marriage and family (Ephesians 5–6), and bearing witness (Acts 1:8). As disciples live into these structures, flexibility remains crucial—some seasons call for intensified focus on urgent ministry work, while others necessitate deeper rest. The rule is not a rigid cage but a scaffolding, stopping drift into unexamined habits. As time, money, and energy align around kingdom priorities, a daily surrender becomes second nature, equipping disciples to embody baptismal identity each moment.

9.2.d Baptismal Remembrance — Daily "Dying and Rising" Practices (Romans 6:3-4) Baptism symbolizes union with Christ in His death and resurrection, not solely as a past event but as an ongoing reality. Paul writes that having been "baptized into Christ Jesus, we have been baptized into his death… so we too might walk in newness of life" (Romans 6:3-4). Daily practices that remind believers of this death-and-resurrection identify include beginning each day with handwashing or water-sprinkling rituals accompanied by the confession, "I died with Christ; today I rise to walk in new life." Some household traditions involve lighting a candle at a baptismal font replica each morning, praying, "As Christ rose, may my heart rise from old patterns." Similarly, before meals, disciples might dip bread in water, symbolizing cleansing, then break bread in remembrance of the body given for them. These embodied acts help the mind and heart grasp that the old self's claims—pride, anger, fear—are forever buried. As the Son commands, "Deny yourself, take up your cross, and follow me" (Luke 9:23), these rituals provide tangible tokens to carry into daily challenges. In seasons of temptation, recalling that one has already died with Christ loosens sin's grip, reminding the will that resistance is not futile. Communities celebrate baptism anniversaries in small groups, sharing testimonies of how reflecting on death and resurrection has reshaped vocational, relational, and personal choices. This daily dying-and-rising practice yields a sustained posture of surrender, bridging internal transformation with external obedience—a foundation for embracing the call to take up the cross daily, as we explore next.

9.3 Obedient Action: Faith Expressed in Works

9.3.a The Call to Take Up the Cross Daily (Luke 9:23) When Jesus urged His followers to "take up their cross daily and follow me," He issued a call that was as countercultural then as it is now. This practice of daily cross-bearing means refusing to let discomfort, fear, or convenience drive our decisions; instead, we choose the way of sacrificial love that Christ embodied. In practical terms, taking up one's cross might involve standing for justice at work when it costs popularity, choosing tough conversations over avoiding conflict, or sacrificing personal comfort to serve those who cannot repay us. When families dedicate moments each morning to reading Luke 9 alongside personal reflections, children learn early that obedience may look different from what peers expect. In communities of faith, small groups can commit to praying for opportunities to bear their cross—perhaps by walking across a neighborhood to offer help to a stranger or by inviting a marginalized coworker to lunch. Refusing to deny self might mean forgoing a lucrative promotion that compromises integrity, trusting God rather than clinging to financial security. Cross-bearing also surfaces when pastors risk unpopular truths in sermons rather than pander to the crowd. The daily modality of this practice trains hearts to see every micro-decision as an opportunity to follow Jesus' pattern, whether saying "no" to petty gossip or giving a portion of the rent money to a family in crisis. As congregations share testimonies of such daily choices, they cultivate courage together, reminding one another that cross-carrying is not a one-time event but a lifelong posture. The gospel's paradox becomes visible: losing our lives to Christ's purposes actually yields life beyond what we can build for ourselves. Over time, what seemed like burdensome imposition transforms into a rhythm that aligns desires with God's redemptive agenda. As disciples internalize this call, the next door swings open to discern the Spirit's timely nudges that guide each step.

9.3.b Listening & Immediate Response — The Spirit's "Nudge" in Ordinary Moments (Acts 8:29–30) Philip's encounter with the Ethiopian eunuch illustrates the power of listening for the Spirit's promptings in real time. While traveling on a deserted road, Philip "heard the voice of the Lord saying, 'Go over and join this chariot'" (Acts 8:29). He obeyed, which led to the eunuch's conversion and baptism. This example shows that discerning the Spirit requires cultivated attentiveness: Philip was not so consumed by his schedule that he missed the divine whisper. Modern disciples can develop this sensitivity through regular silence and introspection—practices like early-morning prayer, where fleeting thoughts are offered to God and the Spirit's impressions are noticed. Practically, someone might feel a sudden conviction to call a friend who has been absent from church, or overhear a co-worker's offhand remark as an opportunity to share encouragement. Churches can teach listening workshops—role-playing scenarios where one partner speaks while the other listens for "God lines," those bits of conversation where divine opportunity beckons. As believers practice journaling these daily promptings, they build records of God's faithfulness, strengthening confidence to obey next time. In neighborhood encounters, a small gesture—buying an extra coffee for a stressed barista—can flow from the Spirit's nudge to extend kindness. When commuters pause before honking at a slow driver, they affirm that patience can reflect Christ's character. These immediate responses, though small, accumulate into a lifestyle where obedience is not deferred but enacted in real time. Listening prayer and simple note-taking apps can help believers track how God speaks through mundane details—texts, conversations, or sudden compunctions. As a result, what began as hesitant listening blossoms into habitual responsiveness, naturally leading communities to partner in justice-shaped obedience.

9.3.c Justice-Shaped Obedience — Loving Neighbor through Structural and Personal Mercy (Micah 6:8) Micah's declaration—"He has told you, O man, what is good; and what does the LORD require of you but to do justice, and to love kindness, and to walk humbly with your God?"—frames obedient action within the broader scope of God's concern for the vulnerable. Justice-shaped obedience means advocating for systemic change while simultaneously practicing personal acts of mercy. In practice, a local church might partner with a legal aid organization to provide pro bono counsel to low-income families, reflecting structural engagement. At the same time, individual congregants can volunteer at food pantries, ensuring that immediate needs are met. Advocating for policy reforms—such as living wages, affordable housing, or equitable healthcare—stems from loving neighbors at a communal level, a natural extension of daily mercy ministries like accompanying a recovering addict to appointments. Bible studies can include the prophetic books—Isaiah, Amos, Jeremiah—so participants grasp how biblical justice intertwines with mercy. When members read Isaiah 58 and see fasting described as "sharing your bread with the hungry" and "bringing the homeless poor into your house," they understand that worship must overflow into social care. In workplaces, followers advocate for transparent hiring practices and equitable pay, resisting the pressure to cut corners for profit. Small groups can host town-hall discussions with local officials to chart civic pathways for justice. Children's ministry can teach stewardship by encouraging youth to donate birthday gifts or chore earnings to causes that feed the hungry. Over time, personal empathy aligns with communal engagement, shaping a consistent vision where obedience of hand—volunteering, volunteering, petitioning—flows from obedience of heart. Insights from social science classes in seminary or lay training equip volunteers to navigate the complexities of systemic injustice without succumbing to cynicism. As justice-shaped obedience unfolds, stories of transformed neighborhoods emerge, reinforcing the pattern of obedience until it becomes reflexive. This seamless movement from personal obedience to structural mercy demonstrates the vibrancy of faith expressed in works, setting the stage for sustaining habits through perseverance in seasons of dryness.

9.3.d Rhythms of Celebration — Remembering God's Faithfulness Fuels Future Obedience (Deuteronomy 16) Israel's liturgical calendar—Passover, Weeks, Tabernacles—served not only as festivals but as communal reminders of God's steadfast love, empowering obedience between seasons. When Miriam led the women in dance after crossing the Red Sea (Exodus 15:20-21), celebration reinforced trust in God's deliverance, making future obedience easier. Modern disciples adopt similar rhythms: annual baptism anniversaries prompt reflection on the Day when sin died and new life began. Quarterly corporate testimonies in worship share stories of God's provision—healing, rescue from addiction, reconciliation—which create a reservoir of faith for times when obedience feels costly. Seasonal communal meals—potlucks during Advent, outdoor gatherings in spring—tie fellowship to storying, as older saints recount how they witnessed God's work in previous decades. Congregational calendars mark Remembrance Sundays where mission partners share reports, inspiring local service. On financial matters, churches practice periodic "vision-driven generosity Sundays," where deacons highlight how past gifts funded community ministries, inviting members to fuel future obedience. Families create "Covenant Breakfasts" on anniversaries, where they revisit commitment prayers and update household mission statements for the year ahead. As gratitude-filled rhythms embed past faithfulness in memory, the church's collective imagination shifts from scarcity—"What if I obey and suffer loss?"—to confidence—"Look how God has prevailed before." This culture of celebration primes disciples to take up the cross again, confident that obedience leads not to defeat but deeper participation in God's unfolding redemption.

9.4 Perseverance: Habits that Survive Dry Seasons

9.4.a Sabbathing in the Storm — Rest as Spiritual Warfare
(Hebrews 4:9-11) Hebrews describes a "Sabbath rest" that still awaits the people of God, urging believers to "strive to enter that rest" (Hebrews 4:9-11). For disciples navigating dry seasons—when prayer feels empty, Scripture seems distant, and worship yields little joy—Sabbathing amid crisis stands as an act of faith. Choosing to rest on Sunday, or the chosen sabbath day, defies the cultural demand to squeeze every ounce of productivity from every hour, proclaiming instead that God's kingdom is not built by busyness. Concrete practices include setting aside a few hours each week with no scheduled tasks—no emails, no errands—just worship, silence, and reflection. In crucible seasons of grief or doubt, Sabbath can feel offensive, yet it serves as sacred refusal to let despair dictate pace. Single mothers who hire a babysitter for a two-hour Saturday prayer retreat model this courage. Small groups experimenting with a "Sabbath journal" record observations of God's provision in the week, transforming rest into an expectant practice. In workplaces, employees negotiate "Sabbath-friendly" contracts—Lapwing's "Calm App" consultants advise firms on implementing email-free days—demonstrating that rest can be systemic resistance. Spiritual

retreats scheduled quarterly provide extended sabbath—a two-day desert experience where participants unplug, worship, and cultivate trust in God's presence. As sleep-deprived church leaders step away for silent retreats, they return not just refreshed but recalibrated, better positioned to guide others through dry seasons. In this way, seasonal rhythms of rest become a form of spiritual warfare, where choosing to cease work undercuts the lies that productivity equates value and that availability equates faithfulness. As believers embed rest in storms, they lay the groundwork for daily practices—examen and fellowship—that sustain them through extended dryness.

9.4.b Prayer of Examen and Long-View Journaling — Tracking God's Quiet Work over Years The Ignatian Examen invites believers to reflect on the day from beginning to end, noticing where God's presence stirred gratitude, where sin provoked confession, and where guidance nudged decisions. During dry seasons, this practice refuses superficial engagement; rather than abandoning prayer because feelings fall flat, disciples patiently review moments—perhaps a consoling sunrise or a word of encouragement from a friend—that signal God's still, small voice (1 Kings 19:12). Over weeks and months, patterns emerge: maybe God's comfort comes most often via Scripture passages, or conviction consistently arises around impatience. Journaling these insights creates a long-view record, countering amnesia when immediate fervor wanes. When a senior saint flips through a decade's worth of journal entries, they see arcs of faithfulness—a conviction during unemployment that led to a deeper reliance on generosity, a season of infertility that birthed new ministries for orphans. Such long-view perspective assures hearts that God's silence today is not absence but a preparation for tomorrow's revelation. Churches can facilitate "examen partners" who meet monthly to share journal highlights, reinforcing that individual dryness is part of a collective pilgrimage. Annual retreats including group artwork reflecting "God at Work" narratives celebrate long-view testimonies: a mural depicting a church's transformation from fifteen regulars to seventy-five monthly participants fosters gratitude. When combined with sabbath rest, these reflective practices make perseverance less about conquering dryness through grit and more about trusting God's ongoing faithfulness. Communities that normalize examen and journaling create cultures where honesty about struggle is welcome and where the Spirit's subtle fingerprints are recognized over time.

9.4.c Fellowship of the Long Haul — Spiritual Friendships and Mentors (2 Timothy 2:2) Paul instructs Timothy to entrust truth to "faithful men who will be able to teach others also" (2 Timothy 2:2), establishing a continuum of discipleship across generations. Dry seasons often feel like desert islands, but mentors and spiritual friends provide lifelines. These relationships thrive when older believers share stories of past trials—perhaps a midlife crisis, a church schism, or a medical emergency—and the ways God sustained them. Hearing how a mentor walked through prolonged unemployment or held onto faith after a child's death inspires younger disciples to persevere. Conversely, mentors benefit from fresh perspectives as younger friends model adaptive creativity for new cultural challenges. Small churches might use a "25/75" rule: prayerfully matching one older woman or man (25+) with a younger adult (75) for monthly check-ins. Accountability circles of four to six, crossing generational lines, meet biweekly to pray, confess, and strategize spiritual growth—these quarters of consistent presence cultivate trust that lasts beyond pastoral changes or ministry disruptions. When spiritual friends face betrayal or burnout, they rely on a mentor who once walked similar valleys, reminding them of God's unchanged nature (Hebrews 13:8). During prolonged grief, companions hold space without rushing to fix, embodying Romans 12:15's call to "weep with those who weep." Fellowship that spans decades undermines the myth that faith is only for the young or flourishing; instead it testifies that endurance emerges in relational soil. Such long-haul connections lay a sturdy foundation for seasons of accelerated ministry or intensified trials, ensuring that disciples do not walk through dry seasons alone but in community that embodies Christ's own relational presence.

9.5 Discernment: Hearing God amid Competing Voices

9.5.a Lectio Divina and Listening Prayer — Scripture as Conversation, Not Data Mining Lectio Divina, the ancient practice of "divine reading," invites believers to slow down and treat Scripture as a living conversation partner. Instead of racing through passages for information, practitioners read a verse or two, meditate on the words, pray them back to God, and rest in the silence that follows. This rhythm mirrors Mary sitting at Jesus' feet rather than Martha's flurry of tasks, emphasizing presence over productivity (Luke 10:39). In listening prayer, disciples pose open-ended questions—"What are you saying to me through this passage?"— then offer space for response rather than imposing their own agenda. Small groups that incorporate Lectio Divina each week report deep shifts: members learn to hear God's voice amid swirling digital noise and ideological clamor. Churches can provide guided meditations on a psalm once a month, encouraging members to carry a phrase in their hearts throughout the week. Over time, listening prayer reshapes interpretive habits: instead of asking "What does this mean?" disciples ask "What is this word doing in me?" This posture trains the soul to recognize the Spirit's gentle promptings, distinguishing them from fleeting desires or cultural pressures. As hearts become attuned to God's cadence, decisions—whether vocational changes or relational reconciliations—flow from clarity rather than confusion. Once the inner ear is sharpened, communal discernment benefits, as participants learn to weigh diverse impressions against the biblical narrative.

9.5.b Communal Discernment Circles — Testing Leadings with the Body (Acts 13:1-3) The Antioch church model exemplifies communal discernment: prophets and teachers fasting and praying in the Spirit, and when the Holy Spirit said, "Set apart for me Barnabas and Saul," the church laid hands and sent them off (Acts 13:2-3). Here, corporate fasting and prayer preceded a collective act of sending, reflecting careful weighing of divine direction. In modern congregations, forming discernment circles—small cohorts committed to seeking God together—enables a similar process. These circles meet regularly, sharing personal impressions, comparing them with Scriptural principles, and weighing them against God's character as revealed in the gospel. When a member senses a call to start a mercy ministry among refugees, others test the intake of that prompting: Does it align with the church's mission? Are there resources? Does the wider body sense affirmation? If the discernment circle discerns coherence, they present the proposal to the whole church for further affirmation. This process prevents unilateral decisions and cultivates unity: no one senses they must single-handedly defend a sense of call. When a circle discerns impending cultural shift—a new issue around digital privacy—quick corporate reflection sets a course for teaching or advocacy before confusion spreads. This communal testing of leadings mirrors the Bereans' model of checking new teachings against Scripture (Acts 17:11), ensuring convictions are not individual eccentricities but Spirit-empowered direction. Through such circles, disciples practice mutual submission, humility, and discernment training, transitioning naturally into evaluating digital inputs that shape everyday thinking.

9.5.c Discerning Digital Inputs — Curating Feeds that Form rather than Deform (Philippians 4:8) Paul's exhortation to focus on "whatever is true, noble, right, pure, lovely, admirable, excellent, or praiseworthy" (Philippians 4:8) functions as a filter for our media diets. In an age of clickbait and viral outrage, curating digital feeds requires intentional discipline. First, disciples evaluate each source: does this blogger's content align with biblical truth, or does it feed anxiety? Do news alerts heighten fear of the future, or do they spur prayerful intercession? Tools such as blocklists, curated newsletters, and limited social media time-blocks help believers control inputs. As an example, some congregations create "kingdom reading lists" together—trusted websites and podcasts that feed the mind with balanced, Scripture-informed perspectives. Instead of defaulting to YouTube rabbit holes, disciples bookmark a few theology podcasts and podcast sermons from global leaders to replace sensational channels. Digital Sabbath practices—turning screens off from

Friday sundown to Saturday sundown—serve as a weekly reset, allowing the mind to digest content without relentless new injections. In group settings, members share one truth or encouragement they discovered online, shifting the focus from entertainment to formation. Over time, these curated inputs shape thinking patterns, making discernment second nature rather than an afterthought. As believers learn to reject unhelpful noise, they gain space for silence, reflection, and genuine openness to the Spirit's voice. With digital feeds rerouted toward the noble and pure, hearts become more receptive to God's guidance, ready to move from discernment into the missional overflow practices that follow.

9.6 Missional Overflow: Practices that Turn Outward

9.6.a Hospitality as Evangelism — Open Tables, Open Lives (Luke 14:12–14) Jesus used meals as the primary venue for kingdom teaching, often dining with tax collectors and sinners (Luke 5:29–32), instructing His followers that true hospitality reaches beyond convenience zones. When the Pharisees grumbled that He welcomed unclean people, Jesus replied that when giving a banquet, hosts should invite the poor, crippled, lame, and blind—those unable to repay—so that in the resurrection the host is repaid (Luke 14:12–14). This counterintuitive model turns family tables into mission fields. Instead of restricting gatherings to like-minded believers, disciples open their homes to neighbors who might never set foot in a church building. A weekly "Bread and Table" practice can involve inviting a different household each Friday night—perhaps a single parent, an immigrant family, or a coworker—to break bread together. During the meal, hosts listen intently to guests' stories, asking open questions about their hopes and struggles rather than launching into a gospel presentation. By creating safe space, hosts demonstrate the incarnational love of Jesus, who dwelt among us (John 1:14), inviting others into belonging before introducing them to belief.

As trust grows, hosts weave prayers for wisdom and occasional readings of hospitality-centered scriptures—such as Romans 12:13, "Contribute to the needs of the saints and seek to show hospitality"—into conversations. Children watching parents bake bread for guests learn that generosity flows from conviction, not compulsion. Multiethnic potlucks reflect the diversity of the kingdom, with menu items and prayers shared in multiple languages, showing that the gospel transcends cultural barriers. Meal invitations also become natural moments to mention congregational activities—an upcoming service project, a community run club—to welcome neighbors into broader community rhythms. When hosts visit guests during illness or job loss, they extend hospitality beyond the dinner table, providing rides to appointments, sending care packages, or sitting vigil through hospital nights. In urban contexts, hospitality may involve hosting international students for weekly study sessions, sharing both academic and spiritual journey. Measures of success shift from counting conversion numbers to witnessing changes in relational dynamics—guests who once felt isolated begin joining worship services or prayer gatherings. Through sustained openness, tables become training grounds for kingdom love, seeding outward faithfulness in homes, workplaces, and social networks. Hospitality practiced in this way naturally flows into vocational witness, as everyday work becomes part of missional overflow.

9.6.b Vocational Witness — Craftsmanship, Creativity, and Integrity at Work (Colossians 3:23–24) Colossians instructs believers to "work heartily, as for the Lord and not for men," reminding them that their daily labor—whether at a desk or in a factory—serves as a platform for gospel witness. Vocational witness begins with craftsmanship: performing tasks with excellence reflects the Creator's intent for stewardship. A carpenter who installs kitchen cabinets with meticulous care, greeting homeowners with gratitude, models the Creator's sustaining work (Psalm 104:24). When medical professionals treat patients with compassion and transparency about treatment options, they embody Christ's healing ministry (Matthew 9:35–36). In offices, Christians commit to honest reporting, shunning inflated metrics, resisting "creative accounting" that erodes trust. When writers craft articles or code developers build software, they pray for the integrity of their work to glorify God, blessing colleagues by delivering quality projects on time. As faith permeates workplace relationships, colleagues appreciate the stability offered by integrity; rumors dissipate, and cohesion increases because one's testimony aligns with practice.

Creativity becomes worship when designers and artists acknowledge that all inspiration is gift from the Spirit (Exodus 35:31–32). Musicians in secular ensembles offer subtle gospel witness through excellence and ethical collaboration rather than overt proselytizing, attracting curiosity about their source of joy. Restaurateurs who name their bistro after biblical themes—"Bread of Life Café"—invite patrons into sacramental memories that connect physical nourishment with spiritual hunger. Freelancers include prayer cards in invoices, letting clients know that their work is dedicated to serving Christ, not solely profit. When financial advisors advise clients to invest ethically, refusing to recommend companies complicit in injustice, they align portfolios with kingdom values. Over time, this integrity fosters invitations to share more explicitly about faith practices, opening doors for deeper evangelistic conversations.

Vocational witness also includes mentoring apprentices, recognizing that training the next generation reflects Jesus sending the seventy-two (Luke 10:1–12). Senior engineers who devote time to teach interns ethical coding practices mirror Paul's relationship with Timothy (2 Timothy 2:2). Organizations adopt servant-leadership models, where CEOs serve kitchen staff and participate in cleaning rather than presiding from ivory towers. This dismantles hierarchical barriers that stifle trust, making faith conversations more organic. As disciples live out their daily vocations, they demonstrate that plural forms of work—cooking, sewing, teaching, accounting, gardening—are arenas of worship, showing how ordinary tasks point to God's artistry and provision. The vocational witness practiced daily sets the stage for testimony sharing, where storytelling invites others into the narrative of God's ongoing work.

9.6.c Storytelling & Testimony — Articulating God's Work to Invite Others In (1 Peter 3:15) Peter instructs believers to "always be prepared to make a defense to anyone who asks you for a reason for the hope that is in you," which calls for building an arsenal of stories that articulate how God's gospel has transformed lives. Storytelling begins with honest self-reflection: keeping a spiritual journal where daily insights, answered prayers, and unexpected provisions are recorded. Years later, these entries become a reservoir for testimony that transcends platitudes. In church gatherings, weekly "Story Seat" slots where one congregant shares a personal snapshot—how they encountered God's forgiveness after addiction, or saw divine provision amidst financial collapse—train the art of narration. Rather than rehearsed scripts, these testimonies highlight vulnerability: "I was afraid of losing my job, but God unexpectedly provided through a neighbor's contact," which resonates because listeners sense authenticity.

Storytelling skills also develop through practicing narrative structure: setting the scene, describing the emotional low point, highlighting the intervention of God or community, and concluding with the present outcome. Youth groups learn how to bridge their story with Scripture, saying, "My experience reminded me of David praising God after Goliath fell" (1 Samuel 17:45), making theological connections accessible. Testimonies take place beyond church walls: at neighborhood block parties, a short story of how prayer guided someone through a dark night can spark curiosity. In workplaces, lunchtime discussions may include simple declarations like, "This promotion came after I prayed for God's wisdom, not for ambition," inviting colleagues to ask follow-up questions. Christians in schools participate in campus forums, sharing how faith helped them navigate peer pressure, thereby modeling where hope comes from. Storytellers avoid jargon—using plain language so evacuees from different backgrounds can follow the narrative thread.

When crisis strikes—health diagnosis or natural disaster—testimonies of God's sustaining presence encourage those going through similar storms. Podcasts and video interviews broaden reach: a mechanic with a compelling story of God's grace after a personal tragedy can touch audiences globally, far beyond local church confines. As believers hone storytelling, they learn to listen for wicket ways God invites others—neighbors, coworkers, or family members—to enter the journey. In this way, testimonies become gospel bridges, not tracts requiring argument but living narratives that incarnate God's love and power. Storytelling flows from hospitality and vocational integrity, creating a panoramic missional overflow where words and deeds coalesce to invite others into the redemptive narrative.

Conclusion

The path of crossing from "fan" enthusiasm into "follower" commitment is paved with more than inspiring sermons; it is mapped by intentional disciplines that incarnate the gospel in every sphere of life. When a person humbly names sin, offers allegiance to God, and moves into acts of mercy and justice, faith ceases to be an abstract category and becomes a force that shapes decisions, relationships, and aspirations. Seasons of doubt and busyness will come, but practices like rooted rest, honest journaling, and loyal friendships anchor the soul when dryness threatens. Listening prayer and communal discernment guard against drifting into cultural conformism, while hospitality and vocational witness ensure that our faith never remains private but overflows in generosity that points toward the kingdom. By integrating repentance, surrender, action, perseverance, discernment, and missional outreach, we shift from merely wanting God's approval to living as fully devoted followers. In embracing these practices, disciples not only "cross the line" themselves but become beacons that invite others into the same pathway of transformative grace.

Chapter 10 — Community of Followers: The Church as Discipleship Hub

True discipleship does not unfold in isolation but within a living network of relationships forged by the Spirit. The church, far from being a mere Sunday gathering, exists as a dynamic fellowship where believers encourage one another, receive grace through shared sacraments, and discover how their distinct gifts contribute to the whole. In this thriving ecosystem, mutual care and accountability replace solitary striving, and diverse generations and cultures learn from one another as they worship, learn, and serve together. When every member—whether newcomer or long-time attender—sees the body of Christ at work in homes, neighborhoods, and workplaces, faith moves from the abstract into hands-on practice. In such a community, patterns of confession and forgiveness shape hearts, shared rhythms of Word and Table affirm identity, and collaborative leadership and missional outreach extend the gospel beyond church walls. Rather than functioning as a consumer venue, the congregation becomes a discipleship hub, equipping followers to walk in Christ's footsteps every day.

10.0 Why Discipleship Flourishes Best in Community

10.0.a Trinitarian Communal Roots — Father, Son, Spirit as Eternal Fellowship Before creation, the triune God existed in perfect, eternal fellowship as Father, Son, and Holy Spirit. This divine communion serves as the foundational archetype for human relationships, revealing that relationality lies at the heart of God's nature (John 17:24). When God determined to create humanity in His image (Genesis 1:26), He invited us into that communal life, not to remain isolated individuals but to participate in a shared, interdependent family. The Father's love for the Son, the Son's obedience to the Father, and the Spirit's mutual testimony (John 5:19–20; John 14:26) model how believers ought to dwell together in harmony. Because the Spirit baptizes us into one body (1 Corinthians 12:13), each follower partakes of this Trinitarian fellowship, enabling us to love one another as God first loved us (1 John 4:11). In practical terms, this means that no disciple lives apart from the mutual indwelling that characterizes community. The Father's will is not to scatter His children but to gather them into a family where grace flows in multiple directions, far beyond a solitary faith. As Jesus said, "Where two or three are gathered in my name, there am I among them" (Matthew 18:20), indicating that Christ's presence is magnified through communal worship, prayer, and mission. This theological truth counters the modern myth of rugged individualism, teaching that personal faith cannot be fully actualized outside of relational networks. When communities gather around Word and Table, they mirror the eternal fellowship, inviting each other to abide in Christ and bear fruit (John 15:4–5). The Spirit's role is crucial here: He convicts individual hearts of sin, but He also knits communities together, enabling them to bear collective witness through unity that transcends human barriers (Ephesians 4:3). In this way, the church becomes a living icon of God's own triune life, drawing outsiders to see the world re-created through community.

10.0.b From Crowd to Covenant — Moving Attendees toward Shared Life Church gatherings often begin as crowds—people who attend services but remain strangers beyond the sanctuary. Transforming a crowd into a covenant community requires intentional structures that foster commitment beyond Sunday morning. In the early church, believers "devoted themselves to the apostles' teaching and the fellowship, to the breaking of bread and the prayers" (Acts 2:42), illustrating a holistic, shared life. Today, churches can mirror that pattern by cultivating small groups that commit to study, prayer, service, and accountability, weaving spiritual rhythms into everyday life. Membership classes that teach congregational covenants—promises to love, forgive, give, and pray for one another—anchor attendees in formal commitments that shape identity. When neighbors see members living out those promises in homes, hospitals, and workplaces, the covenantal dimension becomes visible. Gathering in diverse formats—dinners for eight in living rooms, community service teams that meet weekly—reinforces that the church is not a venue but a visceral expression of God's family. Baptism and membership vows publicly mark this transition, as new members stand before existing members to pledge fidelity to Christ and one another (Acts 2:41–47). From that point forward, a believer's identity is tethered to the covenant community, creating space for mutual encouragement and constructive correction. As shared life deepens, the crowd's loyalty shifts from consumer-driven attendance to covenant-driven belonging, making the church a more effective discipleship hub. This shift in allegiances opens the way for exploring concrete ways members encourage one another and hold each other accountable.

10.1 Mutual Encouragement and Loving Accountability

10.1.a "One-Another" Commands Survey — Love, Bear, Forgive, Spur, Submit The New Testament brims with "one-another" imperatives—explicit commands detailing how believers relate to one another. When John writes, "If we walk in the light, as he is in the light, we have fellowship with one another" (1 John 1:7), he underscores mutual transparency as foundational. Paul instructs spouses to "love one another" (Ephesians 5:28), elders to "shepherd the flock" (1 Peter 5:2), and brothers to "bear one another's burdens" (Galatians 6:2), illustrating that community life demands more than passive presence. Forgiveness is likewise communal: "Be kind to one another, tenderhearted, forgiving one another, as God in Christ forgave you" (Ephesians 4:32), which means every member must cultivate grace rather than judgment. Hebrews calls us to "encourage one another, and all the more as you see the Day drawing near" (Hebrews 10:25), indicating that mutual exhortation sustains perseverance in faith. Submission to one another out of reverence for Christ (Ephesians 5:21) counters the cultural impulse toward autonomy, teaching that humility undergirds unity. Spurring one another on toward love and good deeds (Hebrews 10:24) creates momentum for corporate mission. When congregations systematically review these imperatives—perhaps through a "one-another" sermon series—members internalize community ethics: when Sarah struggles with depression, a sister's exhortation to cling to God's promises (Psalm 34:18) shepherds her through the valley. In conflicts, referencing "one-another" commands guides parties back to biblical patterns. As "one-another" becomes habitual language, it integrates into everyday church rhythms, priming the community for deeper mentoring relationships.

10.1.b Spiritual Friendships & Mentoring Triads — Paul–Timothy–Barnabas Model In Acts 11:25–26, Barnabas journeyed to Tarsus to seek out Saul, bringing him to Antioch for a full year of teaching. This partnership exemplifies how seasoned believers invest in emerging leaders. Paul's adoption of Timothy—calling him "my beloved and faithful child in the Lord" (1 Corinthians 4:17)—highlights how mentoring relationships facilitate transmission of wisdom, encouragement, and doctrinal insight. Triadic structures—where one seasoned mentor coaches two or three younger disciples—create relational triangles that prevent over-dependence on a single leader while multiplying encouragement. Within a triad, the mentor models prayer, Scripture engagement, and missional boldness, while mentees hold one another accountable for spiritual growth. When Lisa, a long-time teacher, mentors David and Maria, she not only shares teaching methods but also invites them into her struggles with burnout, modeling vulnerability. The triad meets weekly for prayer, accountability, and skill development—incorporating teaching from 2 Timothy, where Paul instructs Timothy to entrust to faithful men who will teach others (2 Timothy 2:2). These relationships build trust that makes honesty about sin and struggle safe. When conflicts arise between mentees and their families, mentors guide them toward reconciliation rather than rebellion, embodying Matthew 18:15–17's restorative admonition. As triads multiply, the church's leadership pipeline expands beyond formal hierarchies, ensuring succession and continuity. Spiritual friendships flourish when both mentor and mentees commit to long-term investment, reflecting Jesus' sustained presence with Peter, James, and John.

Building on relationships of friendship and mentorship, the church must also practice loving accountability through guided discipline that restores rather than alienates.

10.1.c Healthy Church Discipline — Restorative, Not Punitive (Matthew 18:15–20) Scripture outlines a process for addressing sin that preserves both truth and love: confronting privately first, involving witnesses if needed, and bringing an unrepentant person before the church (Matthew 18:15–17). The goal is restoration, not public shaming. When Mary spreads harmful gossip, a trusted friend--using gentleness—begins with private conversation, aiming to reconcile (Galatians 6:1). If Mary refuses to listen, a second conversation involving a small group can clarify concerns and pray together. Should she persist, bringing the matter to the congregation serves not as spectacle but as an invitation to mutual prayer and reconciliation. Leaders must rigorously guard confidentiality, ensuring reputations are not ruined by half-truths. Throughout the process, the church offers pastoral care to both the offender—calling them to repentance—and the offended—validating their pain and supporting their healing. In Acts 5, when Ananias and Sapphira lied about possessions, Peter's confrontation led to their deaths; this severity underscores God's holiness but is not normative for church discipline today. Instead, 1 Corinthians 5:5 urges exile of the immoral brother "so that his spirit may be saved on the day of the Lord," demonstrating discipline's soteriological aim. Churches contextualize this by extending sabbatical leaves, counseling referrals, and reconciliatory events that celebrate restored relationships. When policies for discipline are transparent and rooted in Scripture, members do not fear oppressive power but trust that discipline aims at repentance and unity. As healthy church discipline fosters a culture of accountability, small groups and mentoring relationships stand ready to welcome repentant individuals, modeling grace that draws the community closer.

From accountability flows vulnerability, which is nurtured through testimony nights and story circles that normalize transparent confession and mutual care.

10.1.d Story Circles & Testimony Nights — Normalizing Vulnerability Vulnerability grows when people hear others speak openly about failure, doubt, and restoration. Story circles—small group gatherings where each member shares a personal narrative—create safe spaces for honest testimony. Groups might follow a simple pattern: one person speaks for a set time, reflecting on a recent struggle or blessing; the circle then offers empathetic listening without immediate advice. Afterward, they pray specifically for that individual, reinforcing the promise that "the prayer of a righteous person has great power" (James 5:16). Testimony nights at a wider church level feature two or three volunteers sharing six minutes each about how God worked in a crisis. A facilitator ensures that testimonies remain encouraging, focusing more on outcomes of faith than sensational details. As people hear stories of addiction recovery, job loss redeemed, or mental-health battles turned to testimony, it breaks down the illusion that everyone else's faith is more robust. This practice counters perfectionism and fan-culture assumptions that seeing a leader struggle invalidates leadership; instead it illustrates that even leaders depend on grace. Over time, the congregation internalizes that authenticity leads to freedom, not shame. Recording select testimonies—audio or video—creates a resource library that newcomers can access to hear how faith develops in real contexts. Story circles also include dinners, where simple meals become shared ritual, and props like art supplies or journals help participants express their journeys creatively. As vulnerability becomes commonplace, the church embodies Proverbs 27:17's "iron sharpens iron," each story forging resilience in observers. This environment of openness sets the stage for leveraging technology in ways that build up rather than distract.

10.1.e Digital Tools for Mid-Week Check-Ins — Group Chats That Build, Not Distract In an era where digital communication often breeds superficiality, the church can harness apps and platforms to foster meaningful mid-week connection. Creating designated group chats—centered not on event reminders but on check-ins—allows members to post daily highs and lows, praise reports, and prayer requests. Channels labeled "urgent needs," "praises," "Scripture encouragement," and "help offers" help categorize posts, making it easier to respond intentionally rather than scrolling past. Leaders establish norms: no emojis as substitutes for genuine responses, encouraging personal messages when someone shares vulnerability. Phone-based apps like Slack or Microsoft Teams can host "care channels" where members commit to posting at least one devotional thought or prayer prompt each week. When James reports job interview anxiety, at least one person commits to praying and then texting encouragement for three days straight. Such consistent digital rhythms remind members they belong to a community that spans beyond Sunday. Digital platforms also enable mentorship triads to coordinate meeting times, share resource links, and pray over shared prayer lists. Virtual reality prayer rooms can simulate face-to-face presence, offering people in distant locations a sense of communal solidarity. To avoid digital burnout, churches encourage "digital sabbath" windows—a few hours mid-week when no new notifications are sent—allowing members to focus on prayer or scripture reading without distractions. By designing these tools specifically for encouragement and accountability, rather than event promotion or social media-style chatter, the church creates virtual spaces that mirror relational depth. As digital connectivity strengthens mutual care, it naturally leads to sacramental rhythms that shape identity and further solidify community bonds.

10.2 Sacramental Rhythms that Shape Identity

10.2.a Baptism into the Body — Covenant Initiation & Public Allegiance (1 Corinthians 12:13) Baptism is the foundational sacrament that integrates believers into the body of Christ, declaring publicly that the baptized has died to sin and risen to new life in Jesus Christ (Romans 6:3–4). In first-century Corinth, Paul emphasizes that "by one Spirit we were all baptized into one body" (1 Corinthians 12:13), highlighting that this rite is more than a personal experience—it inaugurates communal reality. When a person emerges from the waters, congregants witness the formation of an eternal covenant, pledging to support, instruct, and pray for the newly baptized as they grow in faith. Leading up to the baptism, catechumens undergo instruction in core doctrines—Trinity, Christ's atonement, Resurrection, and the Lord's Prayer—grounding them in the church's shared belief. On the baptismal day, the community gathers around a font or pool, the pastor pronounces the Trinitarian formula ("I baptize you in the name of the Father, and of the Son, and of the Holy Spirit"), and the person is immersed or sprinkled, symbolizing the death and resurrection of Christ. The congregation then welcomes the neophyte, often with the sign of peace and the gift of a white garment or baptismal candle, signifying purity and light. As a covenant sign, baptism anchors identity: the newly baptized becomes "peer," "priest," and "prophet," with specific responsibilities and privileges within the Body. Godparents and mentors accompany the journey, promising to nurture faith through prayer and accountability. When children are baptized, families are reminded that the church shares in their upbringing, echoing Timothy's childhood faith nurtured by Lois and Eunice (2 Timothy 1:5). For adult conversions, testimonies accompany the rite, highlighting God's work before seeing baptismal waters. Post-baptism, integrated steps—such as naming spiritual gifts, assigning small-group mentors, and commissioning for service—ensure the initiate's identity is welded to communal life, seamlessly readying them for participation in the Eucharist.

10.2.b Table Fellowship — Weekly Eucharist as Covenant Renewal & Future Hope The Lord's Supper occupies a central place in the church's liturgical life, reminding participants of Christ's redemptive death and pointing forward to His return (1 Corinthians 11:26). Each week, believers gather around the table—whether in a grand nave, a simple chapel, or a backyard meal setting—to partake of bread and wine that symbolically become Christ's body and blood. The liturgy often begins with a call to confession, allowing congregants to examine their hearts and confess sin collectively, echoing Jesus' warning that eating the bread unworthily brings judgment (1 Corinthians 11:27). After absolution, the pastor or celebrant recites the institution narrative: "On the night when he was betrayed, our Lord Jesus took bread, and when he had given thanks, he broke it and said, 'This is my body, given for you; do this in remembrance of me.'" The congregation responds with "Amen," affirming their faith in the real spiritual presence of Christ. As bread and cup pass from hand to hand, believers approach with reverent expectation, sharing a moment of silent prayer or reciting Psalms that focus the heart on God's covenantal promise (Psalm 34:8). Receiving the elements not only strengthens personal faith but also unites participants to one another as members of the same body—"we, though many, are one body, for we all share in the one bread" (1 Corinthians 10:17). Once the meal concludes, the pastor recites a blessing, sending the congregation into mission: "Go in peace, serve the Lord" (Galatians 6:9). The repetitive pattern of confession, remembrance, and commission forms a weekly rhythm that renews identity: participants remember they belong to Christ and to one another, and they anticipate the marriage supper of the Lamb at the end of time (Revelation 19:9). As the Eucharist is shared, newcomers witness an embodied proclamation of the gospel, priming them to see faith as communal and forward-looking.

10.2.c Confession & Absolution Liturgies — Rehearsing Grace Together While the Lord's Supper includes a preparatory confession, many churches incorporate standalone liturgies focused entirely on confession and absolution, rhythmically rehearsing communal repentance and restoration. In these services, passages such as Psalm 51 and Daniel 9:4–19 provide poetic frameworks for acknowledging sin and pleading for mercy. The congregation stands or kneels as the pastor leads a corporate confession: "Most merciful God, we confess that we have sinned against You in thought, word, and deed, by what we have done, and by what we have left undone." This refrain models David's humility after his own sin (Psalm 51:1–4). Then, through spoken absolution—"Almighty God has promised forgiveness to all who repent; therefore let us confess our sins in penitence and faith" (1 John 1:9)—the assembly experiences tangible assurance that "there is now no condemnation for those who are in Christ Jesus" (Romans 8:1). This gathered liturgy typically concludes with silent prayer, allowing space for hearts to receive solace. Lay leaders sometimes read testimonies of forgiveness, illustrating how grace has broken cycles of shame. Churches with regular confession services report fewer moral blind spots, as individuals grow accustomed to bringing hidden areas into light within a safe, grace-filled environment. When corporate confession is quarterly or monthly, participants who feel stuck in guilt discover pathways to emotional freedom. These liturgies reinforce that forgiveness is not a private transaction but a communal reality, binding participants together through shared vulnerability. With the weight of unconfessed sin lifted, the congregation emerges ready to engage in the fast and feast rhythms that the liturgical calendar provides.

10.2.d Feasts & Fasts in the Church Calendar — Time-Based Catechesis Over centuries, the church developed a liturgical calendar woven with seasons of feasting and fasting—Advent, Christmas, Epiphany, Lent, Easter, Pentecost—that function as time-based catechesis, teaching collective memory and shaping communal rhythms. Advent's four-week preparation encourages expectant prayer and cultural critique, reminding believers to watch for Christ's coming (Isaiah 9:6). Christmas celebrations follow, marking the Incarnation with joy and generosity, echoing Matthew

2:10–11 where magi bring gifts. After Epiphany, the season of Ordinary Time invites reflection on Jesus' everyday ministry—feeding the 5,000, walking on water—modeling a balanced progression into sacrificial simplicity. Lent's forty days mirror Christ's wilderness fast (Matthew 4:1–2), inviting congregants to fast meals or media, substitute alms for treats, and engage in deeper prayer. Ash Wednesday services imprint foreheads with ash—a reminder of mortality and call to repentance—reorienting hearts toward the cross. Holy Week's communal reenactment—from Palm Sunday's processional to Maundy Thursday's foot-washing and the somber silence of Good Friday—immerses participants in the Passion narrative. Easter dawn services herald resurrection with triumphal music and candlelight processions, proclaiming "Christ is risen" (Luke 24:6). Pentecost's eruptions of red banners and wind imagery signal the Spirit's arrival, echoing Acts 2. As the calendar cycles forward, church members internalize the overarching Story, aligning personal time to corporate memory. Fasts such as Good Friday or Daniel Fast weeks amplify dependence on divine provision. Feasts unify resources: Christmas offerings fund local mercy projects rather than consumer indulgence. These temporal markers cultivate shared identity: by celebrating together, believers acknowledge they belong to a people shaped by God's mighty works. When participants observe these seasons with discipline and creativity—children crafting Advent wreaths, families visiting nursing homes on Epiphany—the identity forged in the sacraments becomes visible in homes, streets, and carnival events. This sacramental immersion naturally transitions us into exploring additional embodied symbols—oil, ash, and foot-washing—that further touch the gospel.

10.2.e Embodied Symbols (Oil, Ash, Foot-Washing) — Touching the Gospel Beyond baptism and Eucharist, the church employs other tangible symbols that convey spiritual truths. Anointing with oil—used in the Old Testament for consecrating priests (Exodus 30:30) and in the New Testament for healing (Mark 6:13)—continues in services of prayer for healing. When elders lay hands and anoint with oil, they enact James 5:14's promise that "the prayer of faith will save the sick." The tactile sensation of oil on the forehead grounds prayer in physical reality. During Ash Wednesday, smearing ash in the sign of the cross on foreheads unites congregants in shared mortality and penitence, echoing Genesis 3:19, "For you are dust, and to dust you shall return." This embodied act counters the cultural denial of death, focusing hearts on eternal hope. Foot-washing services, following Jesus' example (John 13:4–5), provide a dramatic, humbling portrayal of servant leadership. When pastors remove shoes and wash parishioners' feet, the congregation sees that Christian leadership mirrors Christ's own humble service. Some churches schedule foot-washing gatherings on Maundy Thursday, allowing times of silence and reflection as participants feel water running over toes—a visceral reminder of Christ's command to love one another (John 13:34). In small group settings, symbolic actions like passing a bowl of water around to invite prayer for one another foster intimacy. Anointing and foot-washing can also take place in hospital chapels when visiting the sick, offering holistic care that ministers to body and soul. Art and architecture reinforce these symbols: fonts carved with waves, stoles adorned with dove and flame, and stained-glass windows depicting the washing of feet visually communicate gospel truths. When congregations incorporate these embodied symbols into regular worship and pastoral care, they provide touchpoints that translate theological concepts into deep emotional and spiritual impressions. As embodied symbols shape identity and discipleship, the church becomes a living sacrament, calling believers into deeper participation in Christ's life and mission. This robust sacramental life now naturally leads us to explore how spiritual gifts are deployed within this community context to advance the gospel together.

10.3 Spiritual Gifts Deployed for Mission

10.3.a Diversity Serving Unity — Equipping the Saints (Ephesians 4:11–16) Paul's vision in Ephesians 4:11–16 portrays a church where Christ gives apostles, prophets, evangelists, pastors, and teachers "to equip the saints for the work of ministry, for building up the body of Christ." This passage underscores that spiritual gifts exist not for individual fame but for communal maturity, reflecting diversity serving unity. Just as a body has many parts—eye, ear, hand—each essential yet distinct (1 Corinthians 12:12–27), so the church flourishes when varied gifts work together. When the evangelist passionately proclaims the gospel, the pastor shepherds new believers into deeper biblical teaching, and the teacher unpacks doctrine, the whole body grows "to the measure of the stature of the fullness of Christ" (Ephesians 4:13). Congregations that recognize and value diverse gifts create environments where introverted administrative gifts stand alongside extroverted evangelistic gifts, honoring both as equally vital. Sunday services can highlight this diversity by inviting multiple gift-ministries to serve: a worship leader's musical gift, a childcare worker's nurturing gift, and a prayer minister's intercessory gift. As each person serves from their unique talent, unity emerges—not uniformity—because the body learns to depend on one another. When conflict arises over gift tensions—perhaps a charismatic leader overshadowing quieter teachers—leaders intervene by reminding the body that every gift originates in the Spirit (1 Corinthians 12:4–6) and must point back to Christ. Training events on gifts help members appreciate how prophecy can function to encourage, not condemn (1 Corinthians 14:3), while teaching reminds teachers to speak in ways that build up rather than confuse. As members grow in their gift awareness, the church's collective witness gains credibility: when gifts align, they demonstrate love in action and doctrinal depth in teaching. This synergy draws outsiders to see a community where mutual support, not competition, shapes mission. From this foundation, the church systematically implements gift discovery pathways to guide individuals into purposeful service.

10.3.b Gift Discovery Pathways — Assessments, Apprenticeships, Coaching Identifying spiritual gifts requires more than one-off quizzes; it calls for layered pathways that combine assessment tools, practical apprenticeship experiences, and dedicated coaching relationships. Initial gift assessments—questionnaires based on biblical categories like wisdom, teaching, faith, healing, and service (1 Corinthians 12:8–10)—provide a starting point by helping individuals recognize potential strengths. Yet assessments alone can mislead without practical validation. As such, congregations establish "Gift Exploration" tracks where participants volunteer in various ministry contexts—leading worship, serving communion, visiting the sick—over a three-month rotation. During this season, participants journal reflections on moments when they felt energized versus drained, paying attention to where they sense God's affirmation. Coaches—seasoned believers trained in gift discernment—meet monthly with explorers to review experiences, ask reflective questions, and offer prayer support. When someone expresses consistent joy and fruitfulness in teaching children's Sunday school classes, the coach might encourage pursuing deeper training or shadowing experienced teachers. Apprenticeships formalize this process: a hospitality apprentice spends six months learning from a veteran host team member, discovering whether relational warmth truly aligns with their gifting. Mentors in pastoral care model active listening and compassion, inviting apprentices into hospital visits to test whether they have the gift of mercy. Regular coaching sessions evaluate growth: if an aspiring evangelist's attempts yield little fruit, coaches help discern whether another gift like encouragement or faith might be more accurate. By combining assessments with hands-on experience, the church clarifies gift identities, reducing frustration from misplaced service. Explored gifts are celebrated in commissioning services, where distinct callings—missions, teaching, administration—are prayed over and affirmed publicly. As gift pathways mature, individuals transition into the marketplace and neighborhood spheres, discovering how their gifts function beyond Sunday contexts.

10.3.c Marketplace & Neighborhood Expressions — Beyond Sunday Roles True deployment of spiritual gifts extends beyond church buildings into workplaces, schools, and local neighborhoods—reflecting Jesus sending His followers into the world (John 17:18). A gifted teacher in Sunday school may also flourish as a mentor for at-risk youth in neighborhood community centers, illustrating continuity between church and community.

When a nurse who demonstrates mercy and compassion on weekends treats patients during the week, she ministers holistically to body and spirit. Similarly, a gifted administrator in church finance may use organizational skills to help low-income families navigate tax filings. Local businesses can partner with the church to offer internships aligned with congregants' gifts—marketing teams train apprentices with communicative gifts, while homeowners with hospitality gifts host trainees in community homes. Neighborhood block parties become fertile ground for gifts of evangelism: individuals with boldness introduce Gospel conversations to curious neighbors over shared barbecues. Those with tongues and interpretation gifts might host intercultural prayer gatherings, bridging language barriers and fostering unity. Marketplaces reflect the priesthood of all believers when accountants, lawyers, engineers, and baristas view their professions as venues to bless customers, coworkers, and competitors. Crucially, the church provides frameworks—like "Marketplace Fellowship Groups"—where Monday-through-Friday believers gather monthly to share how they applied their gifts in real-world contexts, offering encouragement and problem-solving. As members report "Jesus in my cubicle" moments, they learn that spiritual gifting is not confined to Sunday tasks but animates every sphere. This outward focus on neighborhood and marketplace spontaneously seeds collaborative leadership teams to coordinate missional influence on a larger scale.

10.3.d Collaborative Leadership Teams — Flattening Hierarchy for Multiplication The New Testament models leadership plurality: Paul, Barnabas, Silas, Timothy, Prisca, and Aquila operated in teams to plant and nurture churches (Acts 13:1–3; Acts 18:24–26). Contemporary church governance can emulate this by forming collaborative leadership teams that leverage multiple gifts—teaching, administration, pastoral care, outreach—in shared decision-making. Such teams dismantle sole-leadership archetypes, distributing responsibility so burnout and ego-driven mistakes are less likely. Each leader within a team aligns around a common mission statement: to make disciples who make disciples. Roles rotate quarterly, such that one leader chairs meetings, another leads worship planning, and another coordinates community partnerships, ensuring giftedness informs function. When a crisis arises—financial shortfalls, doctrinal disputes—teams convene strategic brainstorming sessions, drawing on varied perspectives to craft balanced responses. Regular team reflections incorporate prayerful inventory against "one-another" commands, affirming where unity thrives and where tensions require reconciliation. As members witness leaders submitting to one another (Ephesians 5:21), it instils a culture of humility throughout the congregation. Collaborative leadership teams also raise up emerging leaders through "leadership internships," where two or three team members mentor an apprentice in administration, teaching, or pastoral care. Once apprentices complete a term, they join a different team, expanding their skill sets and the church's leadership bandwidth. This flattening of hierarchy nurtures multiplication, as more disciples gain hands-on experience in decision-making and service. With robust collaborative teams, the church is better positioned to support missional communities and neighborhood prayer initiatives that require multifaceted leadership.

10.3.e Celebrating Small Obediences — Annual "Gift-in-Action" Stories While big initiatives—church plants, mission trips—rightly draw attention, everyday acts of obedience often go unnoticed. Annual "Gift-in-Action" celebrations spotlight small yet faithful uses of spiritual gifts, reinforcing that every contribution matters. During a special service, the congregation hears ten-minute stories of individuals who, perhaps quietly, used their gift of hospitality to feed a homeless family, or their gift of discernment to mediate a workplace conflict. Visual elements—photographs, short video clips of neighborhood tutoring sessions—underscore the tangible impact. Older saints with gifts of wisdom share how they wrote letters to incarcerated believers, demonstrating discipleship extends through seasons of confinement. Teachers recount how integrating their gift to explain Scripture transformed a weekly Bible study into an intergenerational learning circle. Tech-savvy members describe using their creative gift to design a mobile app connecting local vigil volunteers to police neighborhoods at risk. These micro-testimonies shift cultural expectations: rather than honoring only large-scale ministry milestones, the church values perseverance in small obedience. Post-service, a bulletin insert profiles "Gift-in-Action Champions," individuals who consistently use their gifts in quiet ways, inspiring others to notice siblings whose gifting drives daily ministry unseen. When gifts are celebrated, members feel encouraged to step into new serving opportunities, trusting their actions—however small—participate in God's larger narrative. By honoring faithful service annually, the church nurtures a spirit of thanksgiving and perpetuates a multiplier effect, where small acts become catalysts for greater mission engagement. Having explored how spiritual gifts advance mission internally and externally, we turn next to the intergenerational and intercultural tapestry that enriches community life.

10.4 Intergenerational and Intercultural Tapestry

10.4.a Learning Across Ages — Grandparent Blessings & Youth Vision Intergenerational learning models how older and younger believers mutually shape one another, reflecting Psalm 145:4's promise that "One generation shall commend your works to another, and shall declare your mighty acts." In many congregations, Sunday school is strictly age-segregated, but intentional structures can bridge generational gaps. "Grandparent Blessings" events pair seniors with children and youth, where elders share stories of God's faithfulness—how He provided during economic hardships or sustained churches under persecution—instilling living memory into young imaginations. In return, youth share creative expressions—rap songs, digital artwork, spoken word—interpreting faith through contemporary culture, reminding elders that the gospel remains relevant across time. A monthly "Family Fellowship" service invites families of all ages to worship together, with songs and liturgies chosen to engage both toddlers and retirees. Youth vision workshops involve inviting teenagers to articulate how they see God working in the world—perhaps through environmental justice, refugee support, or social media evangelism—while mentors help them channel this vision into practical projects. In turn, youth mentor older members in digital literacy—teaching smartphone photography for capturing worship moments—enabling elders to share testimonies on online platforms. When intergenerational teams partner to lead community service projects—painting at-risk neighborhoods or hosting multigenerational prayer walks—the church models that faithfulness transcends decades. Over time, bonds form: grandmothers pray for grandchildren's friendships, and grandchildren pray for grandparents' health. This mutual learning breaks down ageist stereotypes: seniors rediscover youthful hope, and young people gain the wisdom to navigate faith's perennial challenges.

10.4.b Hospitality to Immigrants & Refugees — Embodying Ephesians 2 Unity Ephesians 2:14–16 clarifies that Christ "is our peace, who has made us both one and has broken down in his flesh the dividing wall of hostility," creating a new humanity. In increasingly multicultural contexts, the church practices this unity by extending hospitality to immigrants and refugees. A "Welcome Table" program hosts monthly dinners where immigrant families sit alongside long-time residents, sharing ethnic dishes, language lessons, and rhythms of home-country worship. Congregants learn simple greetings—"Shalom," "Salaam Aleikum," "Jambo"—and begin to appreciate linguistic diversity. English conversation groups meet weekly, not just for language instruction, but for sharing testimonies, reading Scripture passages, and praying together. Host families offer spare rooms to asylum seekers, not as an act of charity, but as reciprocal community-building, learning foreign traditions—like Ramadan fast-breaking or Carnival celebrations—in return. Church bulletin boards feature prayer requests from global missions, but local bulletin boards highlight practical needs: legal aid referrals, healthcare clinics offering free check-ups, and job coaching. When immigration policy shifts affect families, the church organizes advocacy teams to write letters to policymakers, exemplifying Ephesians 4:32's call to kindness and mercy within social structures. Seasonal festivals like "Global Gratitude Day" invite congregants to wear native clothing, learn traditional crafts, and hear Bible translators testify to God's provision across nations. As barriers dissolve through shared meals, language learning, and cultural exchange, the church incarnates Ephesians 2 unity, showing that racial and ethnic diversity enhances rather than detracts from gospel witness. This tapestry of cultures strengthens the body and informs worship, bringing us to how shared worship languages and musical styles embody this unity.

10.4.c Shared Worship Languages & Musical Styles — From Mono-Culture to Mosaic Worship that reflects only one cultural expression risks alienating those who do not see their stories honored. Yet incorporating diverse languages and musical styles can cultivate a richer environment where the kingdom comes as a mosaic rather than a monolith. A rotating "Global Liturgy" schedule designates one Sunday each month for worship led by an immigrant community, featuring songs in Swahili, Tagalog, Spanish, or Tamil alongside English translations projected on screens. Worship leaders train the congregation to sing response phrases ("Amen," "Hallelujah," "Hosanna") in multiple tongues, inviting everyone into shared praise. Occasional "Gospel Jazz" evenings highlight how African-American spirituals, choral gospel, and contemporary jazz converge in praising God, educating the wider community about the cultural roots of Christian music. Meanwhile, youth ministries introduce K-pop-influenced dance worship sessions, acknowledging the rhythms shaping teenagers' spiritual expression. To support language integration, the church invests in bilingual bulletins and subtitles for live-streamed services, ensuring that viewers in different time zones can engage meaningfully. Choir directors collaborate with drummers, guitarists, and indigenous instrument players to create worship ensembles that shine a spotlight on global prayer traditions. Singing "Adonai," "Yahweh," "Hosanna," and "Alleluia" in one service creates a tapestry of praise that anticipates Revelation 7:9, where people "from every nation, from all tribes and peoples and languages" stand before the throne. When congregants hear prayers read in multiple languages, they grasp that the Body of Christ transcends personal preferences. Over time, worship balloons into anticipation of heaven's inclusivity, reshaping local church culture away from mono-cultural comfort. This expands our understanding of "one-another" unity and feeds directly into practicing reconciliation when conflicts surface.

10.4.d Conflict as Formation — Practicing Reconciliation Skills
In any diverse community, conflict inevitably arises—miscommunication over cultural norms, differing worship preferences, or generational misunderstandings. The key is not to avoid conflict but to treat it as a formation opportunity. Jesus teaches that friction between brothers requires clear processes: first-person confrontation, then involving witnesses, and finally bringing the matter before the church, always with the goal of reconciliation (Matthew 18:15–17). Practically, the church offers biannual "Reconciliation Workshops" where volunteer mediators train congregants in active listening, "I" statements, and peacemaking prayers. Case studies drawn from New Testament examples—Paul's confrontation of Peter in Antioch (Galatians 2:11–14), the Corinthian calls for restoration after moral failure (2 Corinthians 2:5–11)—provide biblical precedents. When a Latino and a Korean member clash over the appropriate level of musical expression, a volunteer mediator invites each to describe how music shapes their spiritual connection, then crafts a prayer of empathy that honors both perspectives. The congregation supports both parties by fasting and praying, acknowledging that spiritual warfare often underlies cultural friction (Ephesians 6:12). Leaders facilitate guided dialogues that move beyond surface disagreements into the heart-level values driving conflict—perhaps a younger member's desire for authenticity versus an elder's concern for reverence. As church members navigate reconciliation, they learn that peacemaking reflects Christ's reconciling work (2 Corinthians 5:18). Over time, the community recognizes that conflict—handled biblically—grows trust, deepens relationships, and models the gospel to observers. With these reconciliation skills embedded, the church stands prepared to launch missional communities and neighborhood prayer walks that require collaborative resilience.

10.5 Missional Communities and Kingdom Outposts

10.5.a House-to-House Gatherings — Acts-Style Micro-Expressions In Acts 2:46, Luke describes early believers "breaking bread in their homes and receiving their food with glad and generous hearts." House-to-house gatherings recapture this organic expression, where small clusters of 7–12 people meet weekly in a member's living room for worship, Bible study, prayer, and shared meals. This intimate environment fosters deeper vulnerability: strangers in a larger auditorium become friends over potluck dishes and prayer ropes. Families rotate hosting duties based on capacity and gifts—one family skilled at baking might host dessert-themed evenings, while another with a grand piano provides musical accompaniment. Each meeting begins with a shared meal that points back to Eucharistic themes—bread as symbol of Christ's body, wine/juice as covenant blood—reminding hosts and guests that physical hospitality echoes Christ's invitation to table fellowship. After eating, a designated leader facilitates discussion of a gospel-centered passage—perhaps exploring Luke's parables or Romans' theological depth—encouraging participants to ask questions and apply truths to their neighborhoods. Prayer time integrates prayer walks into the room: each person shares a local street or neighbor in need, then they pray interdependently for these concerns. Some house churches practice "Christian Traditions Show-and-Tell," where members bring an artifact—rosary beads, a framed Psalm, a historic hymn—to share how that tradition shaped their faith. This practice enriches awareness of denominational diversity. When a neighbor expresses curiosity, members invite them to a house gathering first, providing a low-barrier introduction to Christian community. Over months, participants form covenant agreements—committing to share resources, welcome strangers, and extend tangible acts of kindness together. As these micro-Expressions flourish, they become launching pads for broader neighborhood engagement, setting the stage for parish mapping and prayer walks.

10.5.b Parish Mapping & Neighborhood Prayer Walks Parish mapping involves dividing a city or town into defined sectors and assigning small teams from the church to take spiritual responsibility for each area. Teams begin by researching demographic data—census statistics on economic conditions, cultural makeup, faith backgrounds—so they understand context before engaging neighbors. Equipped with maps labeling streets and key locations—schools, community centers, grocery stores—teams walk their designated areas regularly, praying aloud for homes, workplaces, and local institutions, asking God to reveal opportunities for friendship and service. Prayer walks might include stopping at community landmarks—parks, bus stops, playgrounds—pausing to pray for the children who play there, local law enforcement, and families who shelter under nearby trees. As team members pray, they remain attentive to spontaneous conversations: a jogger might stop to ask why they are on the sidewalk holding hands and praying, allowing for brief gospel introductions. Teams use notepads (or secure apps) to record prayer points and follow-up visits—perhaps delivering prayer cards or offering practical help like lawn mowing for elderly residents. Quarterly, the entire congregation reviews parish maps in town-hall style meetings, hearing reports from each team about spiritual need, emerging friendships, and signs of hope. Leaders then guide the church in collective prayer for under-reached sectors, aligning corporate fasting or service days with the map's priorities. Over time, neighborhoods once considered "unchurched" gain sacramental presence through distributed small communities, with house gatherings serving as anchors. Parish mapping and prayer walks turn the church's prayers into posture—moving from postures of consumption to patterns of active intercession and relational outreach.

10.5.c Justice Partnerships — Churches, NGOs, City Agencies

In Matthew 25:35–36, Jesus identifies Himself with "the hungry, the stranger, the sick," urging disciples to serve "the least of these." Modern churches translate this into justice partnerships with nongovernmental organizations, social-service agencies, and city offices. For instance, a partnership with a local homeless shelter might involve church members serving meals weekly, providing clothing drives, and hosting job-readiness workshops. Meanwhile, the church collaborates with a nonprofit that supports survivors of human trafficking, offering safe housing, counseling, and reintegration programs. Congregational members learn about systemic issues through consortium meetings where NGO staff present on topics like affordable housing, opioid addiction, or public education disparities. City agencies sometimes invite church leaders to advisory boards on community policing or disaster response, ensuring that faith perspectives inform policy decisions. When winter storms hit, faith-based teams coordinate with emergency management offices to open church buildings as warming centers, demonstrating Christ's compassion in tangible ways. Legal clinics co-hosted by church lawyers and bar associations offer pro bono services to undocumented immigrants navigating immigration courts. As these partnerships deepen, congregations discover that advocacy—writing letters to legislators, attending city council hearings, and mobilizing for policy changes—complements hands-on service. Members trained in community organizing skills lead campaigns for living wages, challenging local businesses to adopt fair compensation practices. These justice partnerships highlight that mission goes beyond spiritual care to encompass holistic well-being, rooted in the biblical call to "seek justice, correct oppression" (Isaiah 1:17). As readers see how justice work intersects with diocesan and civic systems, they prepare to leverage digital missional spaces next, extending community beyond physical borders.

10.5.d Digital Missional Spaces — Online Cohorts for the Unchurched While house gatherings and physical neighborhoods remain vital, digital missional spaces offer unprecedented opportunities to engage people who are far from any church physically or culturally. Thoughtfully structured online cohorts function as "virtual small groups," where participants gather weekly via video conferencing platforms to explore spiritual topics, share struggles, and pray. Adult newcomers might join a "Faith Inquiry" cohort that starts with basic gospel questions—"Who is Jesus?" and "What does it mean to follow Him?"—using interactive polls and breakout rooms to encourage personal engagement. A "Parenting in a Postmodern Age" cohort might include short video teachings followed by moderated discussion boards, allowing busy parents to participate asynchronously. Leaders facilitate digital "Prayer Rooms," where real-time chat threads allow intercessory prayer for global needs—natural disasters, persecuted churches, mental-health crises—embedding participants in a broader Christian network. Online cohorts can bridge time zones: a church in Toronto partners with churches in Nairobi and Manila to run a "Global Perspectives" cohort on racial reconciliation and economic justice, enabling cross-cultural learning. These digital spaces also include resource libraries—sermon archives, eBooks, teaching series—available on-demand, creating a "learning campus" that transcends geographical boundaries. Tech-savvy volunteers moderate forums to ensure respectful, Christ-honoring dialogue, curating content that adheres to Philippians 4:8's emphasis on whatever is true and praiseworthy. As digital cohorts grow, mentors step in to guide individuals toward local expressions—connecting a participant in Tokyo with an online prayer partner in Brooklyn or inviting them to a physical branch church nearby. When digital missional spaces align with house-to-house gatherings and parish mapping, the church emerges as a hybrid network—rooted locally yet globally connected. This layered strategy ensures that community-based discipleship remains dynamic, adaptive, and inclusive, fully utilizing both physical and digital realms to form followers of Jesus.

10.6 Cultivating a Culture of Ongoing Formation

10.6.a Rule of Life for Congregations — Shared Rhythms of Word, Table, Witness A congregational rule of life functions like a scaffolding for collective spiritual growth, establishing shared rhythms that align the community around core practices. The apostolic example in Acts 2:42—devotion to "the apostles' teaching and the fellowship, to the breaking of bread and the prayers"—serves as an early prototype: teaching corresponds to Word, breaking bread to Table, and prayers often fuel outward witness. Modern churches formalize this by drafting a congregational covenant that outlines weekly or monthly anchors: a corporate Scripture reading plan, Sunday Communion, and designated service projects. For example, every Tuesday morning the entire congregation reads a psalm together via text or app, fostering unity in meditation. Wednesdays might be church-wide prayer times, where small prayer cells meet in homes or virtual rooms to intercede for local needs. On

Sunday, worshipers participate in the Eucharistic liturgy, remembering Christ's body and anticipating His return (1 Corinthians 11:26). By synchronizing these rhythms, congregants internalize that personal devotion dovetails with communal formation.

In addition to Word and Table, a rule of life incorporates missional initiatives—quarterly neighborhood cleanups, monthly visits to a local nursing home, or financial gifts to a community scholarship fund. These structured acts of witness prevent service from becoming ad hoc or reactive, teaching that faith always flows outward. The elderly pray for the city council on the first Thursday; youth bring meals to a recovery center on the second Saturday; families volunteer at the food bank on the third Sunday. These recurring patterns weave service into the fabric of community life, creating a sense that discipleship transcends Sunday worship. Embedding formation in time also counters the atheistic drift of busyness: when the calendar highlights corporate rest—such as a monthly "Rest Sunday" with no evening activities—church members reclaim Sabbath as resistance to productivity-based identity. Such rest days reaffirm the Genesis pattern of creation's pause (Genesis 2:2–3) and Jesus' invitation to rest for a while (Mark 6:31).

A congregational rule of life often emerges from a retreat where leaders and lay representatives prayerfully discern values, consult Scripture, and consider local context. They might ask: How can we preserve accessibility for newcomers while encouraging deeper engagement? Answering this shapes practices such as "Stay-and-Pray" Sundays, where after worship service, people linger to pray for one another rather than dispersing immediately. Artistic elements—like posting weekly Scripture verses on campus entrances—reinforce Word rhythms. When the community upholds these shared rhythms consistently, newcomers quickly grasp that Sunday worship is part of a larger discipleship tapestry, not a standalone event. Small groups then structure their gatherings around the same pillars: beginning with a brief devotion, sharing

Communion occasionally, and choosing service projects aligned with the churchwide mission. As these patterns take root, congregants develop an intuitive sense of how to balance personal life and communal commitments, ensuring that transformation happens not in isolated moments but through predictable, Spirit-led rhythms.

10.6.b Feedback Loops — Surveys, Listening Sessions, Adaptive Change A healthy congregation treats feedback as oxygen for growth, creating ongoing loops that capture members' experiences and guide adaptive changes. Since Proverbs 15:22 affirms that "plans fail for lack of counsel, but with many advisers they succeed," modern churches implement annual or biannual congregational surveys to measure spiritual health, program effectiveness, and community needs. These surveys combine quantitative scales—rating satisfaction with worship and small groups—with qualitative prompts that invite narrative responses on prayer life, sense of belonging, and perceived barriers to participation. Survey results are then shared transparently with the congregation, demonstrating that leadership values honesty over appearances.

In addition to surveys, listening sessions facilitate face-to-face dialogue. These sessions might be conducted neighborhood by neighborhood, reflecting parish mapping priorities. A facilitator begins by reading Jeremiah 29:7—"seek the welfare of the city"—reminding participants that their voices shape collective mission. Congregants gather in diverse cohorts—youth, seniors, young professionals, parents, newcomers—to share joys and frustrations, and to propose solutions. Staff and volunteers rotate through sessions to listen rather than defend, asking clarifying questions like "What else?" and "How might we address that?" This listening posture models James 1:19's exhortation: "Be quick to hear, slow to speak, slow to anger."

After gathering feedback, leaders convene working groups to analyze data, identify recurring themes, and prioritize initiatives. If survey feedback indicates that many feel isolated mid-week, the church might launch new community groups or enhance digital check-in tools. If attendees express that sermons lack practical application, teaching teams revisit sermon preparation processes, incorporating more case studies and life-application segments. Implementation plans include measurable goals and timelines—for instance, establishing five new neighborhood prayer cells within six months. As changes roll out, leadership communicates progress through regular "State of the Church" reports, inviting further input.

Feedback loops also encompass spontaneous channels: suggestion boxes in the lobby; a designated email address for prayer requests and ideas; and periodic focus groups for specific demographics—such as young families or recent converts—whose needs may evolve quickly. When a young couple voices difficulty finding childcare during worship, volunteers mobilize to open an additional nursery room staffed by vetted caregivers, ensuring that service barriers do not hinder attendance. Similarly, hearing that older members struggle with digital worship tools, the church organizes "Tech Tutoring Tuesdays" where volunteers teach basic streaming and online giving skills.

Adaptive change emerges not from rigid strategic plans but from iterative cycles of listening, discerning, and adjusting. This approach aligns with Isaiah 1:18's invitation to reason together with God—if a congregation reasons together, it humbly admits areas needing repentance and renewal. By normalizing feedback loops, the church fosters a culture where complaints become opportunities for improvement rather than sources of division. As members witness leadership responding prayerfully and practically, trust deepens, and participation increases. With forms of feedback and adaptation integrated into church life, leaders then turn to safeguarding their own health and ensuring leadership succession, which is crucial for sustainable discipleship hubs.

10.6.c Leader Health & Succession — Guarding Against Burnout and Celebrity The New Testament emphasizes the well-being of those who serve. Paul's instruction to Timothy to "do the work of an evangelist, fulfill your ministry" (2 Timothy 4:5) suggests that ministry requires clear role expectations, support, and rest. Yet many church contexts exalt pastors who display constant availability and charismatic presence, fostering burnout and creating cults of personality rather than healthy followership. To guard against this, churches institute regular health check-ins for leaders—pastors, elders, ministry heads—through pastoral care teams or external mentors. These check-ins include confidential self-assessment tools measuring stress, spiritual dryness, and relational health, combined with peer coaching sessions where leaders candidly discuss struggles.

Leaders also observe sabbatic rhythms: after five to seven years of service, senior pastors take a three-month sabbatical to rest, study, and reflect. During this time, an interim team—composed of elders and staff—leads weekly operations, demonstrating that the church's mission is not pastor-dependent. Sabbaticals emulate the scriptural pattern of periodic retreat exemplified by Jesus (Mark 1:35) and Moses (Exodus 24:18). When sabbaticals coincide with denominational requirements or gift cycles, leaders return energized, with fresh vision and renewed relational bandwidth.

Insulating against celebrity requires fostering collaborative leadership models, as described earlier, and decentralizing decision-making. Churches draft conflict-of-interest policies to ensure that major decisions—like the sale of property or hiring of family members—require board approval rather than unilateral pastoral fiat. Performance evaluations are conducted not by parishioners alone, but by an independent council that includes non-staff members, ensuring accountability to Scripture rather than individual charisma.

Succession planning begins before crises arise. Churches identify potential leaders early through gift discernment pathways and provide training—courses in theology, leadership, conflict resolution, and financial oversight—so second-tier leaders are ready when transition occurs. Rotations in preaching, teaching, and pastoral care duties give aspiring leaders practical experience under the guidance of seasoned clergy. When a senior pastor announces impending retirement, a transitional committee implements a multiyear plan: defining the next pastoral profile, engaging a search team, and providing overlap where the outgoing and incoming pastors co-lead for a season. This transitional overlap mirrors the Moses–Joshua transition (Numbers 27:18–23), where leadership and vision pass smoothly because of intentional preparation.

Leadership health also involves spiritual formation retreats—annual "Leader's Quiet Days" where the entire staff and board convene for prayer, worship, and silent reflection, often at a remote retreat center. These retreats include sessions on resilience, stress management, and spiritual direction, acknowledging that ministry involves spiritual warfare (Ephesians 6:12). Leaders practice confession and lament together, refusing to develop blind spots or unaddressed wounds. Congregational teaching emphasizes the importance of caring for leaders: when the congregation prays for the pastoral team with genuine concern and gratitude, it counters patterns of entitlement that can lead to ministry abuse.

By actively prioritizing leader health and succession, churches safeguard their capacity to serve as enduring discipleship hubs. When parishioners see leaders faithfully rested, accountable, and ready to pass the baton, they internalize that ministry is broader than any single personality. This culmination of formation practices establishes a community resilient enough to sustain discipleship for generations to come, transitioning smoothly into "From Sunday Gathering to Week-Long Embodied Gospel" as the final focus.

Conclusion

As the body of Christ grows into its calling, the blessing of community becomes unmistakable: believers learn to bear each other's burdens, they find strength in shared liturgies, and they see their unique gifts knitted together in service. Intergenerational bonds and intercultural hospitality break down walls of isolation, while sacramental rhythms root identity in Christ's life, death, and resurrection. When the church embraces its role as a training ground—shaping hearts, minds, and hands for kingdom work—discipleship spills over into every sphere of life. Through ongoing formation, honest feedback, and healthy leadership practices, the congregation remains vital and resilient, ready to send forth followers who carry the gospel into homes, workplaces, and neighborhoods. In this way, what begins on Sunday morning becomes a week-long, incarnational witness, demonstrating that the church's true power lies not in its programs but in the transforming fellowship of believers devoted to Jesus and to one another.

www.ingramcontent.com/pod-product-compliance
Lightning Source LLC
Chambersburg PA
CBHW070848050426
42453CB00012B/2086